eLmL 2023

The Fifteenth International Conference on Mobile, Hybrid, and On-line Learning

April 24th – 28th, 2023

Venice, Italy

eLmL 2023 Editors

Daniela Pellegrini, R&D Manager, Piazza Copernico srl., Italy

Samuel Kosolapov, Braude Academic College of Engineering, Israel

Printed from e-media with permission by:

Curran Associates, Inc.
57 Morehouse Lane
Red Hook, NY 12571

Some format issues inherent in the e-media version may also appear in this print version.

Printed with permission by Curran Associates, Inc. (2024)

International Academy, Research, and Industry Association (IARIA)
412 Derby Way
Wilmington, DE 19810

Phone: (408) 893-6407
Fax: (408) 527-6351

petre@iaria.org

Additional copies of this publication are available from:

Curran Associates, Inc.
57 Morehouse Lane
Red Hook, NY 12571 USA
Phone: 845-758-0400
Fax: 845-758-2633
Email: curran@proceedings.com
Web: www.proceedings.com

Table of Contents

eLmL 2023

Forward

The Fifteenth International Conference on Mobile, Hybrid, and On-line Learning (eLmL 2023), held in Venice, Italy, April 24 - 28, 2023, focused on the latest trends in e-learning and also on the latest IT technology alternatives that are poised to become mainstream strategies in the near future and will influence the e-learning environment.

eLearning refers to on-line learning delivered over the World Wide Web via the public Internet or the private, corporate intranet. The goal of the eLmL 2023 conference was to provide an overview of technologies, approaches, and trends that are happening right now. The constraints of e-learning are diminishing and options are increasing as the Web becomes increasingly easy to use and the technology becomes better and less expensive.

eLmL 2023 provided a forum where researchers were able to present recent research results and new research problems and directions related to them. The topics covered aspects related to tools and platforms, on-line learning, mobile learning, and hybrid learning.

We take this opportunity to thank all the members of the eLmL 2023 Technical Program Committee as well as the numerous reviewers. The creation of such a broad and high-quality conference program would not have been possible without their involvement. We also kindly thank all the authors who dedicated much of their time and efforts to contribute to the eLmL 2023. We truly believe that, thanks to all these efforts, the final conference program consists of top quality contributions.

This event could also not have been a reality without the support of many individuals, organizations, and sponsors. We are grateful to the members of the eLmL 2023 organizing committee for their help in handling the logistics and for their work to make this professional meeting a success.

We hope that eLmL 2023 was a successful international forum for the exchange of ideas and results between academia and industry and for the promotion of progress in eLearning research. We also hope that Venice provided a pleasant environment during the conference and everyone saved some time for exploring this beautiful city

eLmL 2023 Chairs

eLmL Steering Committee
Maiga Chang, Athabasca University, Canada
Alexander Mikroyannidis, The Open University, United Kingdom
Daniel Amo Filvà, La Salle - Universitat Ramon Llull, Spain
Rodica Neamtu, Worcester Polytechnic Institute, USA

eLmL 2023 Publicity Chair
Laura Garcia, Universitat Politècnica de València (UPV), Spain
Javier Rocher Morant, Universitat Politecnica de Valencia, Spain

eLmL 2023

COMMITTEE

eLmL Steering Committee

Maiga Chang, Athabasca University, Canada
Alexander Mikroyannidis, The Open University, United Kingdom
Daniel Amo Filvà, La Salle - Universitat Ramon Llull, Spain
Rodica Neamtu, Worcester Polytechnic Institute, USA

eLmL 2023 Publicity Chairs

Javier Rocher Morant, Universitat Politecnica de Valencia, Spain
Laura Garcia, Universitat Politecnica de Valencia, Spain

eLmL 2023 Technical Program Committee

Waqas Ahmed, UniKL Business School (UBIS) - Universiti Kuala Lumpur, Malaysia
Habiba Akter, Universiti Kuala Lumpur (UniKL) Business School, Malaysia
Daniel Amo Filvà, La Salle - Universitat Ramon Llull, Spain
Luis Anido-Rifon, Universidade de Vigo, Spain
Arlette Audiffred Hinojosa, Instituto Tecnológico y de Estudios Superiores de Monterrey (ITESM), Mexico
Regina Bäck, KU Eichstätt-Ingolstadt & KSH Munich, Germany
Shreyansh Bhatt, Amazon.com, USA
Krista Bonello Rutter Giappone, University of Malta, Malta / University of Kent, UK
Abinash Borah, Oklahoma State University, Stillwater, USA
Tina Boyle Whyte, Marquette University, USA
Egle Butkeviciene, Kaunas University of Technology, Lithuania
Mauro Callejas Cuervo, Universidade Pedagógica y Tecnológica de Colombia, Colombia
Djordje Cantrak, University of Belgrade, Serbia
Laurence Capus, Université Laval, Canada
Cristina M.R. Caridade, Coimbra Polytechnic - ISEC, Portugal
Stefano Caselli, Institute of Digital Games | University of Malta, Malta
Maiga Chang, Athabasca University, Canada
Krzysztof J. Cios, Virginia Commonwealth University, USA
Lorraine Cleeton, Northcentral University / Walden University, USA
Aubrey Condor, UC Berkeley, USA
Mike Cosgrave, University College Cork, Ireland
José Paulo Cravino, Universidade de Trás-os-Montes e Alto Douro / CIDTFF, Portugal
Erin Czerwinski, Carnegie Mellon University, USA
Najima Daoudi, École des sciences de l'information, Morocco
Debzani Deb, Winston-Salem State University, USA
Angel P. del Pobil, Jaume I University, Spain
Rafael del Vado Vírseda, Universidad Complutense de Madrid, Spain
Soumyabrata Dev, ADAPT SFI Research Centre, Dublin, Ireland
Federico Diano, University of Naples "Federico II", Italy
Mounim A. El Yacoubi, Telecom SudParis, France

Ke Wang, University of California, Davis, USA
Hironori Washizaki, Waseda University, Japan
Mudasser Wyne, National University - San Diego, USA
Rihito Yaegashi, Kagawa University, Japan
Ahmed Mohamed Fahmy Yousef, Fayoum University, Egypt
Ruochen Zeng, Marvell Semiconductor, USA
Minjia Zhang, Microsoft AI and Research, USA
Yingbin Zhang, University of Illinois at Urbana-Champaign, USA
Jinjin Zhao, Amazon.com, USA

Copyright Information

Active Learning in Teaching Digital Tourism: Preliminary Results Through Online Travel Business Simulation

Michele Angelaccio
Management Engineering Dept.
University of Rome "Tor Vergata"
Rome, Italy
email: michele.angelaccio@uniroma2.it

Lucia Zappitelli
Smartourism Research Lab
University of Rome "Tor Vergata"
Rome, Italy
email: lucia.zappitelli@gmail.com

Abstract—**Today, education requires a constant search of methods and instruments that stimulate student engagement. Active learning methods ensure student activities through their creativeness and reactiveness during educational processes. Simulation techniques have been used as a crucial component of active teaching especially in the context of Business Informatics due to a close relationship between simulated business models and computer technologies and management skills. In this paper, we focus on online Travel Agency Business simulation and show how a real simulation performed through active methodology of web coding results in a complete set of learning outcomes in Digital Tourism and Management education.**

Keywords— Digital Tourism Courses, Active learning, Project-based Learning, OTA Business Simulation

I. INTRODUCTION

Over the last decades, simulation resources have been extensively integrated within teaching programs, especially in engineering. Initially, many strategies have relied on the use of software tools for simulating a wide field of engineering problems [3]. In the last years, a particular attention has been devoted to the programs of business and management engineering for which digital resources for computational problems and simulation have been analyzed also from a learning point of view as usefully employed in terms of active learning methodology [6] [7]. However, in these cases the use of a particular simulation tool is required to involve students in management tasks and strategy building. Often this solution is difficult to implement for students without some technical and digital basic skills. As a matter of fact, Digital Tourism is an example of a business area with the need to teach skills for Online Travel Agencies (OTA business simulation) and often with students with low-level profile of digital skills. Therefore, the main aim of this paper is to describe a simulation based activity to support a complete active learning framework for digital and management competencies for OTA management with a web coding based simulation approach that emulates a simulation scenario of travel business. This is strongly related to the field of Digital Tourism with emphasis on booking data and travel business planning.

In the next section, we describe course organization and the way how web simulation platform has been implemented. Then we analyze the Travel Business simulation process and discuss the advantages. A focus on web coding and its role in active learning strategy it will be discussed in section 4 before the Conclusions.

II. DIGITAL TOURISM COURSES

These specific courses are **Digital Tourism** and **Web Information systems for Smart Cities**. From a general point of view they are organized in agreement with Agile Learning paradigm by following a project based approach (see [5] and [8]). The Digital Tourism course covers, among others, such issues as Digital Tourism fundamentals and software architectures, entrepreneurship, planning of travel business, organizational structures, destination analysis, market research and branding, team building in the modern companies, risk analysis and information gathering.

The teaching methods used so far are: presentations, discussions, case studies, teaching and learning activities, team exercises and web-stories on social platforms.

During the course, students carry out a research project, whose topic is: "Project preparation – Digitalization of a Travel Italian Destination of small scale to be promoted ". The student's task is to develop a model. They should also find examples of interesting business solutions based on a literature review and their observations.

During the classes on the subject "Web Information systems for Smart Cities", students learn about the concept of "Smart City and Data analysis", including the distinguishing factors and consequences of the fourth industrial revolution. In addition, they learn in detail the concepts of the Dashboard and web app for Data analysis and visualization: conditions for the development of this type of web information system, the impact of ICT on the challenges posed by this type of analysis, and aspects related to the sharing of knowledge. The teaching methods used so far in the classes are seminar lectures and exercises: group work, presentations and discussion. Students of this course carry out a research project covering the following aspects:

- development (in a team) of a concept of a digital tourism data model with assumptions and justification/comments on the selection of individual elements of the model;
- preparation of a multimedia presentation on the developed concepts.

As remarked in [6], this activity can be made more attractive by considering business simulation as learning process. In this case this introduction has been obtained by considering Online Travel Agency Business implemented through a complete web platform composed by independent web travel agencies each related to a particular destination assigned to a group of students according to their preferred destination. This differs from [6], meaning that web coding replaces business simulation platform and allows a more complete learning process with respect to the acquisition of digital skills. For example, there is no need to run an external simulation tool to show the elements of business reality because in the case of simulation of online travel agencies , students are able to experiment with real data gathered from the internet the tourism services and corresponding data analysis functions thus emulating tour operators and destination managers behavior. In particular Figure 1 shows the organization of the two courses obtained by considering collaborative platforms for the agile learning process resulting in a set of learning outcomes that are viewed as components of two-levels web architectures BACK-END and FRONT-END used in the Online Travel Agency Simulation Web Platform. In the next section it will be described this type of business simulation solution in more detail and it will be discussed its advantages.

III. OTA Business Simulation Analysis

The Online Travel Agency (OTA) business simulation learning system is implemented through the use of a project based platform (Wordpress PM) syncronized with team collaboration system already used in the class (Microsoft Teams). To engage students in travel business as potential digital tour operator, the project based platform works as multi destination management platform hosting a set of Travel Agencies each assigned to a working group and defined by e-commerce Wordpress CMS with the following plugin extensions:

- BuddyPress plugin for community management [9]
- Project management plugin for the Tour and destination content [10]
- Booking plugin for e-commerce travel simulation [11]

As recognized by [4] and [6], competencies needed in Modern Digital Business society are strongly related to flexible adaptive skills typical of active learning and collaborative frameworks.

In addition, two of the most significant American human development organizations (namely the 21st Century Skills Partnership and the National Council for Social Studies), based on the research and analysis conducted, have introduced a map of social competencies for the challenges of the 21st century. This map contains a catalogue of social skills deemed necessary for full functioning in 21st-century societies. It covers the following areas of competences, i.e.:

- Knowledge and Organizational Competencies,
  - creativity and innovation,
  - critical thinking and problem solving,
  - communication,
  - cooperation within a community group.
- Character Quality
  - efficient use of information and communication technology tools,
  - flexibility and adaptability (the ability to adapt to changing conditions),
  - productivity,
  - leadership skills and responsibility.

The use of this Business Simulation solution in teaching helps each student to develop several competencies relating to a more insightful understanding of reality, its rational transformation, and stimulation of her/his creative activity. In particular, for Travel Business simulation carried out through web platforms, we can summarize the competencies derived from Agile learning activities and learning outcomes in Table I.

With this business simulation strategy, students develop creativity, innovation, and decision-making skills, which are desirable for future roles as needed by new profiles of SMARTOUR OPERATORS emerging in Digital Tourism society.

However, the most innovative contribution of the two courses introduced is that the simulation is obtained through the use of web coding platforms to implement the travel business simulation. In the next section we describe how such OTA Business simulation has been carried out through a specific set of activities.

IV. The Impact of Web Coding

It is interesting to remark the impact of web coding on OTA business simulation to improve learning activity level. Coding laboratories are a very recent learning activity model used in high intensive digital skill course to enhance the competencies on software platforms (cloud, networking, security, algorithms and artificial intelligence). In this case, we apply the same coding approach but shifted at level of WEB-coding laboratory in which the use of web platform is motivated by the fact that in the context of travel business e-commerce they could sufficient to simulate all required digital services (tour data map definitions, scheduling and booking services, etc.) introduced in our courses. This has the potential to extend the capacity skill set towards the education of future digital managers with the inclusion of students incoming also from other different education profiles oriented for example to cultural knowledge.

A. *Agile learning and Web coding for Digital Tourism*

When applied to OTA Business Simulation, web coding has the potential to reach a deeper level of learning activities.

This will obtained by considering that:

- there is no predefined timeline sequence of web coding task to be followed by each student and each group is free to propose an autonomous task definition except the constraint defined by the general travel agency template definition.
- travel simulation and destination definition can be autonomously refined thanks to the online procedures synchronised following agile scrum methodology.
- web output sharing is very natural in the context of Online Travel e-commerce platforms leading to shared data map and services (e.g. booking). A student simulating tour operator on the assigned destination can participate as client visitor for another destination leading to be more productive for future work.
- cross-disciplinary activities are facilitated due to the fact that different digital skilled profiles can benefit from autonomous group coding activity.

B. *Real Business Gaming issues*

In the last session held in spring 2022 at our University of Rome, it has been experimented a real activity in the context of digital Tourism Course composed by an outdoor Smartourism Hackathon. This extra activity has been organized with the collaboration of a real Tour Operator Organization (Tevere Park) with the contribution of students participating in a smartourism gaming learning activity inside a green touristic park located out of Rome and reachable by train. Such gaming learning activity has been performed by exploring real river trekking tours through bike and canoe trips and the associated activities with the assistance of external guides (see Figure 2). The gaming output has been put in the form of web stories including travel data analysis with suggestions and annotations autonomously discussed. In this way, we have confirmed that web coding for Tourism is a framework to enhance digital and business skills in a real world of working activities.

Among the the resulting benefits we remark the following ones:

- Refinement of starting paths is achieved on the field by autonomous interaction between groups and park assistants thanks to a game approach like Hackathon.
- The use of web stories has been made possible in mobile computing mode using socialmedia story editing functions in real time (see Figure 3 in which are listed the web stories collected by students who participated in the game).
- Compared to learning processes conducted only in the classroom or online, team work on the field and spontaneous game processes in the park during the realization of the guided tours, have produced a better level of awareness and self-esteem in students also facilitating teamwork.

V. Conclusions

Digital Tourism competencies are strongly related to the acquisition of experience. Thus, one of the most important elements of education is learning through experience. Business computer simulation currently seems to be the best solution that allows management and digital education in a joint framework but the use of a particular business simulation tool must be replaced with a more user friendly and practical tool due to the increasing number of different sources of touristic data and processes. Therefore, it is important to indicate

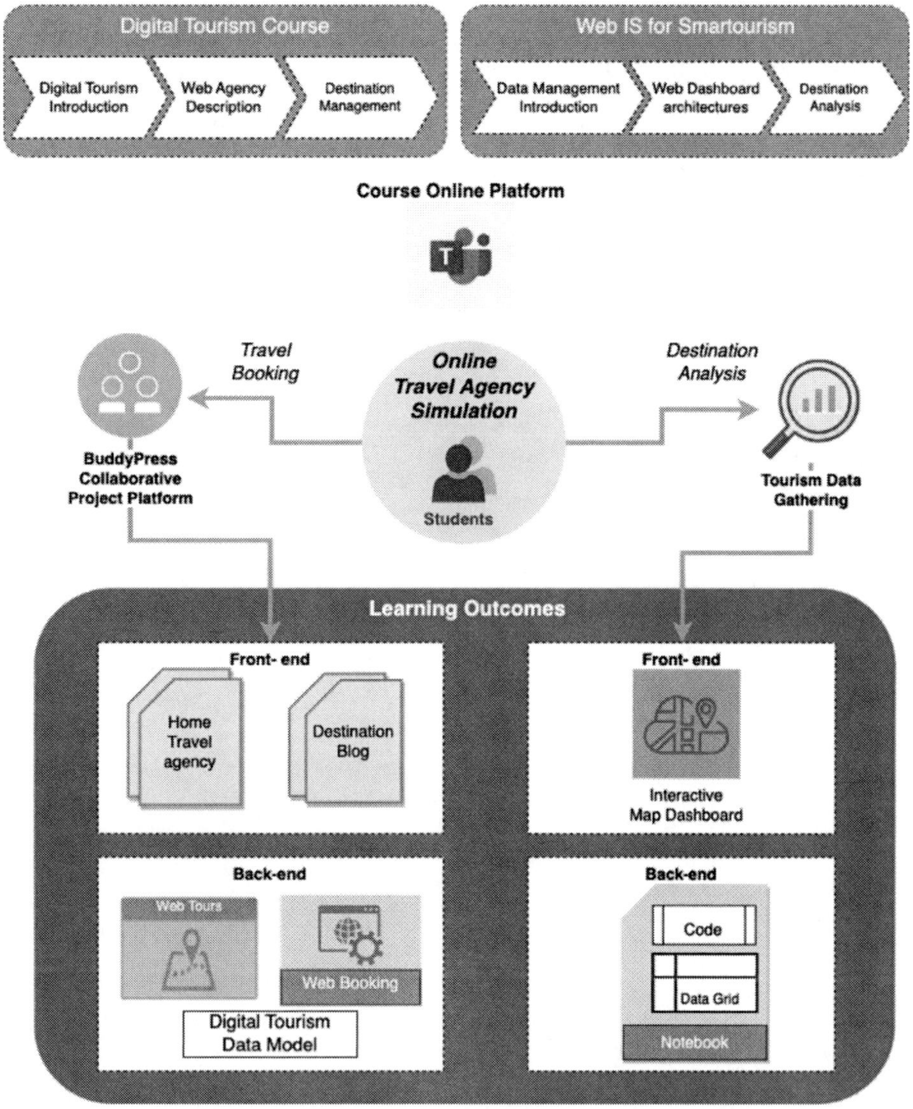

Fig. 1. Agile Learning Organization for the Course **Web for Tourism**

TABLE I
LEARNING OUTCOMES FOR SMARTOURIM COURSE

Cognitive Competencies	Tour and destination discovery web, map and multimedia design Planning and Risk analysis	Digital Competencies Analytical skills
	searching for attractions creativity in content creation innovation in new smartourism experience definition	Creativity
Action oriented Competencies	self management of travel business process time management and task planning	indipendence self learning Flexibility
Social Competencies	Tour integration and comparison Social networking diffusion	Communication and Collaboration Team Working

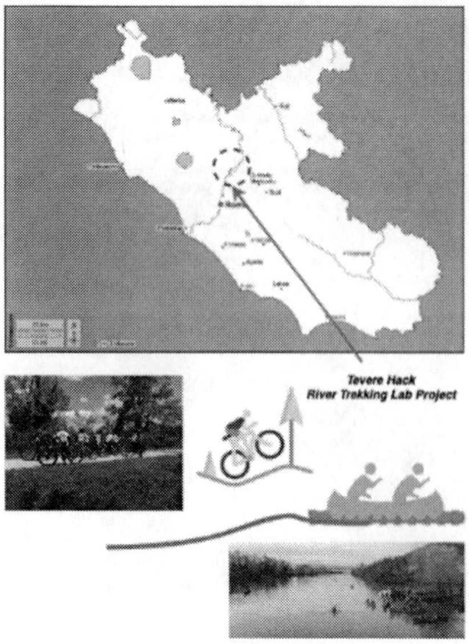

Fig. 2. Smartourism Hackathon Organization

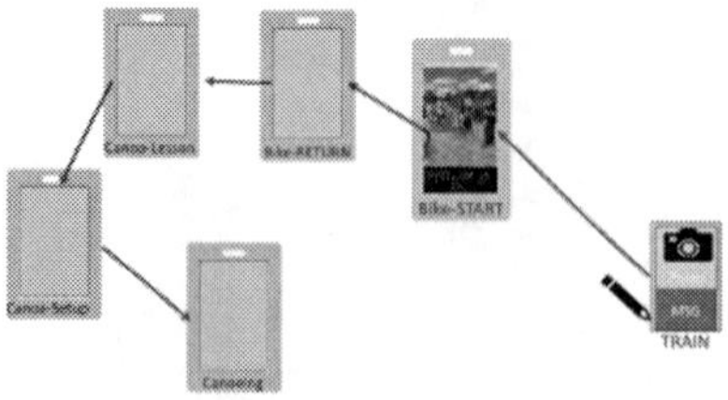

Fig. 3. web stories and student's perceptron

the need to develop students' professional and social competences with the use of a higher level type of business computer simulation strongly related to real cases. In this work we have explored the issues related to a first attempt to learn by means of web coding used in a set of project based courses for smartourism development. A complete organization of the learning web platform with a discussion of the resulting benefits has been given together a first analysis in terms of novel approaches arising from this type of web based simulation leading to the implementation of new game learning particularly suited for OTA business learning.

REFERENCES

[1] Topal, Murat and Karaca, Ozan. , "Gamification in E-Learning", 2022, 10.4018/978-1-6684-3710-0.ch001.

[2] M. Cápay, "Enhancing the Teaching of Informatics through Engaging Experience", *Proceedings Of The 11th International Conference On Computer Supported Education - Volume 1: CSEDU*, pp. 453-460, 2019.

[3] D.Valiente et al., "Active Learning Program Supported by Online Simulation Applet in Engineering Education" *Proceedings Of The 9th International Conference On Simulation And Modeling Methodologies, Technologies And Applications - SIMULTECH*, pp. 121-128, 2019

[4] M. Angelaccio, "Ecopolytechnic: a sustainable and Flexible e-learning system for agile smart learning scenarios", *Proceedings Of The 14th International Conference On E-Learning (EL 2020), pp. 183–186)*

[5] M.Angelaccio, "Design of active learning strategy through agile development methodologies: a technological view", *Proceedings Of The CECIIS 2011: Central European conference on information and intelligent systems, Varazdyn-Croatia, pp. 105-110.*

[6] A. Binsztok, B. Butryn, K. Hołowińska, M. Owoc, and M. Sobinska, "Applying Simulation in Teaching Selected Courses in Business Informatics with the FlexSim Platform" (14th International Conference on Computer Supported Education,pp. 330-337, 2022).

[7] A.Binsztok, B. Butryn, K. Hołowińska, M. Owoc, and M. Sobińska, "Business computer simulation supporting competencies. Potential areas of application and barriers" *Procedia Computer Science*. **207** pp. 3875-3883, 2022.

[8] A. Aji, "The Impact of Active Learning on Students' Academic Performance", *Open Journal of Social Sciences*. **207** pp. 204-211, 2019.

[9] buddypress wordpress plugin, "wordpress.org/plugins/buddypress/"

[10] pm wordpress plugin "wordpress.org/plugins/wedevs-project-manager/"

[11] booking wordpress plugin "/wordpress.org/plugins/booking-calendar/"

Sustainability and Metaverse in Education and Training: Barriers, Opportunities and Environmental Impact

Cinzia Mezzetti
Piazza Copernico srl
Rome, Italy
e-mail: cmezzetti@pcopernico.it

Alessandro Dell'Orto
Piazza Copernico srl
Rome, Italy
e-mail: adellorto@pcopernico.it

Daniela Pellegrini
Piazza Copernico srl
Rome, Italy
e-mail: dpellegrini@pcopernico.it

Abstract— **The proliferation of training experiences and experiments with the metaverse testifies the desire to test new instructional models to increase participant engagement, but also foster situated learning experiences to increase training effectiveness and learning outcomes. However, the creation of training paths in the metaverse is supported by an experimental approach, but also accompanied by curiosity and expectations, as well as by emerging questions about how to combine the opportunities of a new training technology with its adoption problems. In the definitions and experiences, it seems to be a lack of a real educational vision for correctly using this opportunity. In this paper, which is an initial approach to the problem of choosing a new technology, we want to examine the impact both in terms of training and on the environmental dimension, which is a generally underestimated topic in edtech (educational technology) choices.**

Keywords-metaverse; instructional design; sustainability.

I. Introduction

Metaverse is one of current applications that is considered most interesting in edtech landscape and cited in trends of education & training industry observers in recent years. Contextually, both corporate trials and academic studies have been conducted with the aim of demonstrating the usefulness and educational effectiveness of this technology. At the beginning of 2023, however, on the communicative level in industry trends, this topic is found with less centrality in favor of the contamination of methods for a truly individualized (user-oriented) learning.

Since its first definition, Metaverse is considered "*a decentralized network of computer-generated worlds, where users feel a genuine sense of being in these spaces for work, leisure and learning*" [22]. Particularly in recent years with the increasing development of technology capacity, also studies and experimentations increased in a practical use of possible applications of the metaverse in education and training. Authors who are in favor of using metaverse, identify great educational opportunities in creating a virtual and interactive equivalent to the physical world through exploration on Extended Reality (XR) platforms. This definition embraces immersive technologies as Augmented Reality (AR), Mixed Reality (MR) and Virtual Reality (VR). So, there is a spectrum of virtuality, which are already transforming society in technological, industrial, and legal worlds [19].

The ability to act in a virtual and interconnected world to search information, communicate and explore an augmented reality led to imagining a future in which only a reduced and blurred boundary will exist between the virtual and real worlds. As Ng [17] points out, the use of the term metaverse has greatly increased after 2020 to identify technologies that were being discussed even before that year:

- Since the 2000s to the mid-2010s, researchers used the term metaverse to refer to virtual environments such as gamification and avatar-based learning to indicate platforms e.g. Second Life, Digital Virtual World [1] [21]. They emphasized the possibility in building immersive, three-dimensional, multi-user experiences to create authentic learning environments to enrich the educational experience.
- After the mid-2010s, even with a significant improvement of technologies, the definition of metaverse in education didn't change so much, i.e., a 3d simulation environment that encourages communication (with simulated objects/avatars and with other participants), interaction and collaboration by providing active agents to build the learning process was identified with this term [2].
- Since 2020, the term Metaverse has returned to common interest, however, not changing its intrinsic meaning in the educational field. Diaz et al. [5] identify with this term virtual spaces that recreate the real world, learning processes and experiences, through avatars used to interact with other users as in real life. Kye et al. [13] describe the metaverse as a space for a new form of social communication with greater freedom for users to share ideas, thoughts and digital artifacts. Reyes' [20] definition fully identifies the foundational assets of the metaverse:
    - *Interactivity* that facilitates the construction of autonomous and collaborative learning scenarios;
    - *Corporeality* that allows people to represent themselves through avatars;
    - *Persistence* that enables the construction of a virtual world that mimics the real world and keeps people interconnected over time.

In distance learning, this blended approach allows new formal and informal learning modalities emerge, in which physical presence is not a mandatory requirement of the educational experience [13] anymore. Instead, the use of immersive technologies enables educational experiences and allows a deeper and longer learning [16]. Girvan [9] argues that this new learning formula can ensure a democratization of education, allowing access even for people from disadvantaged areas.

We summarize below some emerging indications from the literature in comparison with our own critical reading.

TABLE I . OPPORTUNITÀ SEGNALATE IN LETTERATURA E VALUTAZIONE DELLE POSSIBILI ALTERNATIVE

Opportunity statements	Questions
Metaverse provides more interactive education without compromising the classroom experience [12].	Does interactivity depend on used method or technology?
Applications of the metaverse can provide a more accessible way for communication, improving educational quality [4].	Can training effectiveness also be pursued in other ways?
The teaching process can be managed independently from time and space with enriched teaching experiences.	Can other technologies equally enable the exploration of different worlds (at microscopic or macroscopic level) and eras, depending on the educational objectives?
Metaverse provides immersive, higher participation learning experiences and reducing isolation	But could it be also the other way around? Could it increase the risk of isolation?
Students can become knowledge creators.	Is content creation also possible with other technologies?
Educational resources will be plentiful and increasing	But what will be the necessary investments?
Online 3d metaverse campuses can realize rich, liquid, integrated learning environments and provide rich educational opportunities [3]	What will be the enrollment policies to ensure everyone's right to study?

Possible drawbacks and problems to be addressed are also highlighted:

- Teachers need to learn new methods and acquire digital, design and instructional process management skills in the metaverse. Contact and relationship in presence are necessary in educational and training activities.
- Investments in technology and development of environments and contents with complex, high-quality graphics are required. There is still a low availability of catalogs with digital resources and metavers has high production costs and even access devices are expensive. Privacy and cybersecurity are issues related to the use of digital devices that collect and use data (including biometric data) that must be ensured under a regulatory and informational perspective toward the user. Also a part of little knowledge or confidence in technology and awareness of educational applications persists [16].
- Excessive cognitive load for Extended Reality (XR) experiences that provide many audio-visual stimuli to the user, so it is necessary to identify the correct methods to make this aspect become an advantage for effective learning and retention, rather than instead a barrier. This also requires defining time constraints for these experiences estimated at 10-15 minutes [19].
- The issue of accessibility is very complex under the perspective of used technologies. Increasingly, technologies must evolve to ensure full and equal inclusion and accessibility. [19].

Then there are emerging topics related to the use of technological environments such as [24] those related to Data Management, Digital Copyright, equity and sustainability of education, and the impact of algorithms in educational processes. There are, however, areas and purposes for which experts find the use of Extended Reality (XR) challenging and productive, including:

- increase participant motivation and interest: studies show an increase in self-efficacy through experiential training [14].
- build comprehensive learning environments in which the learner can develop learning through immersive technologies enriched by advanced computing (AI – Artificial Intelligence, data mining, etc.) by developing socialization, collaboration in learning environments and decentralization to increase learning opportunities and technologies [17].

In this scenario and with these available studies, a global consideration about impacts in learning and other impacts must be done. In Section 2 we discuss effective opportunities to implement metaverse solutions in education and training with honest remarks about possible problems and alternatives. In section 3 we provide a wider perspective on the use of technologies in an ESG framework.

II. OPPORTUNITIES FOR TRAINING AND BARRIERS TO ADOPTION OF METAVERSE

Undoubtedly, metaverse appears to be a very interesting chance in the educational and training sector with experiencing worlds and eras other than reality, interacting in complex ways through avatars in contexts even very distant from personal environment, breaking down access boundaries and overcoming distance or language limits.

Metaverse could represent a great opportunity in all those training activities that are difficult to replicate or implying high risk, as for example, in the training of technicians operating in a semi-automated production process. Metaverse offers the possibility to engage in trials with equipment, processing times, and quality control procedures without incurring risks or injuries, even interacting with each other and/or with instructors in real time. Creating a safe and controlled training environment where users can practice and make mistakes without negative consequences is, in our opinion, one of the greatest potentials. In addition, learning can be adapted to users' background and prior skills or specific needs by overcoming barriers to access or habitual behaviors.

It is important to remember that technology is a tool and not a miracle solution [19], that it can support learning processes particularly in so-called Dangerous, Impossible, Counterproductive, Expensive (DICE) situations, and yet it does not solve the problems of a poorly designed or managed training process. The application of metaverse technologies in training, therefore, requires extensive considerations on training objectives and models, user experience, and real training potential. As metaverse will grow, experiences and content will emerge, and even appropriate instructional solutions could be tested to ensure that the tool is not just another expensive and underutilized training application.

III. TECHNOLOGY ENVIROMENTAL IMPACT CONCEPT

It is also important to consider the assessment of the environmental impact of technologies, a factor that is often overlooked when evaluating opportunities and innovations. It is true that calculating the real environmental impact is a huge, if not impossible, problem. It is in fact the sum of a complex series of types of pollution: gas emissions, water consumption, consumption of raw materials, deforestation, urban sprawl, human and animal exploitation, and so on. And this calculation becomes even more difficult for something that does not yet exist: the metaverse. The only certainty we have is that as the number of online events grows, so does the energy demand of the entire infrastructure. According to the Shift Project report [27], digital growth is unsustainable; in fact, the energy consumption of current digital activities is growing at 9% per year, and with the advent of the metaverse, this growth can only continue to grow exponentially. The metaverse will rely on an infrastructure based on cloud computing, blockchain, artificial intelligence and virtual reality. Let's try to analyze them one by one:

- **Cloud Computing**: cloud services are essential for virtual reality and the metaverse. According to a 2020 analysis by Lancaster University, a scenario in which 30% of gamers switch to cloud gaming will lead to a 30% increase in CO_2 emissions by 2030 [28]. Not to be overlooked is the water consumption required by data centers. To get an idea, Google's data centers alone used about 16 billion liters last year, which is comparable to the water consumption of an Italian city with a population of about 185,000 [10] [6].
- **Blockchain**: bitcoins alone have a carbon footprint comparable to that of New Zealand, producing approximately 36.95 tones of CO_2 per year [26]. The use of blockchain is probably the big change and the only real benefit, as the transparency of this technology would force companies to track, submit and manage their green policies [8]. Below are graphs about of the bitcoin network's CO_2 emissions (Figure 1) and energy consumption over time (Figure 2) [27].

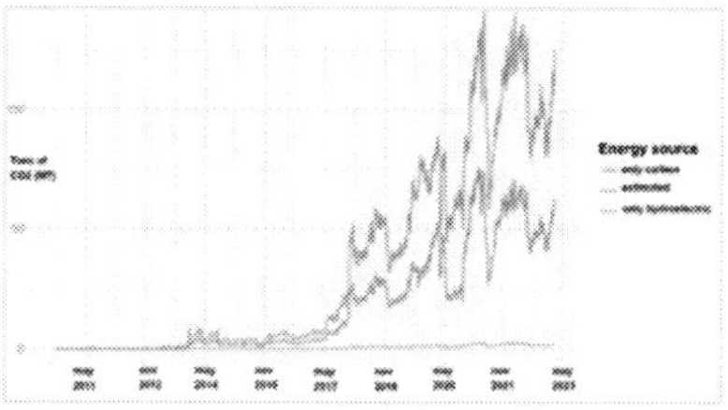

Figure 1. Estimated CO_2 emission (MT) of the Bitcoin network

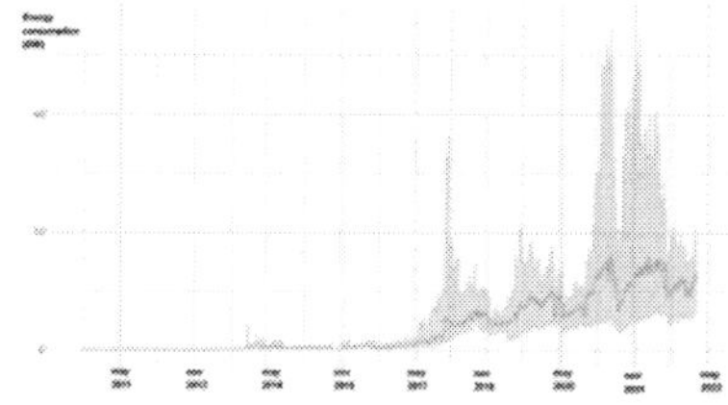

Figure 2. Daily energy consumption (GW) of the Bitcoin network

- **Artificial Intelligence**: according to Strubell et al [23], training a single neural network can generate up to 284 tones of carbon dioxide, which is more than five times the amount of CO_2 emitted by an average car (Table 2). Further confirmation of the order of magnitude comes from Patterson [18], who calculates the emissions for training the model behind OpenAI's famous ChatGPT, GPT-3: 500 tones of CO_2.

TABLE 2. CONFRONTO CONSUMI RISPETTO ALL'ADDESTRAMENTO DI UN MODELLO GPU [19]

Consumption	**CO_2 (Kg)**
Air flight, 1 passenger, NY ⇔ SF	900
Human life, 1 year	5000
Life of an American, 1 year	16400
Car, whole life	57153
Training a model (GPU)	
NLP pipeline	18
with tuning and experimentation	35592
Transformer (large)	87
with neural architecture search	284019

Considering these data, it is possible to conclude that a public access network that connects various devices or terminals throughout, extending the real world, based on the mentioned technologies, can only increase the use of all technologies and consequently also the ecological impact.

Finally, we would like to quote Hwang's definition of the metaverse [11]: *"The metaverse has been recognized as being the next generation of social connection. It refers to a created world, in which people can "live" under the rules defined by the creator. A metaverse could be fully or partially virtual; for example, it could be a fully virtual world like a virtual reality (VR) system, or a partially virtual world like the use of augmented realty (AR) in real-world contexts. In the metaverse space, people can engage in social activities such as discussing an issue, collaborating on a project, playing games, and learning from experiencing or solving some problems."*

But are we sure that all these benefits are not already realized with "the current Internet"?

IV. CONCLUSION

Despite the enthusiasm and clear benefits of using metaverse, we must always maintain a global perspective and consider all the issues associated with the use of technology. Data use, training ethics and environmental impact are just some of the issues that should not be underestimated in the conscious adoption of these innovations for training activities.

Increasingly, companies and training institutions need to understand the global impact of their methodological and technological choices in the virtual world have on the real world. This paper represents the beginning of a corporate consideration of how facing emerging technologies. The next steps of this research will aim to measure the carbon footprint of all digital training products and include it in its quality assurance programs and ESG (Enviromental Social Governance) policy.

ACKNOWLEDGMENTS

Sincere thanks to the management of Piazza Copernico, a digital learning company that decided to adopt a strong ESG policy and supports the prosecution of this research.

REFERENCES

[1] M. A. C. Aguayo, "Democratization of creativity and cultural production in virtual worlds: A new challenge for regulation and cultural management" in: SLACTIONS 2009 International Conference: Life, imagination, and work using metaverse platforms: Proceedingsof the SLACTIONS 2009 International Conference. Universidade de Trás-os-Montes e Alto Douro, p. 53-59, 2009. https://dialnet.unirioja.es/descarga/libro/851957.pdf

[2] B. Barahona, J. Ranilla and E. Gallardo-Echenique, "The communication in simulated learning environments" in Revista Iberoamericana de Educación, Vol. 72, no. 2, 85-101, 2016.

[3] P. Chan, T. Van Gerven, J. L. Dubois, and K. Bernaerts, "Virtual chemical laboratories: A systematic literature review of research, technologies and instructional design" in Computers and Education Open, Vol. 2, no. 100053, 2021.

[4] P. M. Dewantara, I. W. Rasna, and I. B. Putrayasa, "Flexible Learning & Pendidikan Karakter: Refleksi Pembelajaran Bahasa Indonesia di Masa Pandemi Covid-19. Global Aksara Pers, 2022.

[5] J. Díaz, C. Saldaña and C. Avila, "Virtual world as a resource for hybrid education" in International Journal of Emerging Technologies in Learning (iJET), Vol. 15, no. 15, pp. 94-109, 2020. https://www.learntechlib.org/p/217986

[6] C. Firenzani, Average Water Consumption, The Ranking Of Italy's Most Wasteful Cities. Truenumbers, 17 Sept. 2021, https://www.truenumbers.it/consumo-medio-acqua/.

[7] T. N. Fitria and N. E., Simbolon, "Possibility of Metaverse in Education: Opportunity and Threat" in Sosmaniora: Jurnal Ilmu Sosial Dan Humaniora, Vol. 1, no. 3, pp. 365-375. 2022. DOI: 10.55123/sosmanior.v1i3.821

[8] L. Gibbons, 5 Ways the Metaverse Can Help with the Climate Crisis. 4 Aug. 2022, https://www.blockleaders.io/news/5-ways-the-metaverse-can-help-with-the-climate-crisis.

[9] C. Girvan, "What is a virtual world? Definition and classification" in Educational Technology Research and Development, Vol,. 66, no. 5, pp. 1087–1100, 2018. https://doi.org/10.1007/s11423-018-9577-y

[10] U. Hölzle, "Our Commitment to Climate-Conscious Data Center Cooling." Google, Google, 21 Nov. 2022, https://blog.google/outreach-initiatives/sustainability/our-commitment-to-climate-conscious-data-center-cooling/.

[11] G. J. Hwang, and S. Y. Chien, "Definition, roles, and potential research issues of the metaverse in education: An artificial intelligence perspective" in Computers and Education: Artificial Intelligence. Vol. 3, no. 100082, 2022. Elsevier BV. https://doi.org/10.1016/j.caeai.2022.100082

[12] J. H. Kim, B. S. Lee, and S. J Choi, "A study on metaverse construction and use cases for non-face-to-face education" in The Journal of the Convergence on Culture Technology, Vol. 8, no. 1, pp. 483–497, 2022. https://doi.org/10.17703/JCCT.2022.8.1.483

[13] B. Kye, N. Han, E. Kim, Y. Park and S. Jo, "Educational applications of metaverse: possibilities and limitations" in Journal of Educational Evaluation for Health Professions, Vol. 18, pp. 1-13, 2021. https://doi.org/10.3352/jeehp.2021.18.32

[14] A. Lehikko, "Measuring self-efficacy in immersive virtual learning environments: a systematic literature review" in Journal of Interactive Learning Research, Vol. 32, no. 2, pp. 125-146, 2021.

[15] M. Y. Mughal, N. Andleeb, A. F. A. Khurram, M. Y. Ali, M. S. Aslam, and M. N. Saleem, "Perceptions of teaching-learning force about metaverse for education: a qualitative study" in Journal of Positive School Psychology, Vol. 6, no. 9, pp. 1738-1745, 2022.

[16] S. Mystakidis, Metaverse. Encyclopedia, Vol. 2, no. 1, pp. 486–497, 2022. https://doi.org/10.3390/encyclopedia2010031

[17] D. T. K. Ng, "What is Metaverse? Definitions, technologies and the community of inquiry" in Australasian Journal of Educational Technology, Vol. 38, no. 4, 2022.

[18] D. Patterson, J. Gonzalez, Q. Le, C. Liang, L. M. Munguia, D. Rothchild, D. So, M. Texier and J. Dean, "Carbon Emissions and Large Neural Network Training (Version 3)" in arXiv:2104.10350, 2021. https://doi.org/10.48550/ARXIV.2104.10350

[19] D. Pimentel, G. Fauville, K. Frazier, E. McGivney, S. Rosas and E. Woolsey, An introduction to learning in the metaverse. Meridian Treehouse, 2022.

[20] C. Reyes, "Perception of high school students about using Metaverse in augmented reality learning experiences in mathematics" in Pixel Bit - Revista De Medios Y Educación, Vol. 58, 143-159, 2020. https://doi.org/10.12795/pixelbit.74367

[21] E. Schlemmer, D. Trein and C. Oliveira, "The metaverse: Telepresence in 3D avatar-driven digital-virtual worlds" in @ tic. Revista d'Innovació Educativa, Vol. 2, pp. 26-32, 2009. https://www.redalyc.org/pdf/3495/349532298005.pdf

[22] N. Stephenso, Snow Crash (First ed.). New York, N.Y. Bantam Books. 1992.

[23] E. Strubell, A. Ganesh and A. McCallum, "Energy and Policy Considerations for Deep Learning in NLP" in Proceedings of the 57th Annual Meeting of the Association for Computational Linguistics, pp. 3645–3650, 2019, https://doi.org/10.18653/v1/p19-1355.

[24] X. Zhai, X. Chu and M. J.Wang, "Educational metaverse: The shape challenges and reflections of the new generation of internet education" in Open Education Research, Vol. 28, no. 1, pp. 34-42. 2022.

[25] Bitcoin Energy Consumption Index, Digiconomist, 6 Dec. 2022, https://digiconomist.net/bitcoin-energy-consumption.

[26] Cambridge Bitcoin Electricity Consumption Index (CBECI). CCAF.io, https://ccaf.io/cbeci/index.

[27] Digital Sufficiency - Lean ICT: For a Sober Digital. The Shift Project, 5 Mar. 2021, https://theshiftproject.org/en/lean-ict-2/.

[28] "The Metaverse: What Are the Environmental Impacts & Future." Dataquest, 25 May 2022, https://www.dqindia.com/the-metaverse-what-are-the-environmental-impacts-future/

Learning Time Patterns: Many Study Times To Consider When Designing Digital Learning

Sara Zuzzi, Laura Ducci, Claudia Falconio, Daniela Pellegrini
Research and Development Division
Piazza Copernico s.r.l.
Roma, Italy
emails: {szuzzi, lducci, cfalconio, dpellegrini} @pcopernico.it

Mario Santoro
Istituto per le Applicazioni del Calcolo
Consiglio nazionale delle Ricerche
Roma, Italy
email: m.santoro@iac.cnr.it

***Abstract*—One of the most important issues in digital learning is understanding the time dimension and its impact on the design and study of different teaching methodologies. This paper analyses learning time from user data to identify the relationships between performance, methods used and the characteristics of learning materials. This paper investigates aspects oflearning time for three different methodologies: smartlearning; videolearning; tutorial-storytelling. The analysis shows that tutorial-storytelling is an appropriate and effective methodology from multiple perspectives; smartlearning does not guarantee completion or an adequate study pace and uses time; videolearning is positioned in an intermediate level: it performs well, with a more than satisfactory results, but in the face of more difficult and strenuous study, so there is ample room for improvement in this type of course from a technical and a purely methodological point of view.**

***Keywords*—Learning KPI; Learning Times; Digital Learning Design**

I. Introduction

Learning time is a key factor in any training project. In particular, it is crucial in digital learning and all self-led learning projects. In addition, study time also drives in the digital content market, just as it does for the enjoyment of in-depth content (e.g., estimated reading time in newspaper articles, time listening to an audio or viewing a video) and is at the same time also a factor in motivation and engagement. However, there are many dimensions of time in an online course to be taken into account and better investigated (Figure 1):

- technical time, i.e., the running time of an instructional resource measured in minutes/hours;
- organizational time, i.e., availability of teaching resources (time of course opening);
- individual study time (dedicated time) overall and per session, also related to personal characteristics (learning style), availabilities, engagement, and reporting time;
- learning time (related to understanding and acquisition of content);
- commercial time (standard duration).

Therefore, effectively designing the time of a course and defining access rules is a nontrivial problem for the instructional designer.

Another emerging theme is the diversity between intrinsic study times and those provided by teaching materials in different methodologies. Video learning, webinars, and digital materials involve different instructional dynamics specific to each methodology. Investigating time differences means being able to give instructional designers clearer information to design teaching, taking into account cognitive load and usage patterns of training materials. In Section II we briefly review models of learning times in literature. In Section III we describe the courses' data and the methods of analysis. In the following Section IV, we will describe our main results on learning time patterns. Finally, in Section V, we will present our findings and some lines for future works.

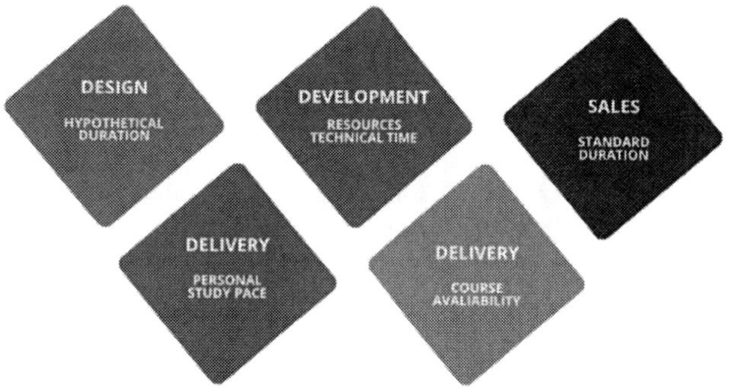

Figure 1: The different dimensions of time.

II. The different times in learning

Time is an essential variable to be investigated in understanding learning processes, as it is an important predictor of learning outcomes. However, it is still little studied [1]. Time patterns are crucial to understanding the factors contributing to effective learning. As collected by Cortès et al.[2], several studies assess the impact of time on:

- outcomes: group exercises or discussions/sharing tend to improve training outcomes [3]. Outcomes include both satisfaction and knowledge acquisition;
- satisfaction: time use is a factor in measuring satisfaction with a course [4][5];
- learning: participants who devote adequate time per week to study have better satisfaction. Knowledge transfer is associated with time spent online per day studying.

Participants who spend more time daily online (social and internet) have more significant levels of learning. Then time spent on academic tasks during the day is associated with more learning (mainly using the morning hours). More digitized users (more hours online) have skills in applying knowledge to different contexts (both academic and work) [2].

According to [6], learning is related to prior experience with distance learning, individual preferences, and average study time. More interest has been devoted to analyzing study hours over available time. Time-of-day (TOD) is a valuable key to understanding differences in use/access to courses and devices.

Some studies delve into learning time patterns, using instructional conditions [7], i.e., the way courses are delivered and the level of autonomy or individual organization [8]. Stockwell [9] highlights how students use different study modes based on other times of the day and devices used. For example, Casany et al. [10] highlighted the greater use of mobile devices at night.

Sher et al. [11] point out that the study and the modes used to depend on the time of day it is carried out. In particular, there are better results for students who used different methodologies to perform the assigned tasks (with a predominance of computer and intensive learner type). Intensive learners, such as users with little use of technology, did not show significant differences in study days but significantly different results. The study showed that computer use for students is related to a meticulous mode of study [9] compared to mobile service for tasks that require precision. Students who used multiple study modes and tools tended to use them during the daytime, preferring the computer during nighttime hours. Online study sessions are primarily performed in the afternoon for all students [10], identifying this behavior as related to students' commuting hours on campus.

The temporal dimension is, therefore, a source of information about learning patterns that can help support learners and improve the accuracy and reproducibility of the predictivity of learning outcomes [1]. These studies are also critical to understanding how to design learning paths, test the most effective and agile teaching methodologies based on content, and make the use of time explicit for the learner to equip themselves with strategies for effectiveness and efficiency in studying.

From the perspective of content creators, the time concerns the commercial duration of the courses and the availability of the license. It follows that it is essential to make explicit all dimensions of time in training to effectively govern this variable in the different steps of the life of an online course. Therefore, time is a very complex variable composed of different measures.

A comparative examination between teaching methodologies of adequate study time (i.e., related to passing final tests) is proposed in this article to investigate whether different patterns of time of use, behavior, and performance are present, the latter analyzed with the LearnalyzeR tool [12]. The findings will be helpful in both the design and organizational phases.

III. Data and Methods

The study involved a sample of different methodologies courses on a client's (insurance company). The courses are delivered over the past year. The data are representative of the types of courses listed in the Piazza Copernico srl catalog.

The teaching methodologies analyzed were:

- **Videolearning**: an effective type of Digital Learning Course designed according to various levels of complexity. Divided into two groups:
  - *Graphic videos*, very suitable for explaining short concepts clearly and simply and creating stories. More or less sophisticated graphic input depending on the client's needs.
  - *Teaching Pills* (videos with actors)video-Lessons with a lecturer or actor playing a lecturer, made at a desk, or otherwise with static filming.
- **Smartlearning**: particularly useful for print and offline study. The development involves transposing the client slides onto SCORM content pages plotted within LMS, using special authoring tools, with an accompanying narrative voice created by a professional (multimedia) speaker.
- **Tutorial_storytelling**: is mainly used for training and updating different types of content, technical manuals, description of procedures, and corporate information. Content pages come with text, images, graphics, and audio. The movement of elements on the page results from animated effects of graphics chosen from an internal library. Games with low-complexity interactions, test pages, and exercises also selected from a predefined internal library can be provided, taking into account customer needs and learning objectives. Similar is the Storytelling version suitable for training and updating on different types of content, soft skills, business processes, corporate reporting, regulations, and safety. This type involves a high level of multimedia, animation of objects and interaction types (SVG), case scripts, and stories that provide concreteness to the content covered.

Twelve courses of the same client of three different types were analyzed: smartlearning (5 courses for a total of 5 editions, 7052 users), tutorial_storytelling (3 courses for a total of 4 editions, 3545 users), videolearning (4 courses for a total 8 of editions, 5605 users); participants took the courses in the year 2022; the selection neglected editions with less than 10 participants.

Starting from the use of the LearnalyzeR tool [12], which analyzes critical issues by supporting tutor intervention on a day-to-day basis and divides the users of a course into performance classes, the present investigation turned toward the study of the Macro Performance Index (MIP) (composite index) by investigating its different aspects (sub-indicators): Results (I_R), Study Pace (I_{SP}), Course Structure (I_{CS}), Computer Adequacy (I_{CA}) (composite sub-indicators), and finally highlighting, with a descriptive analysis, the link between these indicators, time of use and course types.

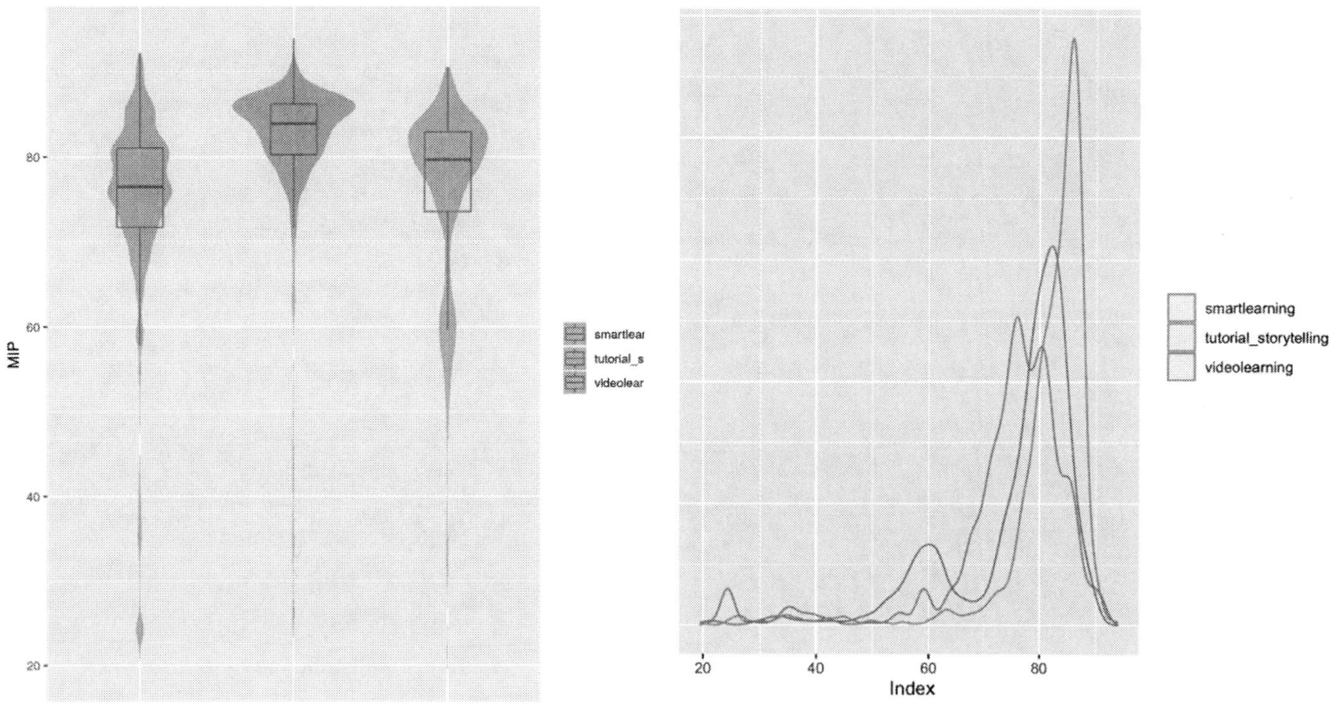

(a) Violin-Box-Plot

(b) Continuos Distribution

Figure 2: MIP distribution by course type.

As mentioned above, the LearnalyzeR tool calculates the MIP and divides users into performance classes: Lukers (MIP=[0;30)), Latecomers (MIP=[30;50)), Regulars (MIP=[50;70)), Hard Workers (MIP=[70;80)), Top Performers (MIP=[80;100]).

The performance index was constructed with the interaction of a group (panel) of individuals (experts) who identified all aspects (indicators) of the phenomenon (the perfomace); using the same method, a set of independent variables were identified for each indicator, which could be obtained from the platform data. Once the indicators and variables were defined, the weighted arithmetic mean was chosen as the aggregation function and the Analytic Hierarchy Process (AHP) [13] was used to calculate the weights. This method makes it possible to understand opinions on a specific topic without complicating matters for the respondent. By processing the answers, it allows the decision-making process of the weights to be constructed.

IV. Results

A first exploration analysis for the relations between MIP and courses type shows:

- **Smartlearning courses**. From Figure 2a, there is a broadened peak around 80 and a few pegs in the left tail (red line); analyzing Figure 2b, the MIP shifted toward performance values below 80, with a median at 76, so at least 50% of users have performance values below that; there is also a long tail down where at least 25% of users have performance below 71. In these courses, at least 50% of users are not at a MIP level above the Regulars class.
- **Storytelling Tutorial courses**. From Figure 2, one can observe a narrow peak above 80 (green line); in Figure 2b, the MIP shifted toward performance values above 80 (median 83) with a fairly homogeneous behavior of the population (narrow distribution); 75% of the users have performance between 80 and 86, so they belong to the Top Performers class.
- **Vidolearning courses**. From Figure 2a, one can observe different levels of performance: a narrow peak around 80 and a second peak around 60 (blue line); analyzing Figure 2b, the MIP is around 80 (median 79), and there is a consistent tail down; however, at least 75% of the users have performance above 73. In this type of course, despite the unevenness of performance, at least 75% of the users are above the Regulars class.

An exploratory analysis was carried out to identify the reasons for the observed performance by relating the sub-indicators, which constitute the MIP, to the type of course. The following was obtained:

Results (I_R)

- **Smartlearning**. From Figure 3, we observe a pronounced problem in the indicator I~R, the behavior of users for this indicator is uneven, and four main types of behavior

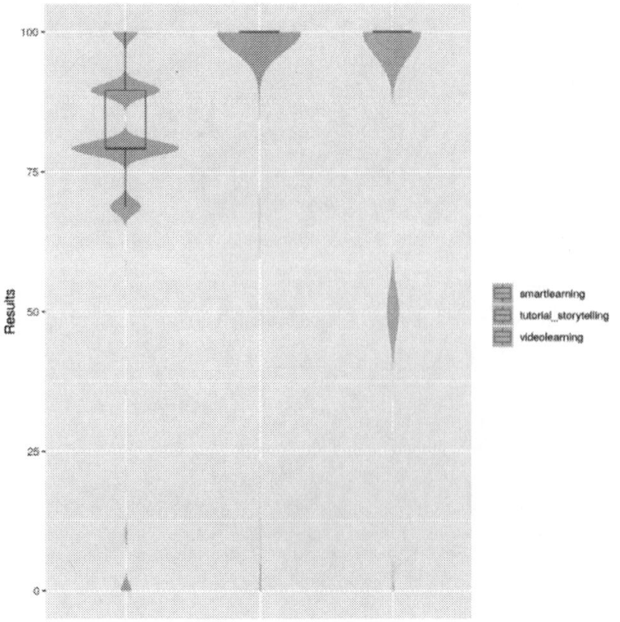

Figure 3: I_R distribution by course type.

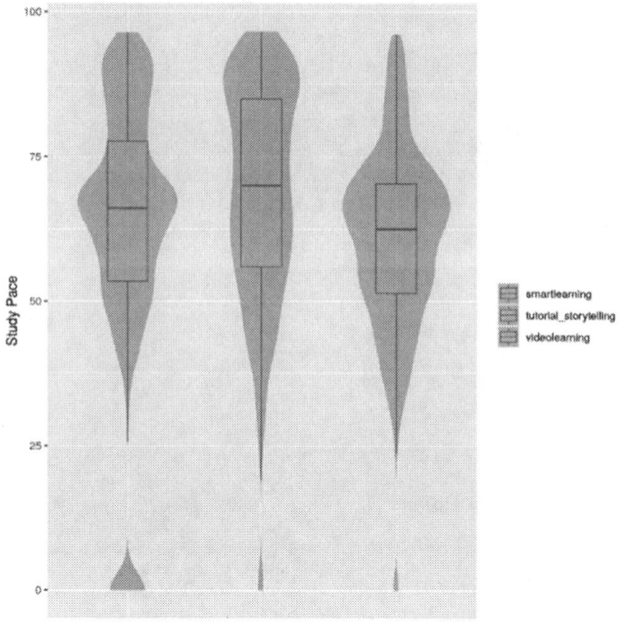

Figure 4: I_{SP} distribution by course type.

are presented. At least 25% of users have an IR indicator value of 79, and only 25% have a value above 89. Only a small number of users (about 8%) reach the value of 100; analyzing the I_R indicator [12], it is observed that this criticality is due to the variable course completion.

- **Tutorial_storytelling**.The participants have homogeneous behavior. At least 75% of the users have an I_R sub-index value of 100 (Figure 3).
- **Videolearning**. Participants have a rather homogeneous behavior. At least 75% of the users have a sub-index value I_R of 100; however, there is a tail downward at sub-index values around 50 (Figure 3), indicating a problem completing the course for a group of users (about 10%).

Analyzing the problems encountered in smartlearning courses for the indicator I_R shows that in all methods of this type, there is a completion problem. In all smartlearning editions, at least 75% of users do not complete the course. While in videolearning courses, there is a problem with one specific edition (361 participants) in which at least 30% of users do not complete the course. So in smartlearning courses, the characteristic of not completing is widely spread in the population under analysis. At the same time, for videolearning, it is a point problem with a single edition.

Study Pace (I_{SP})

From Figure 4, one can observe that:

- In **smartlearning** courses, the median of I_{SP} is 66 with a tail downward.
- In **tutorial_storytelling** courses, the median I_{SP} is 69 with a very elongated distribution structure, but at least 25% of the users have an I_{SP} value above 84 (3rd quartile).
- in **videolearning** courses, the median I_{SP} value is 66 with a tail downward, and only a small number of users have an ISP value above 75 (a tapering upward shape of the blue distribution), at least 75% of users have an I_{SP} value below 70.

All course types have a very uneven behavior for Study Pace, with values tending to the low end, more evident in videolearning.

The sub-indicator I_{SP} is highly dependent on the fruition time, the quantity we want to study. By analyzing the trend of fruition time concerning the expected time of the course structure, it is better to define the *Normalized Use Time* (**NUT** = fruition time/expected time) quantity. One can observe that all three types of the course show uneven fruition behavior (Figure 5), as for the I_{SP} index.

In particular:

- **Smartlearning**, at least 25% of users, in all editions, have a fruition time less than the time assumed in the course structure (the I quartile of NUT per edition varies between 0.7 and 0.9); at least 50% of the users have a fruition time equal to the time assumed in the course structure (median NUT for editions is around 1.02); finally, for two editions (of 516 and 1799 users) at least 25% of the users have a fruition time consistently greater than that assumed (3rd quartile of NUT between 1.6 and 1.7).
- **Tutorial_storytelling**, at least 50% of users have a time roughly equal to that assumed in the course structure (median NUT for editions varies between 0.9 and 1.2), but at least 25% of users have a longer time (3rd quartile of NUT between 1.8 and 2.0). The latter mainly concentrated on two courses (1619 and 1882 users).

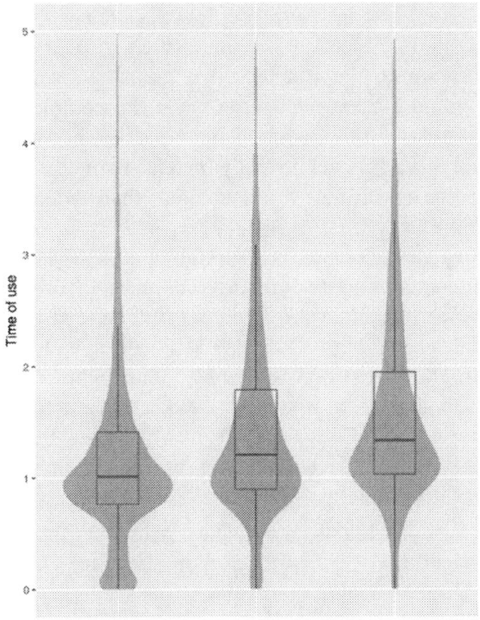

Figure 5: NUT distribution by course type.

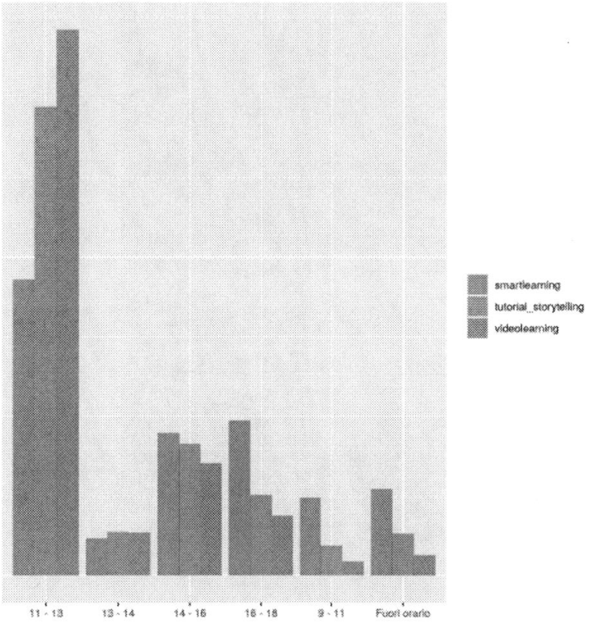

Figure 6: Distribution of connections by time slot and course type.

- **Videolearning**, at least 25% of the users, in all editions, have a fruition time roughly equal to the time assumed in the course structure (NUT varies between 0.9 and 1.2). In contrast, in two editions, the first quartile has NUT values between 1.5 and 1.7 (361 and 302 users, respectively). Looking at the median, 50% of the users have a NUT between 1.5 and 2.8; these participants are in 4 editions (11, 302, 361, and 2565 participants, respectively). For all editions, at least 25% of users consistently use more time than assumed in the course structure (3rd quartile of NUT between 1.6 and 4.3).

To summarize, in all course types, there is evidence of a long time in a significant percentage of the population. However, while it is present in smartlearning and tutorial_storytelling for a few courses/editions, on videolearning, it is widespread across all courses. Finally, in smartlearnig, it is observed that a substantial percentage have a shorter than expected completion time. This fits what was observed in the Results indicator analysis, as course completion is critical for this type of course.

For completeness of analysis, a view of the sub-indices Course Structure (I_{CS}) and Computer Adequacy (I_{CA}) by course type:

- The $\mathbf{I_{CS}}$ indicator in the **smartlearning** type has an identical value of 63 for all editions (medium complexity); **videolearning** also has a homogeneous complexity with I_{CS} between 50 and 57 (medium-low complexity), while the **tutorial_storytelling** editions have a very uneven structure of low complexity (about 55% of users take courses with an I_{CS} value of 39) and medium-high complexity (about 45% of users an I_{CS} value of 75).
- In **smartlearning** and **tutorial_storytelling** courses, there is a good **Computer Adequacy** (I_{CA} greater than 90), only 25% of the users with a value of I_{CA} less than 90 (1st quartile: smartlearning I_{CA}= 89, tutorial_storytelling I_{CA} = 84); while for **videolearning** courses at least 50% of users have I_{CA} values less than 89 and even at least 25% are below 79. The problems relate to linking and uploading videos; those critical issues are present in all the videolearning editions under analysis (except one).

Then, the analysis of the time slots and days of the week by course type give:

- From Figure 6 and Figure 7, for all course types, there is a utilization preference for the 11 a.m.-1 p.m. time slot (the off-hours time slot has a low, but not zero, link frequency), while there is no difference in link frequency for weekdays (holidays have a low, but not zero, link frequency).
- From the exploratory analysis so far, it can be inferred that the videolearnig course type has a criticality of a long time more evident than the other types because it is spread over all editions, with an issue related to linking and video uploading; in a subsequent analysis, it will be investigated whether and how these two criticalities are associated with each other. In contrast, the smartlearnig course type has a widespread completion issue across all editions.

Finally, a heatmap (Figure 8) is presented to get an overview of the above analysis. Looking at Figure 8, patterns between course types emerge:

- **Smartlearning courses:** all have the same complexity (always the exact value of I_{CS}), and, in general, users do

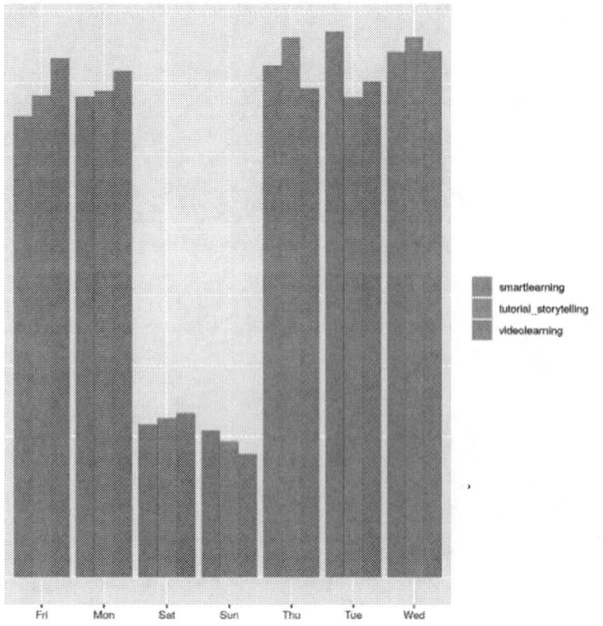

Figure 7: Distribution of connections by day and course type.

not have Computer Adequacy (I_{CA}) problems, but there are different patterns for Performace (MIP), Results (I_R), Study Pace (I_{SP}) and Normalized Use Time (NUT). Low values of MIP are found at dark I_R and I_{SP} (low values) and very dark NUT (less than expected fruition time); therefore, poor performance (MIP with low values) is a consequence of less than expected fruition time. There are bands where I_R and I_{SP} alternate between light and dark. There are good I_{SP} (light bands) at adequate NUT (fruition time around the expected time), but low I_R values (dark bands) or conversely low I_{SP} values (dark bands) at high NUT (fruition time much greater than the expected time), but good I_R (light bands). It can be concluded that to achieve the required results, it is necessary to have a greater fruition time than expected.

- **Tutorial_storytelling** courses users do not have particular Computer Adequacy (I_{CA}) problems, patterns of Performace (MIP), Results (I_R), Study Pace (I_{SP}), Course Structure (I_{CS}), and Normalized Use Time (NUT) can be seen. A very narrow band has low MIP values corresponding to dark I_R and I_{SP} (low values), a very dark NUT (fruition time less than expected time), and low complexity; this can be said to be punctual because this aggregate contains a small number of users. The most full-bodied aggregate is a trend of I_R with good values (users achieve the required results, clear band) but with bands in which I_{SP} and I_{CS} alternate between light and dark. It is possible to highlight that when there is low complexity (low I_{CS}, dark band), there is good I_{SP} (light band) and adequate NUT (fruition time equal to the expected time). In contrast, for more complex courses (high I_{CS}, light band), there are low I_{SP} values (dark band) and high NUT (fruition time much greater than the expected time). We conclude that the results can be achieved within the expected time when the complexity is low. At the same time, when the complexity increases, the required results are achieved by increasing the fruition time from one and a half times to more than twice the expected time.
- The **videolearning** courses have similar complexity (I_{CS}), but the patterns are more confusing. There are cases with low MIP values, despite good I_R corresponding to low I_{CA} and I_{SP} values and a high NUT; low MIP values, with low I_R values (dark bands) corresponding to adequate or too high NUT. In general, compared to the other course types, it is observed that NUT values are much clearer, thus a much longer than expected time of use and Computer Adequacy with problems (low values of I_{CA}).

In Figure 8, we can also observe dendrograms. On the left are aggregations of users by MIP level in the three-course types; at the top are the two aggregates of sub-indexes: I_{CA} with IR and I_{SP} with I_{CS}.

V. CONCLUSIONS

The analysis shows that **storytelling** is an appropriate and effective methodology from multiple perspectives, which performs best regardless of content and editions. One point of attention is the complexity of the structure directly related to the spent study time. It is also clear that smartlearning satisfies the needs for low time-to-market and low impact on the training budget, but it responds less well in terms of results achieved, with lower performance indices (MIP). The simplicity of the course, in terms of instructional design and methodological format, on the one hand,encourages the use of courses outside of working hours, but on the other hand, it does not guarantee completion or an adequate study pace and uses time. The risks associated with using smartlearning in training can be traced to potential problems with staff preparation and additional costs associated with necessary re-training.

Videolearning is positioned at an intermediate level: it performs well, with more than satisfactory results, but in the face of more difficult and strenuous study. In the unevenness of some of the data, there is ample room for improvement in this type of course:

- from a technical point of view, for example, the increasing enhancement of storage and delivery infrastructures for video content, both server-side and client-side, can make the Computer Adequacy values higher;
- from a purely methodological point of view, to manage the high value of uses time, instructional designs can distribute the "weight" of the topics and include more interactions, useful to scan the individual study time and create moments of self-assessment and knowledge reinforcement.

Starting from this analysis on the time issue in e-learning, always open and little explored on data, there emerges the need

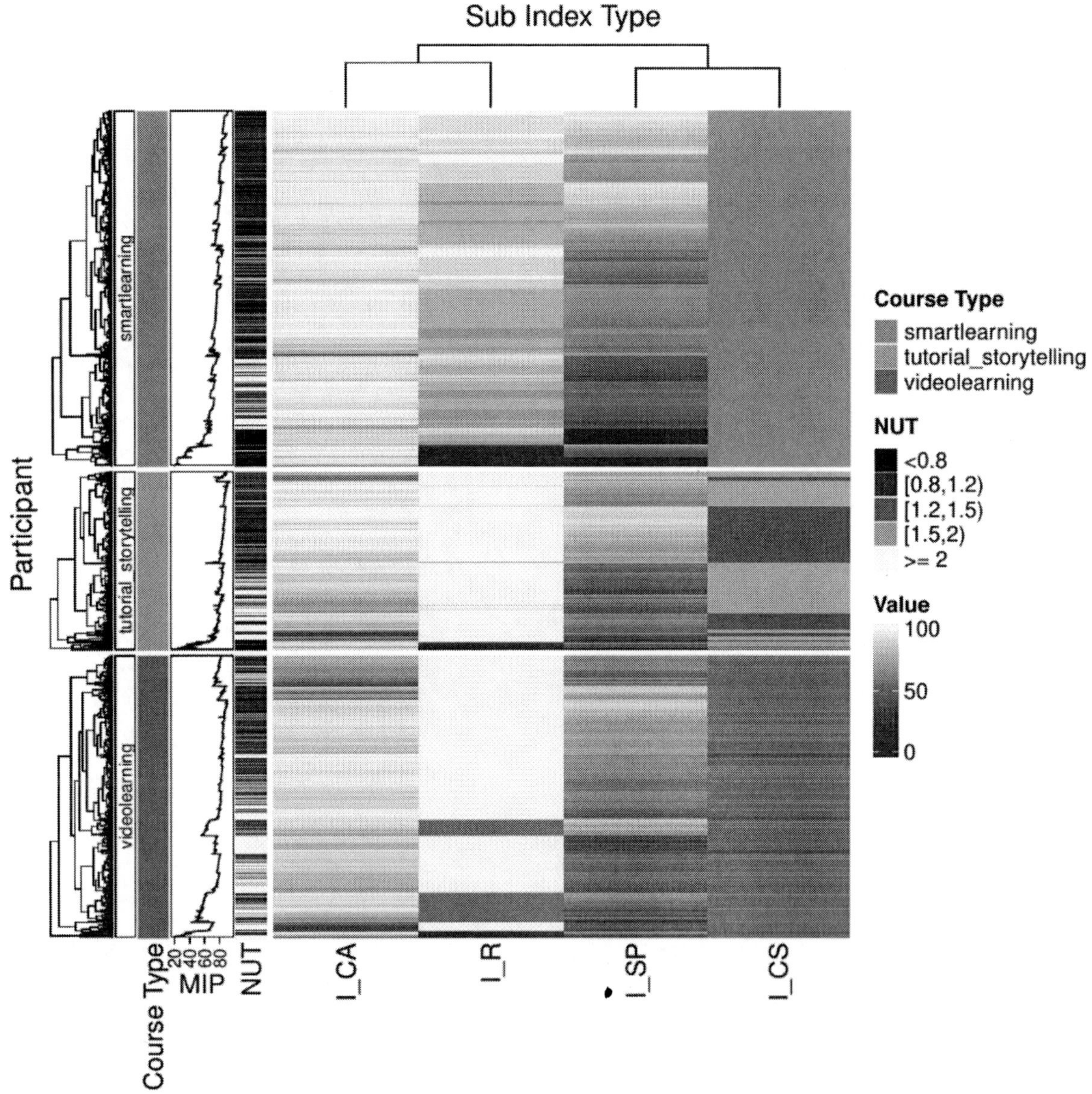

Figure 8: Heatmap. The quantities on the horizontal axis at the bottom are: Course Type (smartlearning, tutorial_storytelling, videolearning); Macro Index of Performance (MIP) is a continuous variable; the scale grows from left to the right, so the (left) peaks represent low values of MIP; Normalized Use Time (NUT), a variable divided into classes as reported in the legend; in the defined intervals the square bracket indicates that the extreme is included, the round bracket that the extreme is excluded. Computer Adequacy (I_{CA}), Results (I~R), Study Pace (I_{SP}), Course Structure (I_{CS}). On the left and top, the observed dendrograms define aggregates of users and sub-indexes, respectively.

to continue the research including in the analysis framework other information, such as the period of fruition; the perceived usefulness to understand the impact of the time learning patterns identified for types and formats of multimedia courses. This analysis will be extended to other instructional methodologies (classroom, game, webinar) because the goal is to give time its proper value for designers, salespeople, and end-users who must have adequate time to learn, i.e, the month of the year in which the course is opened; the characteristics of the target audience; the content, i.e., the thematic area; the connecting device; the perceived usefulness to understand the impact the time learning patterns identified for types and formats of multimedia courses. This analysis will be extended to other instructional methodologies (classroom, game, webinar) because the goal is to give time its proper value for designers, salespeople, and end-users who must have adequate time to learn.

REFERENCES

[1] M. Saqr, J. Nouri, and U. Fors, "Time to focus on the temporal dimension of learning: A learning analytics study of the temporal patterns of students' interactions and self-regulation," *Int. J. Technol. Enhanc. Learn.*, vol. 11, no. 4, pp. 398–412, Jan. 2019, doi: 10.1504/ijtel.2019.102549. [Online]. Available: https://doi.org/10.1504/ijtel.2019.102549

[2] A. Cortés and B. Elena, "Time patterns and perceptions of online learning success factors," *eLearn Center Research Paper Series*, no. 7, pp. 39–48, Jan. 2013 [Online]. Available: https://raco.cat/index.php/eLearn/article/view/272018

[3] C. Zhu, "Student satisfaction, performance, and knowledge construction in online collaborative learning," *Journal of Educational Technology and Society*, vol. 15, no. 1, pp. 127–136, 2012.

[4] P. Arneberg *et al.*, "Analyses of european megaproviders of e-learning," *Megatrends Project*, 2007.

[5] S. Y. McGorry, "Measuring quality in online programs," *The Internet and Higher Education*, vol. 6, no. 2, pp. 159–177, 2003.

[6] D. H. Lim and M. L. Morris, "Learner and instructional factors influencing learning outcomes within a blended learning environment," *Journal of Educational Technology and Society*, vol. 12, no. 4, pp. 282–293, 2009.

[7] A. van Leeuwen, N. Bos, H. van Ravenswaaij, and J. van Oostenrijk, "The role of temporal patterns in students' behavior for predicting course performance: A comparison of two blended learning courses," *British Journal of Educational Technology*, vol. 50, no. 2, pp. 921–933, 2019.

[8] J. Malmberg, S. Järvelä, and H. Järvenoja, "Capturing temporal and sequential patterns of self-, co-, and socially shared regulation in the context of collaborative learning," *Contemporary Educational Psychology*, vol. 49, pp. 160–174, 2017.

[9] G. Stockwell, "Tracking learner usage of mobile phones for language learning outside of the classroom," *Calico Journal*, vol. 30, pp. 118–136, 2013.

[10] M. J. Casany Guerrero, M. Alier Forment, N. Galanis, E. Mayol Sarroca, and J. Piguillem Poch, "Analyzing moodle/LMS logs to measure mobile access," in *UBICOMM 2012: The sixth international conference on mobile ubiquitous computing, systems, services and technologies*, 2012, pp. 35–40.

[11] V. Sher, M. Hatala, and D. Gašević, "When do learners study? An analysis of the time-of-day and weekday-weekend usage patterns of learning management systems from mobile and computers in blended learning," *Journal of Learning Analytics*, vol. 9, no. 2, pp. 1–23, 2022.

[12] D. Pellegrini, M. Santoro, and S. Zuzzi, "Learning analytics and governance of the digital learning process." in *teleXbe*, 2021.

[13] R. W. Saaty, "The analytic hierarchy process—what it is and how it is used," *Mathematical modelling*, vol. 9, no. 3–5, pp. 161–176, 1987.

Accessibility in E-learning: From Inclusive Choice to Universal Training

Saverio Santulli Sanzo, Marta Federici, Silvio Meconi, Daniele Consorti, Alice Antonello, Giuseppina Somma, Antonio L'Abbate, Claudia Falconio

Digital Course Development Area
Piazza Copernico s.r.l.
Rome, Italy
email produzione@pcopernico.it

***Abstract* - This article discusses the topic of digital accessibility as the ability of information systems to deliver usable services and provide usable information, avoiding any form of discrimination, including that oriented toward those who require assistive technologies or special computer configurations due to disabilities or unsuitable environmental conditions. In this paper, the experience of the Piazza Copernico's development team is explained in regarding the implementation of an accessible and usable course. The paper shows the complexity of this topic and the main solutions implemented in a real example to guarantee an effective inclusive learning environment.**

Keywords–Accessibility; Usability; Disability; Inclusion; E-learning; Universal design

I. INTRODUCTION

The topic of accessibility has recently come into the spotlight because, thanks to current regulatory and societal changes globally, more and more people with disabilities can access opportunities that they were previously denied.

The official definition of disability was provided by the World Health Organization (WHO), which defines it as: "any restriction or deficiency (resulting from an impairment) in the ability to perform an activity in the manner and within the limits considered normal for a human being" [1]. However, it is important to emphasize that disabilities should not be regarded as a disease or defect, but a natural part of human diversity. Therefore, individuals with disabilities have the right to take full part in the society that, for a long time, has been structured on standards commonly considered "normal. "Disabilities can be of different types and degrees and may be present from birth or acquired as a result of illness, accident, or aging. Sensory disabilities, such as blindness and deafness, limit the ability to see or hear and consequently may limit the ability to learn and interact. In addition to sense organ impairment, physical, mental, and intellectual limitations are also to be considered.

Respect for and inclusion of all is a social responsibility and, as such, must be made explicit in all contexts of an individual's life. One of the areas to work on to achieve this goal concerns training and, more specifically, e-learning. This area requires special attention to design and develop accessible e-learning training, it is necessary to take into account the many difficulties that any individual may face. For example, those with visual impairments often find themselves in the condition of not being able to enjoy effective learning, either because of the traditional use of images and graphics that are significant for the achievement of training objectives, or because of instructions to be displayed in the interface employed to facilitate navigability in the course. From this and other needs we are seeing a proliferation of accessibility technology regulations and guidelines, which increasingly promote the design of accessible online platforms and content for all users. So, for Piazza Copernico it rapidly became a topic to be studied to promote correct solutions to manage learning and promote inclusive learning digital materials and courses, accordingly to D&I policy in company itself and clients' requirements.

II. ITALIAN REGULATION

The increasingly imminent need to make digital environments accessible is regulated in Italy by Law No. 4 of January 9, 2004 (Stanca Law) [2], which establishes provisions to facilitate and simplify access to digital tools for users in general and people with disabilities in particular. The constitutional framework on which this law is based is Article 3 of the Italian Constitution, as it is based on the principle of equality and social dignity. In Art. 3 of Law 4/2004, moreover, the addressees are specified, namely:

- public administrations.
- public economic entities.
- private companies that are concessionaires of public services.
- public welfare and rehabilitation institutions.
- transport and telecommunications companies with majority public capital participation.
- regional municipal utilities and IT service contractor companies.

Thanks to Law 4/2004, it is possible to obtain a more objective framework regarding definitions, particularly of "accessibility," understood as: "the ability of information systems, in the forms and to the extent permitted by technological knowledge, to deliver services and provide information usable, without discrimination, even by those who due to disabilities require assistive technologies or special configurations" (Law 4/2004) [2]. The law also provides an accurate definition of "assistive technologies" in terms of: "technical tools and solutions, hardware and software, that allow the disabled person, overcoming or reducing the conditions of disadvantage, to access information and services provided by information systems" (Law 4/2004) [2].

III. WEB CONTENT ACCESSIBILITY GUIDELINES (WCAG) AND E-LEARNING STANDARD

The spread of the offer in services and courses delivered largely via the Web and aimed at post-secondary or vocational training rose the need for authorities to adopt recognized standards to enable their quality certification [3][4]. The International Standard Organization (ISO) with the International Electrotechnical Commission (IEC) created an international standard, ISO/IEC 24751 (2008) [5], which considers the accessibility characteristics that "the new training context" must have to be considered accessible [9].

Among the most comprehensive and important guidelines for accessibility, WCAG is a set of international guidelines related to accessibility and usability provided by the World Wide Web Consortium (W3C), an international no-governmental association that has been working for years to further the web. Web Content Accessibility Guidelines (WCAG) 2.1 is the most recent version and was released on June 5, 2018. It is based on four core principles:

1. *Principle of perceptibility, states that all interface elements should be able to be perceived by the user;*
2. *Principle of operability, states that the user must be enabled to effectively use the interface;*
3. *Principle of understandability, states that the content of the interface must be presented clearly and unambiguously;*
4. *Principle of robustness, states the relative importance of an interface's ability to be accessible regardless of the technology used by the user.*

Thirteen criteria are also provided within the Web Content Accessibility Guidelines (WCAG) to determine the level of accessibility of an interface. Depending on the fulfillment of these criteria, the interface can be classified through three levels of accessibility: A, AA and AAA. These levels are progressive, so as accessibility increases as the level advances. It is important to emphasize that the thirteen criteria in no way represent a regulation with normative value, but rather a set of practical and useful guidelines for those involved in making digital environments accessible.

IV. MAIN EXISTING METHODOLOGIES AND THEORIES

Considering the theoretical models and methodologies employed in e-learning, a major contribution to the topic of accessibility comes from Universal Design for Learning (UDL), an approach based on modern neuroscience. Specifically, Universal Design for Learning (UDL) is a framework that addresses the main training difficulties present within still rigid, one-way learning environments, which raise significant barriers in the process of knowledge acquisition by users, not only those with disabilities [6].

The underlying principle is that there is no one type of learner, but everyone learns differently based on multiple factors, from physical to sociocultural, and based, therefore, on different needs [6].

Universal Design for Learning (UDL) aims to help anyone planning lessons or learning units understand how to implement learning pathways. A learning program must be able to meet the needs of all students from the outset, encouraging the creation of flexible, inclusive and customizable designs. In this regard, Universal Design for Learning (UDL) has drafted Guidelines to reduce the obstacles associated with traditional training and to try to reach an increasingly broad range of learners.

The guidelines drafted by UDL are based on the following principle: provide multiple means of representation. This principle is indispensable in the absence of a single, optimal tool for all users. In fact, learning is impossible if the information is not perceivable by the learner, or is perceivable with difficulty (for example, if it is presented in ways that require great effort or extraordinary help). For information to be equally perceivable by all individuals, the Guidelines suggest, for example, providing the same information through different perceptual modalities such as: sight, hearing, or touch.

In addition to multiple representations, another strategy to try to break down barriers in learning is to offer the user information in an adjustable format, such as enlarged text and augmented sound. It is especially important to remark the role of multiple representations of information in learning, as they are useful not only in conveying accessible information to users with particular sensory and perceptual disabilities, but also in facilitating understanding for many other users.

V. CURRENT STATUS OF TECHNOLOGIES

Currently there are many technological achievements to overcome obstacles to the accessibility of e-learning paths, among them we consider:

- the use of special keyboards.
- the presence of a video with a translator who expresses himself through sign language.
- the adoption of joysticks.

In more detail, mainly used technologies for visually impaired people are audio description and image magnification using specific software. A tool that can implement both mentioned solutions for visually impaired people is the multipurpose interface. On the other hand, a tool very useful for trainers is the multi-subject database [8], which makes it possible to shorten the distance between trainers and people with disabilities through a virtual repository that can trace the progress of special education.

Technologies to support the blind are called "assistive technologies" and are based on the use of hearing and touch. Among the various developed solutions, it is important to consider screen-reading software that can convert content in written form present in an interface into audio. Other assistive technologies include alternative keyboards (keyguards, adjustable keyboards, miniature keyboards, programmable keyboards) and Braille displays.

To identify the most promising technologies for people with hearing impairments, Martinsa and al. [8] pointed out that the efforts of industry companies have focused on three key aspects:

- comprehension, as the ability of technological tools to recognize gestures, body movements and facial expressions in order to grasp the message.
- representation, as the ability to create a virtual image that corresponds to the user's communications.
- translation, as the ability of software to convert a message expressed through sign language into written form.

Regarding the first aspect, i.e., understanding, there are two solutions adopted until today:

- the use of cameras that can record movements.
- the use of gloves that analyze the movement of the hand and forearm.

Several difficulties are currently evident with both above-mentioned solutions; on the one hand, the gloves fail to capture the message in its entirety because they exclude important aspects, such as facial expressions and body language; on the other hand, although extremely accurate cameras are available, it is difficult to succeed in developing software that can process and understand all the necessary visual stimuli.

For sign language representation, on the other hand, a tool that has been successful in various areas of communication is adopted: the virtual avatar. However, much research on the subject shown that there are several difficulties [8]. Indeed, making animations capable of reproducing specific and complex movements with high levels of accuracy and fidelity proved to be a more arduous task than expected.

Finally in the case of translation, the greatest difficulty doesn't involve software, but regards hardware; in fact, it is really difficult for modern systems to be able to process hundreds of spoken gestures in a few minutes, understand them, and translate them into a written format. Software based on particularly powerful hardware actually cannot process more than eight signs per minute, certainly not enough considering the communication speed of a possible user.

Despite great efforts by institutions, the world of research, information technology, and new technologies, there are still many steps to take to achieve high-impact inclusive goals and so accessibility can become an established principle in e-learning education. However, future of accessible e-learning is very promising. There are several emerging technologies that are making e-learning increasingly accessible for people with disabilities. One of the most important emerging technologies is artificial intelligence (AI). AI can be used to create personalized and adaptable learning systems to real learner's needs and learning abilities. In this way, it become possible to receive personalized education tailored to each specific need. In addition, there are also emerging technologies, such as portable devices and sensors, that can help interact with e-learning in more intuitive ways. For example, handheld devices such as smartwatches can help students with visual impairments receive haptic feedback to navigate learning content. Then, virtual and augmented reality technologies are becoming more accessible and could be used to create immersive and immersive learning experiences.

VI. PIAZZA COPERNICO'S EXPERIENCE

A. *Accessibility vs. Usability*

The adoption of Web Content Accessibility Guidelines (WCAG) became increasingly important as more and more people use technology to access information, services and products. In addition, accessibility has also become legally mandated in many countries, especially for public service-providing organizations.

Creating e-learning courses that comply with WCAG means creating content that is accessible, but also that is easy to use and navigate. However, the two do not always coincide. With these considerations in mind, the Piazza Copernico's production team started from the question, "Will following the WCAG guidelines allow our products to be truly usable by anyone?" Indeed, accessibility and usability are two different concepts, although they are often confused or considered as synonymous. Accessibility refers to "a person's ability to access online content regardless of his or her physical, sensory, or cognitive abilities.

On the other hand, Usability refers to the ease with which a person can use a website or application, that is, its efficiency, effectiveness, and satisfaction during use. According to the ISO 9241-11 (1998) standard [9], the purpose of usability is to study the interaction between the user and the site, or between the user and the online course, with the aim of highlighting obstacles that prevent effective use of information and services. [10] For example, an online course may be accessible, because it has text alternatives for images and support keyboard navigation, but it may not be very usable if the navigation is confusing and unclear, with menus and submenus that are not well organized and difficult to find. On the other hand, an online course could be very usable, that is, easy to navigate and use, but not be accessible if it does not support assistive technologies or offer text alternatives for images. In the goals of accessibility and usability there is an overlap in some cases, but the differences between the two areas become clearer when considering the entities involved.

To verify that the accessibility requirements of the WCAG guidelines are met, automatic validation of the page code using special software and a series of technical tests are required. The focus of usability, on the other hand, is on the relationship between the product and the end user, and the preferred method of validation is a test conducted directly with human users.

In summary, accessibility and usability are both important for ensuring a positive and inclusive user experience for all users, but they are different concepts and require different design and validation approaches. Therefore, the appropriate test of whether an online course is accessible is whether people with disabilities can use it, not just whether it complies with WCAG or other guidelines. In fact, Thatcher [11] states that accessibility is experiential and environmental and depends on the interaction of the content with the user agent, the assistive technology, and the user. Obviously, one would hope that there would be a high correlation between user performance and usability measures on the one hand and

WCAG compliance on the other. So far, however, there are few studies that have produced evidence underlying this relationship [12].

In the light of these considerations and in response to the specific need expressed by the company Enel Spa to provide training that would consider the obligations of Legislative Decree 2020/76, the production group in Piazza Copernico began to think about how to make its products accessible and usable, developing an e-learning environment suitable for this purpose. The first project to be tested for accessibility was "Being Antifragile": a course consisting of four episodes built on the stories of various characters in different environments; in each episode a typical situation of chaos, stress, risk, error is staged, in which the "antifragile" attitude can make a difference in improving, learning, evolving. The group worked in parallel on the content front and the interface front to produce an easily navigable environment for people with visual and hearing disabilities and normals with suboptimal conditions; the goal was to achieve level AA according to the WCAG guidelines. To do this, several measures were taken.

B. *Taken measures on the web application*

The development of a web application capable of presenting accessible and usable multimedia content required a set of best practices to be followed.

The principles used at this stage followed the guidelines outlined by the W3C on WCAG, which state that for content to be accessible it must be perceivable, usable, understandable, and robust [13]. The robustness of the code and the use of semantic tags [13] enabled assistive technologies for the blind (*screen readers*) to convey the right information according to the order set in the HTML code. The proper use of semantic tags has enabled *screen readers*, for example, to recognize text as a title regardless of how it looks on the screen. The inclusion of detailed instructions for each button and the implementation of keyboard-only interface navigability allowed users with screen readers to operate with the application controls and know what will happen after each button is selected (see Figure 1).

Figure 1. Example of a message read by the screen reader

About course interface, each button, once selected, shows a clearly visible border, allowing users its immediate identification (see Figure 2).

Figure 2. Example of key highlighting

Adaptive (*responsive*) management of the interface allowed the visually impaired to be able to enlarge the tabs and wording present, without having to give up their functionality (see Figure 3 and 4).

Figure 3. Example of focus on

Figure 4. Example of focus on

C. *Considerations on taken measures on the web application*

The software and interface design must focus on the needs of users by providing tools that are pleasant and functional to use, in an effort to provide the best possible experience during use. Designing the commands to be made available and the information to be communicated at each stage of use, presupposes the task of stepping into the user's point of view to help them efficiently and comprehensively achieve their purposes: in our case, education on a given topic.

In the past, the target user of the graphic and functional design of our courses was quite similar in skills and possibilities to the people involved in making the course itself. Making a web application accessible means taking into consideration a multitude of viewpoints or use cases related to the different possibilities of fruition of the product applicable to users with different abilities and limitations. This is not an easy effort that requires specific training on the various usability needs and the use of assistive technologies to test and verify the validity of the solutions adopted. The immediate visual impact of texts and images is no longer the only parameter to be considered; the usability of what is shown after activating the browser's zoom tool or the use of a screen reader also become an integral part of the process of creating our courses.

D. *Taken Measures on content*

To make the media content accessible, synchronized subtitles are included that report, according to the choice:

- the spoken content only, i.e., subtitles for all audio content in real time in the form of synchronized media types.
- the spoken content and textual description of the noises.
- audio description, i.e., audio description provided for all pre-recorded video content in the form of synchronized media types. Such narration describes important visual details that cannot be understood through the main audio and includes information about actions, characters, scene changes, on-screen text, and other visual content (see Figure 5).

Figure 5. Example of audiodescription

Subtitles can be set in 4 different sizes (see Figure 6).

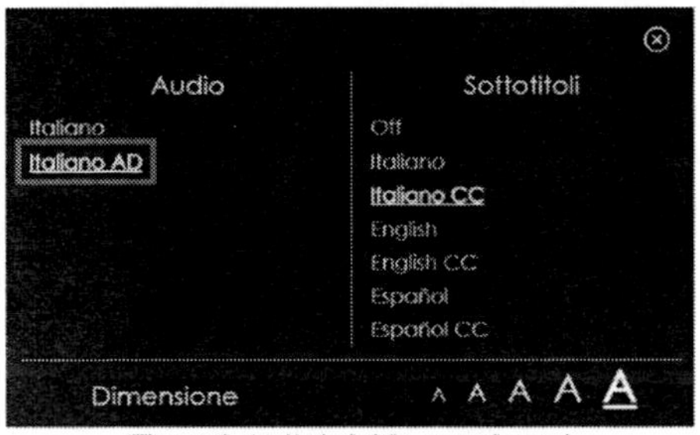

Figure 6. Audio/subtitle control panel

To further support the audience of hearing-impaired people, we have included, on a drag-and-drop panel, the ability to enjoy content through Italian Sign Language (LIS), a natural language conveyed through the visual-textual channel, relying on professional interpreters to literally translate the content of our videos (see Figure 7).

Figure 7. Example of LIS (Italian Sign Language)

E. Considerations on taken measures on content

For years now we focused on the use of video for our training courses, and working on accessibility necessarily means going to work on these as well. After all, we live in a world increasingly dominated by audiovisual content. And access to this content has been declared a fundamental human right by the 2006 United Nations Convention on the Rights of Persons with Disabilities (CRPD). [15] The first key step involved subtitles. Subtitles originated to be aimed at viewers who do not speak the language used in the video. Today the use of subtitles has changed; just look at the wide use of them on social and streaming platforms by all the people who enjoy videos in conditions where audio cannot be heard, such as in public. The use of Closed captioning (cc) or Subtitles for the Deaf and Hard of Hearing (SDH) has since evolved further. SDH includes oralists, as deaf oralists are people educated to speak, lip-read and understand spoken language to the exclusion of Sign Language

This type of subtitles carries over into the written text not only speech, but a whole range of additional information useful to people who are deaf and hard of hearing, such as:

- sound effects (gunshots, dogs barking, phones ringing, etc.).
- identification of the speaker (without a symbol or name identifying the speaker, lines of dialogue follow one another, leaving the viewer confused as to who said what and when, especially for off-screen interlocutors).
- music, the latter being a basic element in identifying the video's tone and atmosphere; it is useful, therefore, to make suggestions as to what type of music is in the field for the deaf.

To support users who have difficulty reading, subtitles are presented as white lettering on a dark background to ensure good contrast no matter what content they are displayed on. A further step toward accessibility is the translation of our videos into Italian Sign Language (LIS), which is increasingly used on TV and in live events to engage the signaling deaf community. If subtitles and LIS help those who have difficulty hearing, audio-descriptions are necessary for those who have difficulty seeing. Audio-descriptions consist of audio commentaries describing scenes that would not be understandable without visual support. The difficulty encountered lies in the fact that the training products produced are not feature films, which have more extended time frames and allow for full and detailed audio-descriptions, but short videos, usually at a fast pace, that require a specific study of best formula for effectively describing a scene.

F. Results

Once the "Being Antifragile" course was made accessible, with the described changes on the web application and content, it was sent to the client for consulting by Salvatore Scaldaferri - Digital Accessibility Specialist of Global Digital Solutions of the Enel Group. This collaboration allowed us to test and verify the effectiveness of the measures undertaken in line with accessibility guidelines and to implement them in terms of usability. The Digital Accessibility Specialist's main observations concerned:

- the correct reading sequence of on-screen elements.
- the overlap of the audio description with respect to the narrative voice of the video.
- the clarity of the instructions regarding the choice of subtitles.
- some redundancies in the functionality of the buttons.

The feedback allowed us to refine the functionality of the interface and calibrate content interventions according to the learning patterns of Enel users with disabilities. Changes were subsequently validated by the client, who confirmed that the course was usable according to his needs and that there were no anomalies that would affect compliance with WCAG level AA.

VII. CONCLUSIONS AND FUTURE WORK

What we have seen is confirmation that beyond the adoption of accessibility guidelines, only the human user is the true test of the usability of an e-learning course. Indeed, in this context, usability is important because students must be able to easily access learning materials, navigate between different sections of the course, and interact with the available tools and resources. Reflection should also be extended to the existing correlation between instructional design and usability since a well-designed e-learning course should also be easy to use. In fact, it is important to remember that when we talk about accessibility in e-learning we should not refer exclusively to the idea of making the platform and learning objects universally usable, but we should be aware that the content should also be conceived and designed in an accessible and usable way. In this regard, there is a lack of guidelines that give guidance on how to design in an accessible and inclusive way for all users, thus addressing the issue of accessibility from a methodological-didactic point of view. Next steps for producing highly and globally inclusive educational products involve new studies to identify standardizable design patterns to ensure full accessibility for all types of content while also taking into account the cognitive engagement required of the user.

ACKNOWLEDGEMENTS

Many thanks go to Salvatore Scaldaferri, *Digital Accessibility Specialist*, and the Enel Group Global Digital Solutions team for their support in improving the usability and accessibility of the courses. Thanks also to the entire Piazza Copernico instructional design and development team for their efforts in implementing the interface and content to make them accessible and usable: Claudia Falconio, Silvio Meconi, Daniele Consorti, Alice Antonello, Saverio Santulli Sanzo, Marta Federici, Thomas Mezzetti, Teresa Orlando, Alessia Francocci, Giuseppina Somma, and Antonio L'Abbate. Thanks to Daniela Pellegrini and the entire R&D group at Piazza Copernico for their support, motivation and stimulating exchange. Special thanks to Oliviero Vittori (*President*) and Marco Luzzatto (*Administrator*) who made this possible and to all the staff of Piazza Copernico who enthusiastically joined the project.

REFERENCES

[1] OMS, International Classification of Functioning, Disability and Health (ICF), 2001

[2] L. 9 January 2004, n.4, Dispositions to promote the access of people with disabilities to information technology tools.

[3] U. Ehlers, L. Goertz, B. M. Hildebrandt and J. M. Pawlowski, Quality in e-learning: use and dissemination of quality approaches in European e-learning. European Centre for the Development of Vocational Training (Cedefop) in "Panorama Series", pp. 116, 2005.

[4] N.K. Parker The quality dilemma in online education revisited in T. Anderson, The theory and practice of online learning, 2nd edition. Edmonton, Canada: AU Press, Athabasca University, 2008.

[5] ISO/IEC 24751 Information technology-Individualized adaptability and accessibility in e-learning, education and training, 2008.

[6] H. David Rose and J. Grave, Universal Design for Learning (UDL) Guidelines version 2.0. CAST, 2011.

[7] A. Savidis and D. Grammenos, C. Stephanidis, Developing inclusive e-learning systems, Springer-Verlag, 2006.

[8] P. Martinsa, H. Rodriguesb, T. Rochaa, M. Franciscoc, L. Morgado, Accessible options for Deaf people in e-Learning platforms: technology solutions for Sign Language translation. In "Procedia Computer Science", Vol. 67, pp. 263 – 272, 2015.

[9] SO 9241-11, Ergonomic requirements for visual display terminals, 1998.

[10] P. Ghislandi and F. Cumer, Accessibility for quality e-learning in "TD Tecnologie Didattiche", Vol. 21, no. 3, pp. 153-160, 2013.

[11] J. Thatcher, Prioritizing Web Accessibility Evaluation Data. Proceedings of CSUN, 2004.

[12] B. Kelly, D. Sloan, L. Phipps, H. Petrie and F. Hamilton, Forcing Standardization or Accommodating Diversity? A Framework for Applying the WCAG in the Real World. Conference: W4A, 2005

[13] https://www.w3.org/TR/WCAG21

[14] https://www.w3schools.com/html/html5_semantic_elements.asp

[15] Booklet_All the Same: Layout 1 (esteri.it)

Back to Normality - Changes in Time-Effective Logistics of Project-Based Course Electronic Instrumentation after COVID-19 Limitations Release

Samuel Kosolapov
Department of Electronics
Braude Academic College of Engineering
Karmiel, Israel
e-mail: ksamuel@braude.ac.il

Abstract—**The classic course Electronic Instrumentation was based on analog electronics - analog sensors, actuators, and amplifiers, and, in most universities, was taught as the theoretical course followed by a specialized and expensive laboratory. The appearance of inexpensive microcontrollers changed the way sensors and actuators are used; hence, our days, Electronic Instrumentation can be taught as "a classic course in the modern envelope": by using as analog as digital elements and by using special programming techniques needed to program microcontroller effectively. This presentation describes changes in the time-effective logistics which was used for eight years to teach this course in the "normal time", in "COVID-19 time", "in the Hybrid time" and, again in the "normal time" by using real electronic components and kits, and by using TinkerCad simulations.**

Keywords-project-based learning; time-effective logistics; electronic instrumentation; TINKERCAD.

I. INTRODUCTION

The course "Electronic Instrumentation" is one of the basic courses in the curriculum of an electronic engineer. Most classical books dedicated to this course describe the operation, design, and parameters of different sensors and actuators – for example, temperature sensors and electrical heaters. A significant part of those books discusses analog devices (like analog voltmeters and ammeters) used to measure different physical parameters by using specialized sensors [1] [2]. Books for advanced students additionally discuss calibration procedures, errors, and the reliability of the measurements [3]. Some books provided a detailed description of the full-fledged analog systems designed to control relevant parameters by using specialized sensors and actuators and electronic amplifiers and filters.

In the past, the classic course Electronic Instrumentation was based on analog electronics - analog sensors, actuators, and amplifiers. Hence, in many universities and colleges, this course was taught as a theoretical course – mostly due to the high cost of the real-life systems used in the industry. For example, the description of the course "ENT353 Electronic Instrumentation Systems" claims that "At the end of this course students will be able to demonstrate the ability to design instrumentation system suitable for required parameter measurement, understand the working principle of instrumentation system, and describe the working principle of various sensing devices" [4].

Many educators in the field of electronic instrumentation have emphasized the importance of practical training: "In most of the following steps: conceive, experiment, design, build, test, improve – practical aspects are critical for understanding the items learned" [5].

Leading educational institutions like MIT [6] and others includes in their curricula of electrical engineering set of laboratories in which basic electronic equipment and real electronics components are used.

Starting from the 80s, electronic analog systems were gradually replaced by digital systems containing "the wonder chip Micro-processor" [7] [8]. Large control panels packed with analog voltmeters, ammeters, and mechanical switches were gradually replaced by small-size digital systems with human-friendly displays. Additionally, the appearance of inexpensive microcontrollers changes the way sensors and actuators are used. Hence, our days, the course Electronic Instrumentation can be taught as "a classic course in the modern envelope": by using as analog as digital elements, plus using special programming techniques. Thus, our days, the programming of Micro-processors has become an important part of the education of electronic engineers.

Online technologies were used by many educators long ago, but these technologies have become vital because of the COVID-19 situation: the situation in education, which is seriously dependent on the epidemiological situation, makes educators look for new ways of education [9]. It became a must to provide a way to carry out electronic experiments and assignments, as in a real laboratory, as in a student's home. An interesting option was to use the online platforms for implementing elements of the Electronics Laboratory by using online electronic simulation platforms like TinkerCad [10] [11].

An additional idea was to lease to each pair of students a specially prepared kit containing real electronic components and an inexpensive microcontroller development board. Then, students would be able to execute assignments at their homes – by using the kit and PC. Some elements of this idea were partly described in [12] [13]. This article describes additional details of the practical implementation of this idea.

Section II describes "Elements of the Course": lectures, exercises, non-obligatory "in-class Micro Exams", "Home Works" and "Micro Projects", including practical details of how they were provided in "regular times" (when lectures and exercises were provided physically at the campus), in "COVID19" time (when lectures and exercises were provided by using online ZOOM services), in a "hybrid" situation (when some students were physically visited lectures and exercises, while others were used ZOOM translations), and, finally – last semester – "back to normality" – when lectures and exercises were provided physically at the campus.

Section III describes the implementation details of Gmail Protocol which is an important element of time-effective logistics.

Section IV describes details of the logistics of "Micro Exams", "Home Works" and "Micro Projects". The logistics of "Micro Exams" are described in subsection 'A'. The logistics of "Home Works" are described in subsection 'B'. The logistics of "Micro Projects" are described in subsection 'C'.

An important part of any "time-effective" logistics of that kind is time-effective and fair grading. Details are described in Section V named "Time-Effective logistics of reports checking".

Section VI shortly summarizes the results of student pools (partly published in the previous publication [13]) and provides some conclusions.

II. Elements of the Course

Course Electronic Instrumentation in the new format was provided at the Department of Electronics of Braude Academic College of engineering every semester starting from 2015. Important elements of this course: 13 two-hour frontal in-class lectures, 13 one-hour in-class exercises, three "Home Works", two "Micro Projects", and 10 non-obligatory "in-Class Micro Exams" (provided during exercise hours).

"Home works" and "Micro Projects" are executed by pairs of students, whereas "Micro Exams" are individual assignments.

In the "normal pre-COVID-19 years" (from 2015 to 2020), the course "Electronic Instrumentation" was provided on campus. During three semesters starting from March 2020 to August 2021, this course was provided under strict COVID-19 restrictions by using online tools only: ZOOM, TinkerCad, and Gmail. Specifically: lectures were provided by using remote ZOOM sessions, and assignments were executed by using TinkerCad simulations instead of using real components. Starting from October 2021, the course was provided in a hybrid way: lectures were provided at the campus, but with ZOOM "on", so that students have a choice: to visit the campus or listen to the lectures by ZOOM from outside the campus. "Home Works" and "Micro Projects" were executed by using the kits, but in some situations, students were asked to provide simulations by using TinkerCad and/or MultiSim simulation applications. From October 2022, the course is provided in a "normal in-class" way. However, the practice of using TinkerCad and other simulations in combination with using real components and development boards was found useful for the goals of the course, hence, currently, this practice is continuing to be used.

III. Gmail Protocol

In prehistoric pre-computer times, students' assignments were prepared by using pen and paper. At due time, students put their papers on the educator's table. Then, the educator physically took those papers to his/her cabinet, checked and graded those papers by using pen and paper, and returned the graded exams to the students. This outdated procedure created a lot of logistics problems and conflicts (like lost papers, non-consisting grading, problems with grades appeal, and others), and, what is more important, it was not time-effective from the point of view of the educator – it was not an easy job to read handwritten texts.

When personal computers became available, students started to print their assignments, but this solved only the problem of reading handwritten texts.

Email services, from their origin, were found instrumental in many businesses in documenting different stages of routine operations. Gmail services were pioneers by implementing some obvious today ideas like online access to all emails from any computer, usage of multiple labels, and simple and fast search in the emails. Hence, free Gmail services were selected for collecting student assignments. It is known that for security reasons, many educational organizations effectively forbid using Gmail services by enforcing the usage of special educational platforms like "MOODLE". In order to comply with those security requirements, the Gmail protocol described never uses the full names and full IDs of the students. Additionally, for every course, a dedicated Gmail address is used.

From 2015 this Gmail protocol was evolutionarily modified. Currently, the following rules are used.

The dedicated Gmail address is used to collect and store students' assignments only. Discussions are provided by using official college communication means only.

When the specific assignment is ready, one of the students fills the standard fields of the email:

"To": in this field, only the address of dedicated to the specific course Gmail must be written.

"CC": email address of the second student. This requirement is very important as proof that the assignment was sent at due time and to the correct address. Additionally, the second student may validate that the correct version of the assignment was sent.

The "Subject" field was filled by a specially designed alpha-numeric descriptor – "Report ID". In order to find an optimal format, its structure was modified in some semesters. In the last semester, the following format of the "Report ID" was used:

ABCD-EFGH-Z-YYYY-MM-DD

Where: token "ABCD" contains the last 4 digits in the ID of the first student, and token "EFGH" - contains the last 4 digits in the ID of the second student. In order to prevent ambiguity, it was requested that numerically ABCD < EFGH. This rule, in a pseudo-random way, automatically defines who is the first student, and who is the second student (the first student signs on the kits leasing form). Token "Z" equals to "HW01" for the "Home Work 01", "HW02" for the "Home Work 02", and "HW03" for the "Home Work 03". Homework items were the same for all pairs of students. For "Micro Projects 1", token "Z" was equal to "MP1V", where V was the number in the first list of assignments to be executed. Those numbers were set in a pseudo-random way in the range {1..6}. For the "Micro Project 2" token "Z" was equal to "MP2N", where N was the number in the second list of assignments to be executed. Those numbers were set in a pseudo-random way in the range {1..5}. "YYYY-MM-DD" stands for the year, month, and day of the report. Delimiter "-" was used to make the "Report ID" more readable for humans and to make a search by tokens plain and simple.

The "Text" field was used only to comply with the Gmail rule to fill it in some way and not to send Gmail with this field void. So, students were asked to write there at least two letters, or, some very short text.

The attachment was a PowerPoint file named exactly as described before "report ID":

ABCD-EFGH-Z-YYYY-MM-DD.pptx

In some cases, students were asked to attach ZIP file, named as

ABCD-EFGH-Z-YYYY-MM-DD.zip

This strong naming policy enabled a simple search by the tokens of the "Report ID". Two examples of search are presented in Figure 1. On the left is presented an extract of the result of the search of all reports of "Home Work 03" by using the token "*-HW03-*". On the right is presented the extract of the result of the search of all assignments of the specific pair of students by using the short ID token of the first student: "*-1608-*".

IV. Logistics of "Micro Exams", "Home works", and "Micro Projects"

The logistics of "Micro Exams" are described in subsection 'A'. The logistics of "Home Works" are described in subsection 'B'. The logistics of "Micro Projects" are described in subsection 'C'.

A. *Logistics of "Micro Exams"*

Originally, "Micro Exams" were executed in class, during the time of the exercises. In the frames of those micro exams, students were asked to solve on paper a short clearly defined problem, technically close to one of the problems solved during previous lectures and exercises. After a short time (say, 5 minutes), an educator collected papers from the students. The exact time of the start of the specific "Micro Exam" was set by a lecturer in a way unknown to the students.

Later, the logistics of the micro exams was changed. Students were still asked to write the solution on paper, but then they were asked to take a photo of their solution by using a smartphone and email the photo to the lecturer by using the subject field "ABCD-MEZ", where Z is a number of the "Micro Exam". It is clear that only emails sent immediately after the "Micro Exam" finish were graded. When the COVID-19 restrictions were enforced, these logistics was used without changes. During the hybrid semesters, the administrative decision was to permit participation in micro exams only to the students technically present in the class. Hence, it was "return" to the "collection of the papers" logistics. This old and non-reliable practice is still in usage after "back to normality". Surprisingly, many students started to ask if it is possible to use tablets to solve problems by using handwriting tools (like S-pens). So, considering that nearly all students have advanced tablets, it can be predicted that in the nearest years, paperless logistics will be used for "Micro Exams".

The first goal of those "Micro Exams" was to provide minimal feedback to the lecturer: what is the level of the student's understanding of the material learned? The second goal was to provide minimal feedback to the students: do I understand the material learned? This is why during "Micro Exams" students were permitted to use computers and the Internet, and even ask neighbor students for assistance. All the above were permitted because the additional goal of these exams was to enforce students to learn critical staff (for example: correct usage of timers and hardware interrupts) now, and not closer to the end of the course.

Participation in the "Micro Exams" is not a must, however, presenting the solutions to the lecturer may result in some improvement in the final grade. Typically, nearly 50% of students participated in the Micro Exams and nearly 25% of all the students enrolled in the course have got maximal grade improvement.

B. *Logistics of "Home Works"*

At the beginning of the "normal" semester, pairs of students get from the lecturer a specially prepared kit to be used at their homes to practically implement "Home works". Specifically, in the frames of the course Electronic Instrumentation, students get: a 37-in-one Sensor kit, an Arduino UNO R3 board, a small-size breadboard, a shield with a small breadboard, a short USB cable, a set of wires, and a plastic box to store relevant staff.

As it was mentioned above, during three semesters starting from March 2020 to August 2021, this course was provided under COVID-19 restrictions. During those semesters, the distribution of real electronic components became at least problematic, but working in pairs with real components became impossible.

The selected solution was to use online TinkerCad simulations. An important feature of this simulation is that it is a free cloud service, without the need for installation or license.

During the exercises provided by ZOOM, the lecturer periodically provided live demonstrations of the TinkerCad operation.

So, during "normal" semesters, students were asked to implement "Home Works" by using real components, prepare a report containing photos of the assembly (step by step) and testing the system in accordance with the lecturer's requirements, and, to demonstrate the operation of the system physically in the class.

In the "COVID-19" semesters, students were asked to do with TinkerCad simulation actually the same steps as with real components: to position modules and to connect them by wires, but, instead of photos of real components, screenshots of the simulation screens were used. Students were requested to include the link to their TinkerCad simulation in the report so that the lecturer was able to check the layout, the code, and the operation of the system developed by students. The same link was used by students to demonstrate the operation of their system during the ZOOM session.

Figure 2 demonstrates typical extracts from the student's reports. On the left, the screenshot of the TinkerCad simulation is presented. An educator may immediately see that wire from the button is connected to the inappropriate pin – which is a severe error – hardware interrupt cannot be used as required. On the right, a photo of a real board with real modules and wires is presented. An educator may immediately see that the photoresistor is not in line with LED, which is a problematic layout – leading to a significant error in measurement.

It is clear that if some pair of students had "copied" photos and "code" from the report of another pair of students, this would be immediately revealed. During eight years, such "illegal copying" was revealed less than 10 times.

Figure 3 presents a simplified flowchart of the steps expected to be executed by the educator and by pair of students in the frames of the described logistics for the different situations.

C. *Logistics of "Micro-Projects"*

In the frames of the course, students were asked to prepare two "Micro-Projects".

The first micro project was about different types of motors (6V DC, Servo, Stepper, and Brushless). Each pair of students prepared a PowerPoint presentation dedicated to a specific type of motor and to a specific type of electronic controller and, present it in the class (in case of the "regular" semester) or by ZOOM (in case of "COVID-19" semester). In these presentations, students were asked to explain the physical principles of the specific motor operation and explain how this motor can be controlled electronically by presenting the exemplary circuit needed to control this motor from a microcontroller.

The second Micro Project was about the design of an Automatic Measurement System (AMS). However, considering the tight timetable, the quality of those Micro Project reports was not as good as expected. Hence, in the last years, a simpler Manually Controlled Measurement System (MCMS) was asked to be designed and implemented only by using simulations. Each pair of students was asked to develop a different type of MCMS: an MCMS for measuring DC voltage in different voltage ranges, an MCMS for measuring AC voltages in different voltage ranges, etc. Students were asked to prepare the electric circuit of the MCMS, provide relevant calculations, and prepare a simulation of the analog part only. In this case, each pair of students was asked to send a PowerPoint presentation close to the end of the semester. Grading was provided by evaluating the quality of the report and simulation.

V. Time-Effective Logistics of Reports Checking

It is clear that checking 12*(3+2) reports is a time-consuming job. Hence, significant efforts were made to develop time-effective logistics (a set of formal rules) describing how exactly students must prepare and send their assignments.

Figure 4 presents an extract from the specially prepared Excel template. To make grading fast and consistent, a relatively large number of items to be checked are listed in column 'B'. While grading the specific report, an educator in a very short time finds in the student's report a slide labeled as in column 'A' and, by looking at the photos or screenshots very fast validates if all the requirements were implemented. In case of errors, an educator sets a comment in the relevant cell. To make this process fast, in column 'J' typical errors relevant to the specific item and "their price" are summarized, so that the educator puts in the comment only the number of the relevant error. Grading by template was proven as fast and consistent.

VI. Conclusions

During 10 years, different variants of this time-effective logistics for the different electronic engineering courses were tested. Some results were published before in [12] [13] and reported at a number of international conferences. Unfortunately, in recent years the participation of the students in the students' pools was minimal or even zero. Considering the semesters when student' pools were provided, grades provided by students for this course were in the range {4.23...4.94} (by using 1-5 scale) and were in most cases by 0.5 higher than the mean department' courses grade. In the written comments, most of the students' remarks were positive, and, the median grade for this course in most of the semesters was 5.0. Additionally, we may evaluate the opinions of the students by using the number of students enrolled in this course. This course is not obligatory course. The number of students that can be enrolled is 24. During nearly all semesters the number of students that were registered for this course was 24, and, in most semesters, a number of students registered themselves on the waiting list. Obviously, not all students have got grades at the end. The numbers for the semesters {2019-03 .. 2022-10} are {24, 24, 23, 18, 21, 23, 22, 24}. By analyzing the number of students that have got grades, one can conclude that the organization and outcome of this course are attractive enough for the students.

Manual management and grading of the student's reports (by using grading templates) was found simple and time-effective, as for the students, as for the educators. An indirect parameter that can be considered as an indirect argument taken into account is a low number of grade appeals – less than 3 per semester.

REFERENCES

[1] A. K. Sawhney, "A Course in Electronic Measurements and Instrumentation", Dhanpat Rai & Co, 19th Edition, 2015.

[2] W.D. Cooper & A.D. Helfrick, "Electronic Instrumentation, and Measurement Techniques", Prentice Hall, 3 rd revised Edition, 1985.

[3] B. G. Liptak, "Process Measurement and Analysis", Chilton Book Company, 4 th Edition, 2003.

[4] N. Damle "ENT353 Electronic Instrumentation syllabus". Available from https://www.udemy.com/course/electronic-instrumentation/ [retrieved: 01,2023]

[5] D. R. Ramos and F. Alonso-Fernandez, "A practical Electronic Instrumentational course for engineering students" IEEE EDUCON Education Engineering 2010 – The Future of Global Learning Engineering Education, April 14-16, 2010, Madrid, SPAIN, pp. 1181 – 1188.

[6] G. Hom, "Hands-On Introduction to Electrical Engineering Lab Skills". [Online]. Available from https://ocw.mit.edu/courses. 2008-01. [retrieved: 05, 2022].

[7] R. Gopalakrishnan, "Electronic Instrumentation for Control", IETE Journal of Research, vol. 27, issue 2, pp 53-60, 1981

[8] O. Pandey, "Electronics Instruments", chapter in the book "Electronic Engineerings", Springer, 2022.

[9] D. Luchaninov, R. Bazhenov, V. Sabirova, M. Mamyrova, and Z. Zholdosheva, "Online training of students of applied physics in the field of circuitry", ICMSIT-II 2021 pp 1-6.

[10] F. Jacob, A. Alberto, and P. Guimaraes, "Use of Tinkercad platform for Teaching Electronics Subject in Post-Secondary Technical Courses", TEEM21, October 2021 pp. 543-547, Available from https://doi.org/10.1145/3486011.3486517 [retrieved: 05, 2022].

[11] E. A. Juanda, and F. Khairullah, Tinkercad Application Software to Optimize Teaching and Learning Process in Electronics and Microprocessors Subject", Proceedings of the 6th UPI International Conference on TVET 2020 (TVET 2020), pp. 124 - 128.

[12] S. Kosolapov and N. Sabag, "Logistics of Electronic Home-Project-Based Course", International Journal of Information and Education Technology", vol. 9 no. 6, pp. 445-448. 2019.

[13] S. Kosolapov, "Time-Effective Logistics of Project-Based Course Electronic Instrumentation", eLmL 2022: The Fourteenth International Conference on Mobile, Hybrid, and On-line Learning, pp 35-41, IARIA 2022,

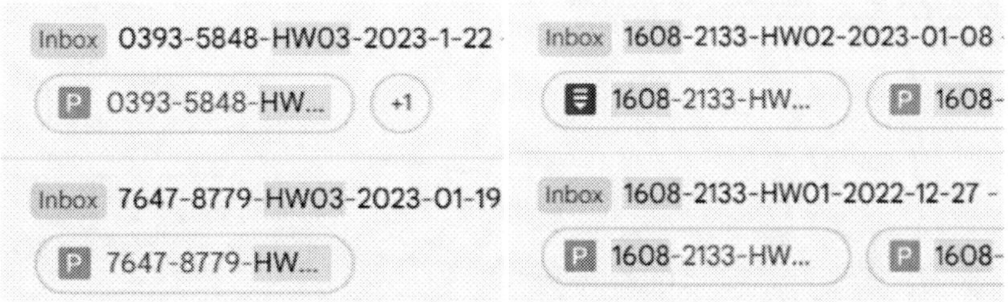

Figure 1. Screenshots of the lecturer's Gmail.
Left: Extract of the result of the search of all reports of "Homework #03" by using token "*-HW03-*"
Right: Extract of the result of the search of all assignments of the pair of students by using the short ID token of the first student "*-1608-*"

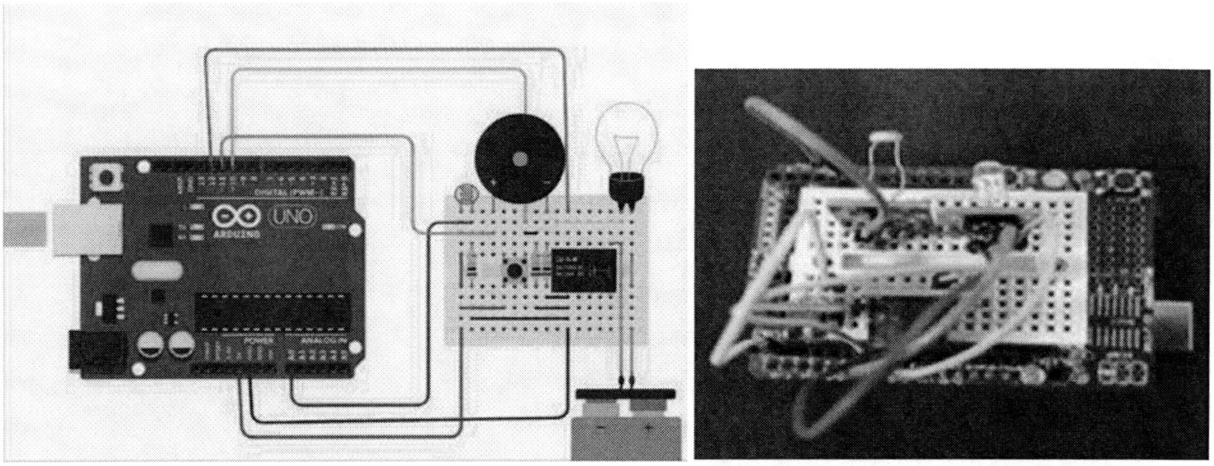

Figure 2. Easy grading.
Left: Screenshot from Version 1 of the Homework 01 report as implemented by pair of students by using TinkerCad simulation.
An error in the wiring can be seen: the pin in the button module is not connected to pin 2 or pin 3 of the Arduino UNO R3 Board.
Right: Screenshot from Version 1 of the Homework 03 report as implemented by pair of students by using a hardware kit.
An error in the layout can be seen: the photoresistor and LED are not in line.

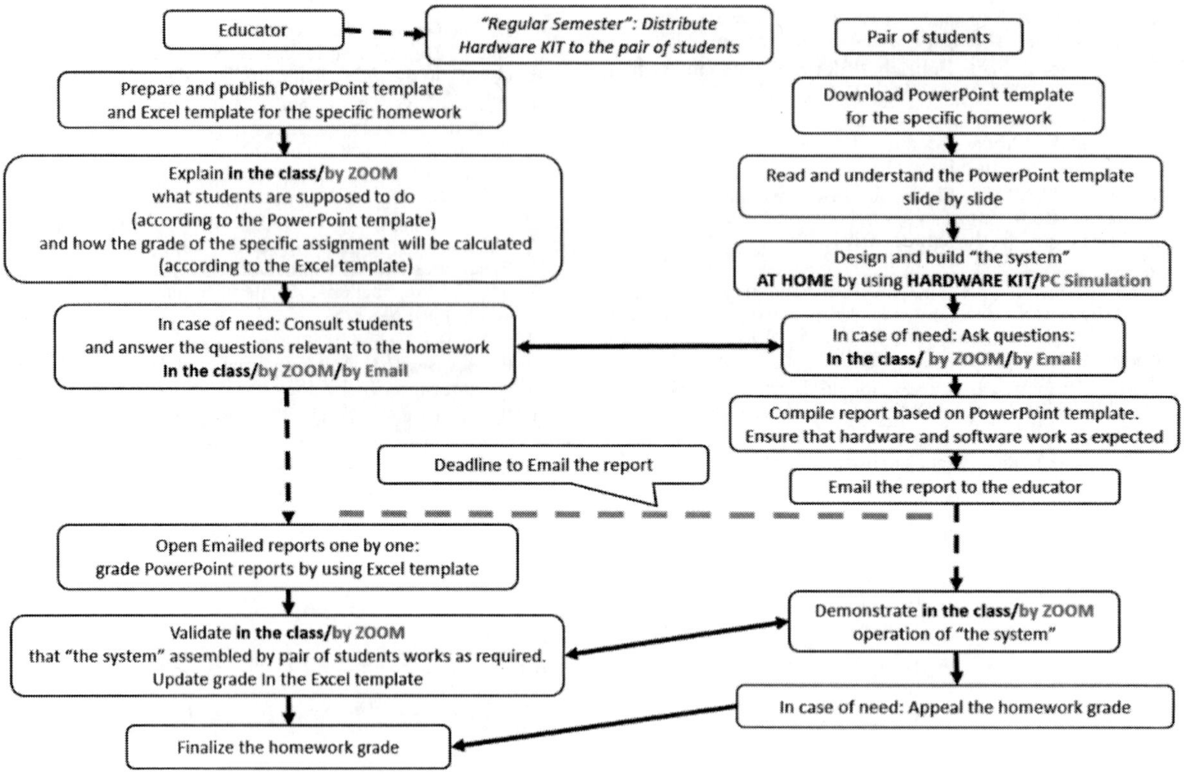

Figure 3. Simplified flowchart of the exemplary homework roadmap.
Left: actions of the educator. Right: actions of pair of students

	A	B	C	D	E	F	G	H	I	J
1	Code	Item	Max Grade		7647-8779	3810-7278	1608-2133	0393-5848		Typical Errors
8										
9	P1V.11	Mechanical and Electrical Elements of the motor (drawings with numbered list of parts and explanations)	3		3	3	0	3		
10	P1V.12	Physical principles of the motor operation (drawings, equations and explanations)	3		3	3	0	3		
11	P1V.13	Photos (from Internet) of at least TWO commercially available motors from different companies and with pins explanations	2		2	2	0	2		
12	P1V.14	Important parameters of above two motors (names and typical values and graphs with VALUES) + explanations & comparisons; recommendations which motor to select when and why	4		4	4	0	4		
13	P1V.21	Full Electrical circuit of a motor controller (in case of IC – what exactly is inside IC)	4		4	4	1	2		
14	P1V.22	Photos (from Internet) of at least TWO commercially available motors controllers with pins explanations	2		2	2	2	2		
15	P1V.23	Full electric circuit of the working motor system: containing Arduino, Controller, Motor, External Power supply (if relevant)	4		4	4	4	4		
16	P1V.24	Explanation: how speed and direction of a rotation can be changed by Arduino Commands	4		4	4	0	2		
17	P1V.25	Evaluation of speed (RPM) limits. Explanation of a typical torque behavior	2		2	2	2	2		
18	P1V.3	Numbered List of sources IEEE style	2		2	2	2	2		
19										
20		**Total**	**30**		**30**	30	**11**	**26**		

Figure 4. Extract from Excel template for grading Micro Project 1.

Impact of Introducing E-learning in Secondary Education During Pandemic

Case study of a tutoring school in Northeast Greece - Teachers' perspective

Kosmas Iatridis
Department of Informatics
Linnaeus University
Växjö/Kalmar, Sweden
email: kosiatridis@gmail.com

Sarfraz Iqbal
Department of Informatics
Linnaeus University
Växjö/Kalmar, Sweden
email: Sarfraz.iqbal@lnu.se

Abstract — **Covid-19 pandemic affected educational organizations to adopt new educational delivery models. The use of digital tools has been common in universities and in adult education. However, the adoption of e-learning in secondary education for minors has been a new phenomenon. This article intends to elicit information about the challenges that students, teachers and organizations faced during the pandemic, when e-learning was introduced as the only means to teaching minors. The challenges were investigated by performing an exploratory case study at a European School. The findings were classified into three categories: students' challenges, teachers' challenges, and organizational challenges. Furthermore, the positive and the negative effects of the introduction of e-learning were investigated.**

Keywords - E-learning; Secondary Education; Organizational learning

I. Introduction

Information Technology is influencing every aspect of modern life and the way organizations operate and interact with their stakeholders. Due to the Covid-19 pandemic there was a significant increase in the demand for e-learning tools to facilitate the teaching procedures during the school closures [1]. During the pandemic 90% of the education ministries globally implemented some form of e-learning, involving the internet and in some cases the television and the radio. Approximately, 1.2 billion children in 186 countries were affected by school closures between 2020 and 2021 [2].

This research explores the challenges and the impact of e-learning introduced in secondary education during the pandemic. The study is based on the experiences of e-learning from the perspective of teachers. The study is conducted at a tutoring school named "Orosimo 2001" in northeastern Greece. The courses offered are Mathematics, Physics, Chemistry, Economics, Informatics, Business Administration, History, Ancient Greek language, Modern Greek language, and Latin language. The organization also offers vocational guidance and psychological support services to students. During the academic year 2020-2021, which is the time period under investigation, there were 23 teachers and 250 students.

Following research questions are explored in this study: 1) What were the challenges faced by students, teachers, and the organization in introducing e-learning during the pandemic, according to teachers' opinion? 2) What was the impact of the introduction of e-learning after the return to face-to-face teaching?

The rest of the article is arranged as follows: Section 2 presents literature review, Section 3 portrays methodology, Section 4 describes findings, Section 5 discusses the results and concludes the article with further research suggestions.

II. Literature Review

A literature review was conducted using Scopus and IEEE Xplore. The keywords were "e-learning" AND "impact" OR "challenges" OR "obstacles" OR "barriers". The articles were limited to those published between 2015 and 2022, while the first 5 pages of each database were examined, containing 10 articles each. Inclusion criteria were based on selecting articles about the impact and the challenges faced when introducing e-learning during the pandemic. Findings were evaluated by title and abstract relevance. E-learning challenges were categorized into those related to students, those related to teachers and those related to educational organizations (Table 1).

TABLE 1: SUMMARIZED LITERATURE REVIEW FINDINGS

Students' challenges	Teachers' challenges	Organizational challenges
Poor internet coverage	Lack of training in ICT technologies	Culture reluctant to changes
Poor internet speed	Reluctance to change	Lack of financial sources
Limited internet data packages	Lack of online time management skills	Electricity shortages
Lack of electronic devices	Low motivation	Issues with the internet connection coverage and speed
Lack of ICT knowledge	Feeling of loneliness	Inadequate coordination
Variation of different educational platforms	Maintain the balance between the working and the personal life	Lack of digital skills by the staff
Lack of technical support	Maintain students' attention and engagement	Resolve members' technical issues
Lack of sense of learning community	Conducting online assessments	Distribute information about e-learning to staff
Absence of physical presence of the	Observing the students	Choosing software application

teacher		
Low motivation and ineffective communication	Higher workload	
Anxiety and depression caused by the pandemic	Development of course content & learning activities	
Time waste due to technical issues	Adopt online pedagogical approaches to students' demands	

A. *Students' challenges*

Major issues for students when using e-learning environments are those related to technical infrastructure and internet connectivity [3]-[5]. In many cases, students do not possess the essential devices in order to have access to the internet [3]-[5]. Other barriers are related to the lack of ICT knowledge and the variation of the different online platforms that students have to use, as they find it confusing to adapt to different electronic environments [3]. Many students do not have essential technical support, due to lack of resources [6]-[8]. In addition, the time that students devote to technical issues limits the learning processes [9]. Other challenges are related to English language skills, which in some cases are essential in order to operate e-learning applications [10]. Students who are not familiar with e-learning applications are unlikely to engage in activities and can easily drop out [11].

Lack of sense of the learning community is an emotion that makes it difficult for students to participate in e-learning, while the absence of physical presence of the teacher is another barrier [8][12]. Low motivation and ineffective communication with other students and the management staff are some more obstacles [7][12]. Other challenges are related to the anxiety and the depression caused by the sudden change and the uncertainty during the pandemic [13]. Especially, children whose family income and living standards are dropped due to Covid-19 are found likely to suffer from anxiety and stress, which in turn affects dropout rates [13].

B. *Teachers' challenges*

Moving on to teachers, a main challenge is the lack of proper training in ICT, as the instructors' teaching skills are usually limited to face-to-face classroom experiences. Moreover, they may feel that e-learning environments are psychologically unsafe [14]. Many times, they have a strong will to stay in the comfort zone, while factors, such as the age, might enhance the reluctance to change [15] Lack of online time management skills is another barrier, while low motivation and the feeling of loneliness are common among the instructors [4][12]. Another crucial factor is the difficulty to maintain the balance between working and personal life [4].

Teachers find it challenging to maintain students' attention and engagement during the lesson [4][12]. More instructional time is needed in order to effectively teach the students, explain their questions, and guide them through their assignments. Conducting online assessments might be a challenging task for instructors, particularly on how to avoid plagiarism during the exams [12]. The workload is much higher, as teachers have to build new e-learning teaching material [12]. Moreover, there are issues regarding the arrangement of online classes and the selection of the online platform [16]. Challenges related to the development of course content and learning activities are common among the instructors. Course design challenges consist of issues concerning online curriculum, subject content, teaching and learning activities, localization of the content, pedagogical model and flexibility [15]. Instructors may fail to provide differentiated e-learning environments, adapt their pedagogical approaches to students' demands, localize the content to local cultures and explore new teaching methods for their courses [11].

C. *Institutions' challenges*

Implementation of e-learning initiatives is related to organizational challenges and the relationship between teachers, students, and educational organizations [11]. Challenges faced by educational organizations have a significant impact on users' interaction with technology and their struggle to adapt with new electronic environments [11]. Stakeholders without essential digital skills might doubt the benefits of e-learning which causes unwillingness to use electronic tools [17]. Furthermore, organizations may lack the financial resources in order to upgrade the technical infrastructure, the internet connection, and to upskill their staff [6]. Organizations might face electricity shortages and issues with the internet connection coverage and speed [10]. A major obstacle to implementing e-learning initiatives is the inadequate coordination between organizations, students, and teachers [10]. Unclear plan of e-learning implementation negatively affects educational services [17]. Furthermore, the administration should support instructors to overcome technological problems [10]. However, the support should not be centered only on technical aspects of e-learning, but it should also consider course design issues and information distribution [11].

Existing culture and educational policy are key challenges [18]. The cultural aspects influencing e-learning environments can be measured by the attitudes, beliefs, and roles of organization's members [18]. Many attempts to adopt e-learning solutions could fail because learning and teaching settings are not contextualized [11]. Choosing a software application with the appropriate learning system and interface design is another issue for educational organizations [15]. E-learning applications should guarantee the privacy and the security of the participants, while access should be given only to authorized users [19].

D. *Theoritical Framework*

Additionally, a theoretical framework was developed to assess organizational learning. Argyris and Schon [21] made a distinction between two different types of learning: a) the single-loop learning, which relates to changing theories of action by refining them, and b) the double-loop learning, which relates to changing theories of action by questioning the shared beliefs, norms, and assumptions to reach a new set of theories-in-use. Single-loop learning is the way of learning that it is adopted when following specific instructions faithfully, without further examining the procedures and the causes of problems [21]. These processes are repetitive routine behaviours and involve adapting to the circumstances, without worrying about long-term solutions. They solve the problems without altering the organization's fundamental processes and nature [21]. Double-loop learning is the procedure of comparing the norm with the situation, questioning the appropriation of the norm, and justifying whether the selected method is the best way of doing things [21]. New set of norms are established to adapt to the environment, which means that an organization might change its policies and its objectives [21]. Figure 1 depicts the usage of Single-Loop and Double-Loop Learning in this article.

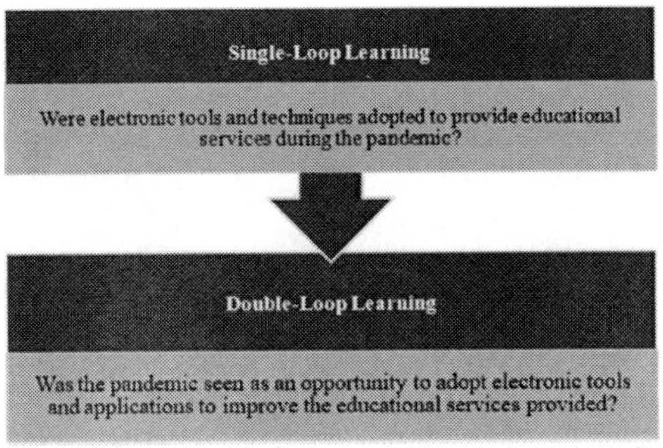

Figure 1. Applying Single-Loop and Double-Loop Learning

III. METHODOLOGY

Following qualitative research methodology, Semi-structured interviews were selected, as they provide a wealth of information, while the data can be compared more easily [22]. The interviews were conducted in the organization, while the snowball sampling was selected. In total, 9 teachers participated in the interviews. Each interview lasted for approximately 30 minutes. Interviews were recorded in Greek and later transcribed to English. Teachers were asked about their experience in e-learning during the academic year 2020-2021. Two of these teachers were also the administrators of the organization, so the input was valuable in order to investigate the organizational challenges from a broader scope.

Thematic analysis was utilized to analyze the collected data [22]. Thematic analysis consists of the systematic identification, organization and understanding of repetitive patterns within data. In the first step the researcher becomes familiar with the data, identifies, and collects excerpts corresponding to each research question. The next stage is the interpretation of the data, which is called coding. Then, the transition from codes to themes takes place. Themes are more abstract and conceptual constructions generated from codes, and finally the findings are presented [22].

IV. FINDINGS

The following are the themes that emerged through the thematic analysis of the interviews:

- The adaptation procedures to e-learning
- Students' challenges in e-learning according to teachers' perspective
- Teachers' challenges in e-learning
- Organizational challenges in e-learning according to teachers' perspective
- Impacts of e-learning

The findings are summarized in table 2.

TABLE II: SUMMARIZED INTERVIEW FINDINGS ABOUT E-LEARNINGS CHALLENGES

Students' challenges	Teachers' challenges	Organizational challenges
Poor internet connection	Poor internet connection	Technological upgrade
Lack of electronic devices	Lack of electronic devices	Additional financial cost
Lack of sociability	Lack of sociability	Solve students' and teachers' technological issues
E-learning did not give them any pleasure	Need to adopt new educational approaches	Coordinating the educational processes
Difficulty to understand the content of the course	Motivating the students	The reluctance to adopt e-learning by a portion of the members of the organization
Sense of indifference	Supervising children	The pricing of e-learning services
	Physical fatigue	

A. *The adaptation procedures to e-learning*

The first theme describes the adaptation procedures to e-learning. To facilitate adaptation to e-learning during the pandemic the Greek Ministry of Education and the organization provided the children with tablets and laptops in order to participate in electronic lessons. Although the curriculum remained the same, the teachers had to digitize the teaching material and to adapt their teaching in order to be able to distribute it electronically to their students.

B. *Students' challenges in e-learning according to teachers' perspective*

The second theme consists of students' challenges in e-learning. Students faced several technical, emotional, and cognitive challenges. The pandemic reduced the social relations among the children. Students could not meet their friends and participate in their hobbies. E-learning classes did not provide them with the opportunity to socialize, a fact that enhanced the feeling of loneliness.

Attending face-to-face lessons was more enjoyable, as it was a chance to meet their friends and contact with the teachers. Furthermore, it was difficult for the students to understand the content of the course in e-learning environments, a fact that reduced their performance. Moreover, they felt indifferent about their homework obligations, and referred to technological issues to avoid participating in e-classes.

C. *Teachers' challenges in e-learning*

The third theme is related to teachers' challenges in e-learning. The teachers faced challenges similar to the students. The teachers needed to find new educational approaches in order to teach into electronic environments. They had to obtain new skills in order to motivate the students to participate, keep their interest and explain the course content. Moreover, supervising students was a challenge for the teachers, as it was difficult to know what the children had written and felt insecure about what children had really learnt. Furthermore, the teachers felt physical fatigue when working long hours on computer.

D. *Organizational challenges in e-learning according to teachers' perspective*

The fourth theme is about organizational challenges. These challenges were related to the technological upgrade, the financial costs, the coordination of the educational procedures and the reluctance to adopt the e-learning tools by some members of the organization.

E. *Impact of e-learning*

The fifth theme is related to the impacts of e-learning introduction. The interviewees found that e-learning had some positive impacts on the educational processes. The organization reached new customers and its members became more adaptable. The financial procedures were digitized and children with special needs benefited from e-learning applications. However, there were some negative aspects of the e-learning introduction during the pandemic. E-learning had a negative impact on students' social skills and on their interest to learning processes.

V. DISCUSSION AND FURTHER RESEARCH

The research questions are answered in this section to discuss the results of the study.

A. *The challenges faced by students, teachers and the organization in introducing e-learning during the pandemic, according to teachers' opinion*

Regarding the students, technical issues were major challenges for them. Many children had poor internet connection at home, and they lacked the essential electronic devices in order to participate in lessons. Especially families with many children did not have enough devices for every child to participate in the learning processes. According to the interviewees, the pandemic reduced the social relations among the students. Students could not meet their friends and participate in their hobbies. E-learning classes did not provide the students with the opportunity to socialize, a fact that enhanced the feeling of "loneliness". Attending face-to-face lessons was more enjoyable for children, as it was a chance to meet their friends and contact with the teachers. A new challenge that emerged from the interviews and was not mentioned in the literature review was the difficulty for the students to understand the content of the course in e-learning environments, which reduced their performance. Moreover, the students felt indifferent about their homework obligations, and referred to technological issues to avoid participating in e-classes.

Regarding the teachers, they faced difficulties in using the new electronic tools and applications to deliver the lessons. Moreover, the poor internet connection and the lack of the essential electronic devices to deliver the lessons were some technical challenges they faced initially. The teachers needed to find new educational approaches to teach in new electronic environments. They had to obtain new skills in order to motivate the students to participate, keep their interest and explain the course content. Moreover, supervising students was a challenge, as teachers could not know what the children had written and felt insecure about what children had really learnt. Additionally, the interviews showed that the feeling of "loneliness" and "the lack of sociability" during the lockdowns had a negative impact on teachers' psychological mood. A new challenge that emerged from the interviews was the "physical fatigue" that teachers felt when working long hours on computer.

Moving on to the educational organization, there was a need to buy new technological devices due to the growing demand for laptops and tablets, as many teachers used organization's classrooms to deliver the lessons. Furthermore, the organization had to upgrade the internet connection. These needs brought additional financial costs to the tutoring school. A major challenge for organization was the coordination of the learning processes. The secretariat had to organize e-classes in Skype, handle information about students' absences and grades, scheduling the exams and receive payment of the tuition fees. Furthermore, the secretariat had to give instructions to students and teachers about how to overcome the technological issues that they faced.

Another challenge for the organization was that a portion of the teachers was reluctant to adopt e-learning during the pandemic. However, the young teachers and the board were supportive in adopting e-learning tools. There was a new challenge that emerged during the interviews The School had to decide whether it should continue to charge the parents the same amount for e-learning services. The parents might have not realized the value of e-learning and the effort made by the organization and the teachers. However, the organization chose to keep the amount at the same level, as it continued to pay the teachers regularly.

B. The impact of the introduction of e-learning after the return to face-to-face teaching, according to teachers' opinion

According to the interview findings, teachers and students became more adaptable to the environmental changes gradually. While many instructors transformed the way they delivered their lessons. The organization continues to use electronic tools that have brought some benefits in the delivery of educational services even after the return to face-to-face teaching. With the use of electronic tools children do not miss lessons, even if for some reason they cannot attend face-to-face classes. The learning experience is enhanced even more, as the lessons can be recorded and watched whenever and wherever the students want to. In e-learning, the lessons are delivered regardless time and place. Hence, students and parents can save time and money from the trip to educational facilities, while the organization can save money from operational costs. Many interviewees mentioned that they continue to use PowerPoint and projectors to present teaching materials in a more interactive way. Videos, interactive maps, and digitally enriched material are used to make the lessons more student-centered. Furthermore, during the pandemic the teaching staff digitized the educational material, while the organization and the parents digitized the payment transactions. After the return to face-to-face teaching, the students continued to use online messaging tools to keep in touch with the teaching staff and solve questions about the lessons.

Finally, there were some positive impacts and opportunities in e-learning regarding secondary education which were not mentioned in the literature review. Students with special needs are benefited as e-learning environments provide their users with audio media interactive systems and visual stimuli. Furthermore, by using e-learning tools the educational organizations can approach new clients, as students from different places can attend online courses. In addition, an important element that emerged from the interviews is that e-learning is just as effective as face-to-face teaching if the students are willing to participate.

On the other hand, some teachers did not continue to use electronic tools after the return to face-to-face teaching, remaining unaffected by the changes brought by e-learning during the pandemic. Moreover, the adoption of e-learning tools had a negative impact on some aspects of educational processes. E-learning had a negative impact on students' social skills, as the children lost significant time from their adolescence. The students did not come in real life contact with their friends, teachers, did not participate in social activities, sports, hobbies, which is devastating for the behavior and social life. In addition, during the pandemic, many students felt indifferent to e-learning, and this attitude continues into the current academic year. The children are less committed to their lessons, they participate less, their effort is reduced, and they consider the learning processes as something not important. In addition, the use of e-learning as the main tool for teaching delivery has created many learning gaps, which is an obstacle in dealing with new educational material. Finally, children who had significant problems with e-learning felt disadvantaged, an emotion that negatively affects them.

C. Using the theory of organizational learning to assess the impact of e-learning on the educational organization

According to the interviews, the organization was ready to adopt electronic tools, as from the third day of the national lockdown. The school provided e-learning services to the students. The electronic rooms that included the students from each class were already organized before the school closures, while the organization provided additional electronic devices to teachers and students, who were in need. The internet connection was also upgraded as many of the organization's teachers continued to use the school classrooms to deliver their lessons. Tuition payments were digitized, a fact that facilitates financial transactions even today. The organization also adopted electronic tools, such as video calls for students to attend the lesson, in case for some reason they could not attend face-to-face teaching.

The organization provided complete freedom in the choice of teaching methods and tools to teachers. Thus, the teachers had the opportunity to choose whether to continue using e-learning tools after the return to face-to-face teaching. The teachers that teach mathematics, physics and chemistry adopted e-learning tools during the pandemic, while after the school closures did not continue to use them. During the present academic year these teachers continue to teach in the way they did before the school closures. They use just some social media platforms to communicate with children and inform them about the schedule and solve potential questions about the lessons. According to organizational learning theory, these teachers adopted specific tools, without worrying for long-term solutions. They did not perceive the pandemic as an opportunity to reflect and transform their educational methods, by using the electronic tools for the enrichment of their teaching. As Argyris and Schon [22] mentioned, the adopted activities solved the problems without altering the fundamental processes. Therefore, these teachers fall into the category of Single-loop learning.

On the other hand, the philologists who teach Ancient Greek, Latin, Modern Greek Language, History and Literature adopted the use of electronic tools even after returning to face-to-face teaching. These teachers continue to use chat applications to communicate with students, but they also use electronic tools, such as PowerPoint, video, and other multimedia, to make their lessons more interactive and student-centered. The pandemic crisis was seen by philologists as an opportunity to adopt electronic tools and enrich their teaching. The members understood the problem, changed their attitude, and chose the appropriate strategy for long-term solutions. Therefore, these teachers fall into the category of Double-loop learning.

The research aimed to investigate the challenges faced by students, teachers, and organizations in introducing e-learning in secondary education during the pandemic, an area of concern that lacked sufficient prior studies. The findings were classified into three categories: students' challenges, teachers' challenges, and organizational challenges. In addition, the positive and negative effects of the introduction of e-learning were investigated. In this study organizational learning theory was utilized in order to examine whether the introduction of e-learning during the pandemic was the occasion for the teachers of "Orosimo 2001" to transform their educational practices. This research work contributes to the existing literature by describing the challenges and impact of e-learning in secondary education during the pandemic, a topic that has not been sufficiently investigated. The findings of the research can be used as a tool for educational organizations in order to mitigate the negative impact of e-learning. Furthermore, the data of this study can be used in order to define the training needs of the teaching staff and structure training programs.

As a suggestion for future research, it would be useful to explore the views of students and other members of educational organizations about the challenges they faced during the pandemic. This could help identify differences and discrepancies with teachers' views.

REFERENCES

[1] E. Edelhauser and L. Lupu-Dima, "One year of online education in COVID-19 age, a challenge for the Romanian education system," Int. J. Environ. Res. Public Health, vol. 18, no. 15, p. 8129, 2021.

[2] J. M. Donohue and E. Miller, "COVID-19 and school closures," JAMA, vol. 324, no. 9, pp. 845–847, 2020.

[3] Al-Balas, M., Al-Balas, H.I., Jaber, H.M., Obeidat, K., Al-Balas, H., Aborajooh, E.A., Al-Taher, R. and Al-Balas, B., 2020. Distance learning in clinical medical education amid COVID-19 pandemic in Jordan: current situation, challenges, and perspectives. BMC medical education, 20(1), pp.1-7.

[4] F. Farooq, F. A. Rathore, and S. N. Mansoor, "Challenges of online medical education in Pakistan during COVID-19 pandemic," J. Coll. Physicians Surg. Pak., vol. 30, no. 6, pp. 67–69, 2020.

[5] W. Hassan, "COVID-19 pandemic: Langkawi vocational college student challenge in using Google classroom for teaching and learning (T&L)," Int. j. adv. trends comput. sci. eng., vol. 9, no. 3, pp. 3299–3307, 2020.

[6] M. A. Almaiah, A. Al-Khasawneh, and A. Althunibat, "Exploring the critical challenges and factors influencing the E-learning system usage during COVID-19 pandemic," Educ. Inf. Technol., vol. 25, no. 6, pp. 5261–5280, 2020.

[7] P. Sahu, "Closure of universities due to Coronavirus disease 2019 (COVID-19): Impact on education and mental health of students and academic staff," Cureus, vol. 12, no. 4, p. e7541, 2020.

[8] N. A. M. Zulkefli, H. Hashim, and S. Syahrin, "Evaluating e-learning google classroom tools for computer science subjects during covid-19 pandemic," International Journal of Advanced Trends in Computer Science and Engineering, pp. 6251–6258, 2020.

[9] S. Windiarti, N. Fadilah, E. Dhermawati, and B. W. Pratolo, "Teachers' perception toward the obstacles of E-learning classes," Ethical Ling. J. Lang. Teach. Lit., vol. 6, no. 2, pp. 117–128, 2019.

[10] Naveed, Q.N., Qureshi, M.R.N., Alsayed, A.O., Muhammad, A., Sanober, S. and Shah, A., 2017, November. Prioritizing barriers of E-Learning for effective teaching-learning using fuzzy analytic hierarchy process (FAHP). In 2017 4th IEEE international conference on engineering technologies and applied sciences (ICETAS) (pp. 1-8). IEEE.

[11] H. Aldowah, H. Al-Samarraie, and S. Ghazal, "How course, contextual, and technological challenges are associated with instructors' individual challenges to successfully implement E-learning: A developing country perspective," IEEE Access, vol. 7, pp. 48792–48806, 2019.

[12] M. Rannastu-Avalos and L. A. Siiman, "Challenges for distance learning and online collaboration in the time of COVID-19: Interviews with science teachers," in Collaboration Technologies and Social Computing, Cham: Springer International Publishing, 2020, pp. 128–142. .

[13] Cao, W., Fang, Z., Hou, G., Han, M., Xu, X., Dong, J. and Zheng, J., 2020. The psychological impact of the COVID-19 epidemic on college students in China. Psychiatry research, 287, p.112934.

[14] A. Tooq, Z. Cadiente, D. Ligawen, and S. Mendaje, "Readiness, Challenges, and Satisfaction in the New Paradigm of Teaching and Learning: An E-Learning Evaluation," in 2020 Sixth International Conference on e-learning (econf), IEEE, 2020, pp. 6–11.

[15] Hamdan, M., Jaidin, J.H., Fithriyah, M. and Anshari, M., 2020, December. E-learning in time of COVID-19 pandemic: Challenges & experiences. In 2020 sixth international conference on e-learning (econf) (pp. 12-16). IEEE.

[16] P.-S. Goh and J. Sandars, "Rethinking scholarship in medical education during the era of the COVID-19 pandemic," MedEdPublish, vol. 9, no. 1, p. 97, 2020.

[17] Sabr, D.S. and Neamah, A.F., 2017, September. Notice of Violation of IEEE Publication Principles: Challenges and Opportunities of E-Learning in Iraq. In 2017 International Conference on Computer and Applications (ICCA) (pp. 259-265). IEEE.

[18] L. Shahmoradi, V. Changizi, E. Mehraeen, A. Bashiri, B. Jannat, and M. Hosseini, "The challenges of E-learning system: Higher educational institutions perspective," J. Educ. Health Promot., vol. 7, p. 116, 2018.

[19] S. Shivshankar and S. Paul, "E-Learning Environment-The Security and Privacy Challenges Focusing on the Counter Measures," in 2015 International Conference on Developments of E-Systems Engineering (DeSE), IEEE, 2015, pp. 176–179.

[20] A. Al-Azawei, P. Parslow, and K. Lundqvist, Barriers and opportunities of e-learning implementation in Iraq: A case of public universities. The International Review of Research in Open and Distributed Learning. 2016.

[21] C. Argyris and D. A. Schön, "Organizational learning: A theory of action perspective," Reis, pp. 345–348, 1997.

[22] M. Denscombe, EBOOK: The Good Research Guide: For Small-Scale Social Research Projects. UK: McGraw-Hill Education, 2017.

Education 4.0 Supporting Remote, Hybrid, and Face-to-Face Teaching-Learning Systems for Academic Continuity during the COVID-19 Global Pandemic

The Mechatronic Product Design Course in Higher Education as Case Study

Jhonattan Miranda
School of Engineering and Sciences
Tecnologico de Monterrey
Mexico City, Mexico
e-mail: jhonattan.miranda@tec.mx

Donovan Esqueda-Merino
School of Engineering and Sciences
Tecnologico de Monterrey
Mexico State, Mexico
e-mail: donovan.esqueda@tec.mx

María Soledad Ramírez-Montoya
Institute for the Future of Education
Tecnologico de Monterrey
Monterrey, N.L. Mexico
e-mail: solramirez@tec.mx

Abstract—**The COVID-19 global pandemic provoked the emergence of new teaching-learning systems necessary to guarantee academic continuity at all levels, resulting in remote, hybrid, and face-to-face teaching-learning processes becoming more robust and efficient. However, higher education faces a significant challenge because, in many cases, the physical infrastructure with face-to-face access to specialized laboratories must have integrated, functional, and practical learning to train disciplinary competencies. Consequently, it is required to implement new pedagogical procedures and remote technologies to compensate for the lack of face-to-face access to laboratories. This study examines Education 4.0, the intersection of technology and pedagogy in today's higher education landscape. A case study is presented to provide a comprehensive comparison of remote, hybrid, and face-to-face learning modalities, illustrating their unique features and effectiveness in different educational contexts.**

Keywords-Education 4.0; Higher Education; Educational Innovation; Engineering Education.

I. INTRODUCTION

The global pandemic caused by the coronavirus (SARS-CoV-2) has resulted in the most significant health crisis of the modern era, causing social and economic devastation worldwide. One of the most affected sectors was education at all levels. During 2020 and 2021, face-to-face academic activities were suspended worldwide due to prevention and mitigation measures to contain the spread of the virus. For several months, the uncertainty and prolongation of the health crisis forced educational institutions to develop various short, medium, and long-term solutions that incorporated new pedagogical models, learning methods, delivery modalities, and teaching-learning programs powered by 4.0 technologies. These solutions aimed to guarantee academic continuity at all levels and make remote teaching-learning processes more robust and efficient. In 2021 and 2022, the return to face-to-face instruction occurred mainly in hybrid and face-to-face teaching-learning modalities. However, the courses had to be flexible enough to adapt to the possibility of returning to a remote education format at any time. These activities were accompanied by implementing safety measures such as mask-wearing, social distancing, best practices, and knowledge gained during the crisis.

During academic continuity efforts amidst the pandemic, various challenges arose, including infrastructure issues such as access to platforms and devices, stable electricity and connectivity, training stakeholders in Information and Communication Technologies (ICTs), and designing new pedagogical procedures to maintain student engagement and assess their knowledge effectively. Higher education faced unique difficulties, particularly with face-to-face access to specialized labs needed for practical learning and developing disciplinary competencies. To address these challenges, the educational sector embraced Education 4.0, a combination of technological advancements and pedagogical procedures [1].

The implementation of existing and emerging ICTs, including virtual classrooms, virtual labs, and remote labs, played a vital role during the pandemic. Studies showed that students could learn and develop disciplinary competencies with favorable outcomes using these technologies [2][3]. Virtual laboratories utilized traditional multimedia resources, 2D simulations, and immersive 3D environments, incorporating Virtual Reality (VR) and Augmented Reality (AR) techniques. Successful examples of these technologies were seen in teaching basic sciences, such as physics, chemistry, and mathematics [4][5].

In higher education, VR and AR have also been observed in various implementations, for instance, during the design process and development of technology-based products. Furthermore, the combination of virtual environments with hardware systems employing haptics and joysticks has made the learning experience highly relevant, as students can combine tactile sensations, vision, and proprioception during their learning process. Examples can be observed in physics [6], medicine [7], and engineering [8], among others. Most recently, the integration into higher education of Natural Language Processing (NLP) systems based on Artificial Intelligence (AI), such as those developed by the OpenAI company, has the potential to significantly improve the efficiency of tasks, such as grading and content creation [9].

In the case of engineering education programs, the use of Learning Management Systems (LMSs) has enhanced their capabilities to provide access to specialized virtual laboratories in engineering. For example, specific features have been included to support Computer-Aided Design, Manufacturing, and Engineering Systems (CAD, CAM, CAE) and other more complex and robust systems, including Product Lifecycle Management (PLM) software and

Supervisory Control and Data Acquisition (SCADA) systems [10]. Also, Engineering Education has implemented simulations of manufacturing plants and industrial robotics, the latter using software for simulating discrete events and digital twins' techniques [11].

On the other hand, remote laboratories have grown exponentially due to technological advances in communication and connectivity. Today, Cyber-Physical Systems (CPS) laboratories are a type of laboratory where physical elements and software components intricately intertwine. Remote laboratories allow the experience of telepresence in physical laboratories, carrying out practices and remote experiments with actual equipment with the advantages of flexibility in time and place [12].

This work uses the concept of Education 4.0 to design new teaching-learning systems and pedagogical procedures, with a case study on the "Mechatronic Product Design" course demonstrating the application of ICTs and learning methods for remote, hybrid, and face-to-face dynamics.

The rest of this paper is structured as follows: Section 2 introduces the concept of Education 4.0. In Section 3, the Education 4.0 Reference Framework is presented as a conceptual foundation for designing teaching-learning systems in higher education. Section 4 provides a case study illustrating the design, development, and implementation of a new teaching-learning system within the context of Education 4.0, using the "Mechatronic Product Design" course as an example. Finally, conclusions are drawn in Section 5.

II. EDUCATION 4.0 IN HIGHER EDUCATION

The Education 4.0 concept has been implemented in various contexts and described by different authors. Therefore, the education sector has been evolving and leveraging particular technologies of the fourth industrial revolution, such as generic technology for connectivity, datafication, digitalization, smartification, and virtualization. The combination of these technologies with active learning methods and professional instruction to train key competencies in students today is known as Education 4.0. Also, Education 4.0 can refer to the training and development of core competencies in engineering education for Industry 4.0 [13], according to the Education 4.0 Framework proposed by the World Economic Forum. The Education 4.0 framework is characterized by critical shifts in learning content, the development of essential skills and competencies, and experiences to redefine quality learning in the new economy [14]. In addition, the fostering of self-learning (heutagogy), collaboration (peeragogy), and the highlighted use of ICTs (cybergogy) is included in Education 4.0.

This work considers the use of 4.0 Technologies with current techniques and methods in education for the development of desirable competencies in the profile of today's students. We use the following concept of Education 4.0 applied to higher education as a reference: "Education 4.0 is the period in which the education sector takes advantage of emerging ICTs to improve pedagogical processes that are complemented by new learning methods and innovative didactic and management tools, as well as smart and sustainable infrastructure used during current teaching-learning processes for the training and development of key competencies in today's students" [1].

Therefore, identifying the key enablers to achieve the Education 4.0 vision is crucial to guide educators during teaching-learning. Additionally, designers, researchers, and specialists in teaching-learning programs and instructional design should refer to these key enablers.

Six categories of key enablers are used in the design and implementation of today's teaching-learning systems, and Figure 1 summarizes the key enablers of Education 4.0 [15].

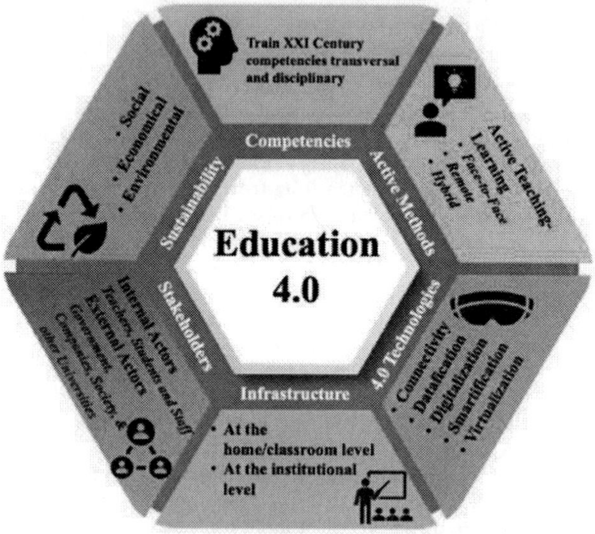

Figure 1. Six key enablers of Education 4.0, adapted from [15].

1) Training key competencies, covering both soft and hard competencies for students.

2) Applying active teaching-learning methods with various modalities, such as problem-based learning, project-based learning, experiential learning, and gamified learning.

3) Utilizing 4.0 Technologies, which involve connectivity, datafication, digitalization, smartification, and virtualization.

4) Implementing innovative infrastructure, including services, facilities, devices, and physical-virtual environments to enhance teaching-learning processes.

5) Involving relevant stakeholders, such as internal actors (teachers, students, staff) and external actors (government, industry, society, other universities) in the teaching process.

6) Considering sustainable impacts by aligning with the UN Sustainable Development Goals (SDG) to create positive social, economic, and environmental effects.

III. THE EDUCATION 4.0 REFERENCE FRAMEWORK FOR DESIGNING TEACHING-LEARNING SYSTEMS

The Education 4.0 Reference Framework for designing teaching-learning systems was used in this work [15]. This reference framework allows designers to be guided during the design and development processes of new educational products, teaching-learning processes, and educational infrastructure, considering the concept and vision of Education 4.0.

This reference framework is justified by the need to create integrated systems where product, process, and infrastructure interact for improved performance. Additionally, these systems must adapt to existing contexts and environments while considering the key enablers of Education 4.0. The reference framework incorporates the six key enablers of Education 4.0, enabling resources to support training in transversal and disciplinary competencies through active teaching-learning processes in various delivery modes (face-to-face, hybrid, remote). This innovative infrastructure, with the participation of key stakeholders and the support of 4.0 Technologies, facilitates positive social, economic, and environmental benefits. It is, therefore, necessary to have an integrative vision that can offer a new education product, a new teaching-learning process, and the necessary infrastructure to achieve more efficient and effective processes and a better user experience. Although this framework allows an integrated design (product-process-infrastructure), it can also facilitate the design process for individual entities, as presented in the case study section for the design of a "teaching-learning process."

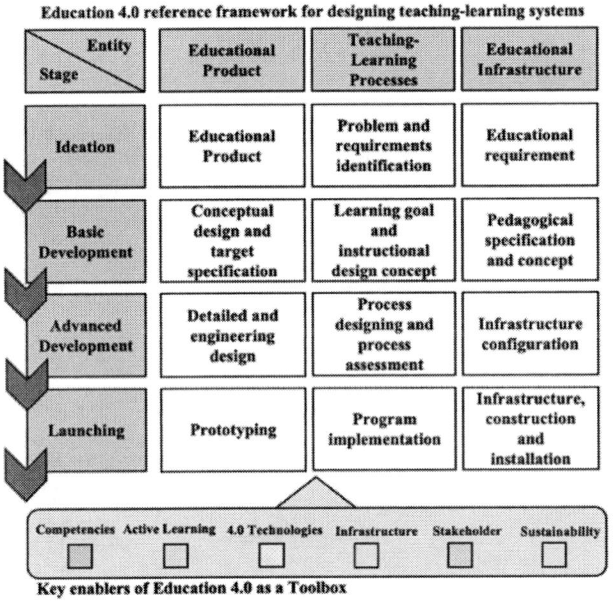

Figure 2. The Education 4.0 reference framework for designing teaching-learning systems.

This reference framework comprises four design stages of the product development lifecycle in a systematic design process: (i) Ideation, (ii) Basic development, (iii) Advanced Development, and (iv) Launching. Figure 2 presents the general model of the Education 4.0 Reference Framework for designing teaching-learning systems.

IV. CASE STUDY: THE MECHATRONIC PRODUCT DESIGN COURSE IN HIGHER EDUCATION

Innovation and entrepreneurship among today's students lead to creative, efficient, and practical solutions to society's challenges and problems and achieving sustainable goals. However, the current social context, technological advances, necessary processes of digital transformation, and new paradigms in education bring challenging teaching-learning scenarios for educators. The lack of specialized guides and resources to address these challenges is a current problem. In addition, engaging and motivating students in current teaching-learning processes is necessary. Consequently, efficiently teaching and inspiring the next generation of students/entrepreneurs is challenging for educational institutions. Therefore, access to high-quality, innovative, and affordable teaching-learning systems is needed to contribute to forming highly competitive professionals.

The course "Mechatronic Product Design" is presented as a case study to illustrate the design, development, and implementation of new teaching-learning systems in Education 4.0 to design teaching-learning processes. This course is among the academic offerings in the mechatronics engineering and mechanical engineering careers at Tecnologico de Monterrey in Mexico. Implementing this course was justified as part of the emerging programs to ensure academic continuity in this institution during the 2020 - 2022 global health crisis.

Tecnologico de Monterrey implemented a strategy to redesign its face-to-face courses in a remote-hybrid format applying a flexible-digital model [16]. Online resources and 4.0 Technologies were primarily implemented to carry out this transformation. Also, national and multi-campus courses were opened to optimize resource use and leverage the benefits of distance formats. Therefore, students attending the 26 Tec campuses in Mexico enrolled in these courses.

In engineering education, teaching-learning processes require physical infrastructures, including specialized laboratories and tools, because they are necessary for training disciplinary skills/competencies and experiential and practical learning.

Mechatronic engineering was a challenging area because it encompasses various disciplines such as mechanics, software, electronics, and control systems and is also one of the engineering areas most impacting industry thanks to the implementation of emerging technologies in new products and the generation of best practices in current production systems.

In addition, the emergence of smart and sustainable products and processes has assumed significant relevance in recent years. That is why holistic designs of new products, manufacturing processes, and production systems are necessary for mechatronics. Therefore, distance teaching and practical activities in this field have become challenging.

The Education 4.0 Reference Framework for designing teaching-learning systems was taken in this work's redesign process, and particular requirements were considered. In addition, the four stages of transformation from traditional courses (face-to-face) to online distance "remote" and "hybrid" courses (flexible-digital) as part of the program designing activities were also used: (i) planning, (ii) synchronous elements, (iii) asynchronous elements, and (iv) preparation for delivery. Figure 3 summarizes the four implemented stages during the transformation process. Table I summarizes the application of the four design stages of the Education 4.0 Reference Framework for designing teaching-learning systems. Table II presents the teaching-learning process, highlighting how the Education 4.0 enablers shaped the "Mechatronic Product Design."

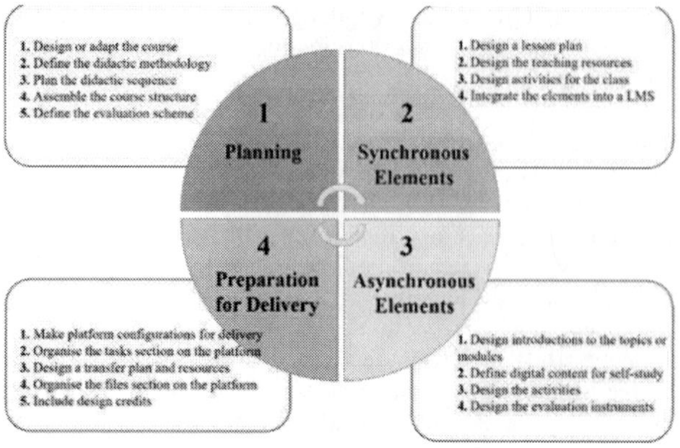

Figure 3. The transformation model from traditional courses to remote and hybrid courses.

TABLE I. SUMMARY OF THE DESIGN PROCESS, TEACHING-LEARNING PROCESS ENTITY

#	Activities	Particular Model
1	***Problem and Requirement identification specification***	**Problem:** Redesign the "Mechatronic Product Design" course from face-to-face to remote and hybrid delivery modalities and provide adequate training and development of key transversal and disciplinary competencies considering experiential and practical learning as core issues. **Student profile:** Undergraduate Mechatronics Engineering and Mechanical Engineering students at Tecnologico de Monterrey, Mexico. **Semester:** 8 or 9. **Previous knowledge:** Embedded systems, computerized control, and machine analysis and synthesis. **Duration:** 22 sessions (2 hours per session), 44 hours for summer sessions. And 16 sessions (3 hours per session), 48 hours for a semester session. **Delivery Modality Goal:** Remote (synchronous and asynchronous) and Hybrid. **Academic periods to be implemented:** Summer courses and Semestral courses.
2	***Learning goals definition and instructional design concept***	**Learning Outcomes:** At the end of this program, participants learn best practices and apply the appropriate tools of technology-based and mechatronic product, process, and manufacturing systems designs, create working prototypes, identify market segments, and define business models and manufacturing systems.
3	***Process designing and process assessment. Program assessment***	**Process designing:** Application of the transformation model from traditional courses to remote and hybrid courses: (i) Planning, (ii) Synchronous elements, (iii) Asynchronous elements, and (iv) Preparation for delivery. **Assessment Instrument:** The "i-Scale" was implemented [17]. This tool covers qualitative evaluations for learning outcomes, the nature of innovation, growth potential, institutional alignment, and financial viability. This evaluation indicated that this course has few or no drawbacks to be implemented.
6	***Program implementation***	**The number of students and delivery modality:** 28 students from 7 campuses across Mexico (Summer 2020, Remote). 56 students from 2 campuses in the Central Mexico region (February-June 2021, Hybrid and Flexible). 50 students from 2 campuses in the Central Mexico region (February-June 2022, Face-To-Face and Flexible). **Students' assessment method:** Mixed method analysis applying surveys about the perception of the transversal competencies trained and a qualitative evaluation of the working prototypes. **Research question for quantitative analysis:** What is the student's perception of the training of transversal competencies in these courses? **Research question for qualitative analysis:** What are the results of developing mechatronic working prototypes in these courses?

TABLE II. THE MECHATRONIC PRODUCT DESIGN COURSE CONSIDERING THE EDUCATION 4.0 ENABLERS

Modules	Education 4.0 Enablers	Goal
1. Introduction to innovation and new product and process design Key concepts related to innovation and methodologies for new product and process design and development.	**Main Competencies:** *Soft: Critical Thinking; Hard: Methodologies Design* **Main Active Methods:** *Active Learning and Flipped classroom* **Main 4.0 Technologies:** *LMS, Web-conference platform, and instant message systems.* **Main Infrastructure:** *At institutional, access to remote labs and virtual classrooms* *At home, connected and connectivity services* **Main Stakeholders:** *At least two teachers were involved* **Sustainability:** *SDGs were promoted*	• Identify types and sources of innovation. • Identify the methodolog y and techniques to be used.
2. Mechatronic Product Design Design and development of a mechatronic product through four stages: (i) Conceptual design, (ii) System design, (iii) Engineering and detailed design, and (iv) Prototyping and validation.	**Main Competencies:** *Soft: Collaboration, Cooperation, Creativity & Innovation.* *Hard: Mechatronic principles and integrated product design* **Main Active Method:** *Blended-based Learning and Learning by Doing* **Main 4.0 Technologies:** *LMS, Virtual labs for simulation, and 3D modeling systems* **Main Infrastructure:** *At the institution, access to physical and remote labs and virtual classrooms* *At home, connected and connectivity services* **Main Stakeholders:** *At least two teachers and one specialist from the industry were involved* **Sustainability:** *Design for Sustainability (DfS) and Life Cycle Assessment (LCA)*	• Identifying opportunity areas • Understandi ng painful situations and customer/us er requirement s. • A prototype of the proposed mechatronic product. • Evaluation of the mechatronic working prototype.
3. Manufacturing Process Design	**Main Competencies:** *Soft: Collaboration, Critical Thinking.*	• Definition of materials

Design and development of a manufacturing process through three stages: (i) Conceptual design, (ii) Technology selection, (iii) Production Plan.	*Hard: Process Design, Production Scheduling, and Virtual Commissioning.* **Main Active Method:** *Blended-based Learning and Learning by Doing* **Main 4.0 Technology:** *Spreadsheets, Software for Plant Design, Project Management, and Plant Simulation* **Main Infrastructure:** *At institutional, access to remote labs and virtual classrooms.* *At home, connected and connectivity services.* **Main Stakeholders:** *At least two teachers and one specialist from the industry are involved.* **Sustainability:** *Design for Sustainability (DfS) and Life Cycle Assessment (LCA)*	and processes to be used. • Organization of the plant and schedule of activities. • Analysis of main costs and projected sales.
4. Business Model and Launching Define and validate the value proposition of the product/process/business and product pitch.	**Main Competencies:** *Soft: Communication.* *Hard: Enterprise creation and marketing principles* **Main Active Method:** *Blended-based Learning and Learning by Doing.* **Main 4.0 Technology:** *LMS, Virtual Classroom, and Collaborative Virtual Platforms.* **Main Infrastructure:** *At institutional, access to remote labs and virtual classrooms.* *At home, connected and connectivity services.* **Main Stakeholders:** *At least two teachers and one specialist from the industry are involved.* **Sustainability:** *Business sustainability assessment (short-medium-long term).*	• Product market-fit • Product pitch • Product business model

Building upon the Education 4.0 concept, this study utilizes the Education 4.0 Reference Framework to design teaching-learning systems that cater to the evolving needs of the education sector. By incorporating the four stages of transformation (planning, synchronous elements, asynchronous elements, and preparation for delivery), this research effectively adapts traditional face-to-face courses to the online distance "remote" and "hybrid" formats, which are better aligned with the flexible-digital approach in Education 4.0.

Figure 4 presents the results of an applied survey about the perception of the trained transversal (soft) competencies during the impartation of this course. The graphics compare both surveys, a pre-survey based on the perception of how often these competencies are trained during their classes and a post-survey based on the perception of how often the competencies were trained during the boot camp. These surveys were applied during three periods (2020, 2021, and 2022) to analyze how the three different delivery modalities impacted the designed course. The presented results show that most of the students perceived that the promoted key competencies were trained during the activities of this course. Figure 4 shows a significant increase in the feeling of accomplishment of the students regarding the soft competencies that were designed and implemented in the course. Additionally, general satisfaction with the course experience was positive in 75% of the cases.

Also, in this course, the students were encouraged to develop collaborative and cooperative mechatronic projects; then, group activities were promoted, and teams were formed. For the case of the remote course, the teams were integrated by students from different campuses; for hybrid and face-to-face, the teams comprised students from different areas in the mechatronics and mechanics fields. Therefore, the formed teams allowed students to propose various new mechatronics products and their manufacturing processes and business models. These products aimed to address current social needs, pursue sustainability, and follow technological megatrends to be updated and remain competitive in the marketplace.

For this study, 16 new mechatronic products were evaluated. The projects presented corresponded to 3D models accompanied by simulations, Apps, and in some cases, rapid prototyping through 3D printing methods and rapid prototyping with Arduino boards. It was possible for the three formats (face-to-face, hybrid, remote) thanks to the provision of physical and virtual infrastructure at both levels, institutional and home. The positive results obtained highlight the potential of these new teaching-learning systems and modalities in fostering essential skills and competencies required for the new economy.

V. CONCLUSIONS

Due to global lockdowns resulting from the COVID-19 pandemic, institutions have rapidly transitioned to digital education models, supported by diverse ICTs, leading to the emergence of Education 4.0. Through this paper, a framework for designing courses within the context of Education 4.0 is presented.

The framework introduced is explained with a case study of an engineering course involving the process and design of a mechatronic product. This course was chosen as a practical example of implementing a highly complex course on multi-campuses and surveying students in the same major but with different educative backgrounds. Moreover, the course format facilitated interaction among students from different campuses and disciplines, creating active learning environments with synchronous and asynchronous teamwork activities.

Throughout the three different delivery modalities (face-to-face, hybrid, remote), the course demonstrated adaptability and flexibility in response to varying circumstances. The consistent positive outcomes across modalities indicate that the Education 4.0 framework is robust enough to accommodate diverse teaching and learning needs while maintaining high-quality education.

The results showed that aligning the learning goals with the key competencies to be trained and applying correct learning methods supported by adequate ICTs of 4.0 Technologies and infrastructure made it possible to generate product ideas and conceptual products and create physical and working prototypes. It demonstrated that students could implement the acquired knowledge and integrate core concepts in this engineering area. Likewise, this new class format allowed students to interact with others from different campuses and disciplines and generate active learning environments with synchronous and asynchronous teamwork activities.

Finally, this paper encourages further investigation of the Education 4.0 framework across various disciplines, levels, and cultural contexts. By examining the framework in diverse environments, researchers and educators can enhance understanding of its potential and limitations, ultimately guiding best practices and policies for future teaching and learning.

ACKNOWLEDGMENT

The authors acknowledge the financial and technical support of Writing Lab, Institute for the Future of Education, Tecnologico de Monterrey, Mexico, in the production of this work. Also, the authors appreciate the financial support from Tecnologico de Monterrey through the "Challenge-Based Research Funding Program 2022". Project ID # I004 - IFE001 - C2-T3 – T.

REFERENCES

[1] J. Miranda, et al., "The core components of education 4.0 in higher education: Three case studies in engineering education," Computers and Electrical Engineering, vol. 93, pp. 107-278, 2021.

[2] D. Keddi, and S. Frerich, "Enhancing Engineering Education by Virtual Laboratories," International Conference on Remote Engineering and Virtual Instrumentation, Springer, Cham, pp. 359-365, 2022.

[3] E. García-Morán, et al., "Industry 4.0 Competencies as the Core of Online Engineering Laboratories," Design and Technology Education, vol. 26, no.3, pp. 30-51, 2021.

[4] O. C. Agbonifo, O. A. Sarumi, and Y. M. Akinola, "A chemistry laboratory platform enhanced with virtual reality for students' adaptive learning," Research in Learning Technology, pp. 28, 2020.

[5] N. Ahmad, and S. Junaini, "Augmented Reality for Learning Mathematics: A Systematic Literature Review," International Journal of Emerging Technologies in Learning (iJET), vol. 15, no. 16, pp. 106-122, 2020.

[6] L. Neri, et al., "Improving the learning of physics concepts by using haptic devices," IEEE Frontiers in Education Conference (FIE), pp. 1-7, 2015.

[7] D. Escobar-Castillejos, J. Noguez, L. Neri, A. Magana, and B. Benes, "A review of simulators with haptic devices for medical training," Journal of Medical Systems, vol 40, pp. 1-22, 2016.

[8] R. L. Williams, X. He, T. Franklin, and S. Wang, "Haptics-augmented engineering mechanics educational tools," World Transactions on Engineering and Technology Education, vol. 6, p. 27, 2007.

[9] D. Baidoo-Anu, and L. Owusu Ansah, "Education in the Era of Generative Artificial Intelligence (AI): Understanding the Potential Benefits of ChatGPT in Promoting Teaching and Learning," SSRN 4337484, 2023.

[10] X. L. Liu, W. M. Wang, H. Guo, A. V. Barenji, Z. Li, and G. Q. Huang, "Industrial blockchain-based framework for product lifecycle management in industry 4.0," Robotics and Computer-Integrated Manufacturing, vol. 63, p. 101897, 2020.

[11] D. Chavarría-Barrientos, et.al., "A methodology to support manufacturing system design using digital models and simulations: an automotive supplier case study," IFAC-PapersOnLine, vol. 51(11), pp. 1598-1603, 2018.

[12] C. Terkowsky, S. Frye, and D. May, "Using Constructive Alignment to Evaluate Industry 4.0 Competencies in Remote Laboratories for Manufacturing Technology," International Conference on Remote Engineering and Virtual Instrumentation, Springer, Cham, pp. 603-613, 2020.

[13] S. Das, D. K. Kleinke, and D. Pistrui, "Reimagining engineering education: Does Industry 4.0 need Education 4.0?," Virtual Annual Conference Content Access, 2020.

[14] World Economic Forum, "Schools of the Future, Defining New Models of Education for the Fourth Industrial Revolution," Geneva: World Economic Forum, 2020.

[15] J. Miranda, M. S. Ramírez-Montoya, and A. Molina, "Education 4.0 reference framework for the design of teaching-learning systems: two case studies involving collaborative networks and open innovation". Smart and Sustainable Collaborative Networks 4.0: 22nd IFIP WG 5.5 Working Conference on Virtual Enterprises, Springer International Publishing, vol. 22, pp. 692-701, 2021.

[16] Tecnológico de Monterrey, Educational Innovation Department, "Report FDM," 2020.

[17] C. S. López-Cruz, and Y. Heredia, "Escala i, Guía de Aplicación," Tecnológico de Monterrey, México., 2017.

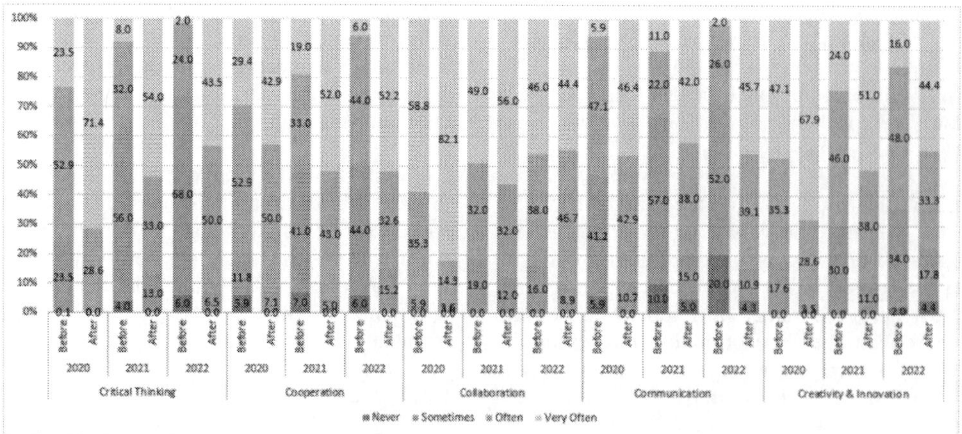

Figure 4. Survey results comparing the key transversal competencies trained before and after the course (2020 – 2021 - 2022).

Architectural Design of an Adaptive, Structure-Aware Intelligent Tutoring System

Sebastian Kucharski
Chair of Distributed and Networked Systems
Faculty of Computer Science
Dresden University of Technology, Germany
email: sebastian.kucharski@tu-dresden.de

Tommy Kubica
Chair of Distributed and Networked Systems
Faculty of Computer Science
Dresden University of Technology, Germany
email: tommy.kubica@tu-dresden.de

Iris Braun
Chair of Distributed and Networked Systems
Faculty of Computer Science
Dresden University of Technology, Germany
email: iris.braun@tu-dresden.de

Abstract—**Intelligent Tutoring Systems (ITS) for Learning Management Systems (LMS) combine the benefits of user-centered learning and the provisioning of easy-to-use learning content in one place. They typically have two major drawbacks. First, they are LMS-specific (i.e., not adaptive). Thus, many LMS do not include an ITS because existing solutions cannot be reused. Second, they lack in a didactically usable representation of the structure of the learning content (i.e., they are not structure-aware). Therefore, the learner may get lost during the provision of assistance. Overcoming both of these drawbacks at once is a desirable objective, because it allows the learner to take advantage of personalized learning in diverse LMS while accessing a large amount of available learning content. In addition, it allows an ITS to use cross-plattform analytics (CPA) to improve assistance. The main challenge in achieving this objective is dealing with the heterogeneous approaches to structuring learning content used by different LMS. For this purpose, an adaptive, structure-aware ITS is proposed that can work with diverse LMS by using a generic data structure that can represent and process the required learning knowledge data in a system-independent way. The focus of this paper is to outline the architecture of this system.**

Keywords-personalized learning; technology-enhanced learning; learning analytics; educational data mining.

I. INTRODUCTION

The purpose of integrating *Intelligent Tutoring Systems* (ITS) [3] into *Learning Management Systems* (LMS) is to combine LMS-specific advantages (e.g., easy-to-use provision of a large amount of learning content in one place [2]) and ITS-specific benefits (e.g., adaptation of learning content to the user's needs [5]). There are typically two major drawbacks to combining ITS and LMS.

1) The ITS are designed for a specific LMS only (i.e., they are not *adaptive*) such as the one developed for Moodle [13].
2) The LMS lack in a didactically usable (e.g., graphical) representation of the learning content structure that can be controlled by the ITS (i.e., they are not *structure-aware*) [14].

The former causes that neither implemented didactic concepts can be reused nor derived user assistance profiles can be considered in different LMS [5]. The latter can result in the user not being able to follow the assistance that is related to the structure of the learning content, and subsequently getting lost in the learning space during the guiding process [7]. This is due to the fact that ITS are intended to guide the learner through the learning content, while LMS are mainly designed for self-employed learning. To bring the two together, the ITS must be coupled with the content structure of the LMS in a way that is comprehensible to the user.

Related work addressing these two drawbacks and the corresponding research challenges is summarized in Section II. In Section III, an adaptive, structure-aware ITS is proposed that overcomes both drawbacks at once.

II. RELATED WORK

Previous work on ITS adaptation has been primarily concerned with adapting these systems to the learner [12], and rarely with adapting these systems to different learning environments in which they might be integrated. Thus, the ITS developed so far are usually independent systems [11] that cannot make use of the large amount of learning data that is available in the established LMS.

The research that has been done to integrate intelligent tutoring mechanisms into learning environments [1], has mainly focused on developing learning-environment-specific systems that are limited to working with environment-specific data. To overcome this limitation, Mangaroska et al. investigated how learning data from different e-learning systems combined in a learning ecosystem can be represented and processed system-independently [9]. For this purpose, the authors proposed a cross-platform architecture [10] that includes three e-learning systems from which learner-generated data is collected. This data is converted into the unified *Visualized Education NTNU System Object Notation (VSON)* and processed by a visualization dashboard. The main focus of this research is the generic integration of learning-analytics in e-learning systems and the investigation of what *cross-platform analytics* (CPA) means for learning design research [8]. As far as known, it has not been investigated how an ITS integrated into an LMS can make use of the collected data, while the purpose of the proposed system is to provide didactically traceable assistance functionalities based on this data in a system-independent way. Thus, the focus of this research is on how to generically provide assistance functionalities and the corresponding system-specific assistance components of the ITS LMS independently.

How to integrate ITS functionalities into arbitrary LMS was investigated by Palomino et al. [4, 6]. For this purpose, a system was developed that is LMS-independent by using a generic data structure for the learning content and that enables learning sequences piecewise conditional on the learner's performance measured by grades [5]. A prototype editor for defining these sequences has been implemented in Moodle. As far as known, there has been no investigation of the possibility of creating or generating a structured visualization of the learning content from the generic data structure. Furthermore, although the data structure is system-independent, the ITS parameterization component (i.e., the path specification editor) and the ITS assistance component (i.e., the learning sequence mechanism) are currently dependent on Moodle. The focus of this research is therefore on what kind of assistance can be provided system-independently and how the corresponding components can be built and automatically provided for diverse LMS.

III. ADAPTIVE, STRUCTURE-AWARE ITS

Overcoming the two drawbacks mentioned in Section I is particularly challenging due to the heterogeneous approaches to structuring learning content used by different LMS. For this purpose, a structure-aware ITS is proposed that can be used for diverse LMS by the utilization of a generic, LMS-independent learning knowledge data model. As shown in Figure 1, this system includes two assistance components that have to be integrated into the considered LMS and that are described in Section III-A and III-B. Both of these components can be provided automatically in order to make the ITS as system-independent and thus as adaptive as possible. The data that is required for the generation and dynamic parameterization of these components is stored in a generic data structure presented in Section III-C. This data is retrieved from the diverse LMS using a thin adaptation layer which is described in Section III-D.

A. Knowledge Graph Editor

The first assistance component, called the *knowledge graph*, is a graphical representation that visualizes the learning content. It is embedded in the *knowledge graph editor* which is integrated with the considered LMS. The editor can be used in two different modes. One is intended to support the learner and is called *read-only mode*. The other one is intended to support the configuration of the ITS by the teacher and is called the *editing mode*. In the *read-only mode* the *knowledge graph editor* can support the learner in the following ways.

1) It provides an overview of the learning content, it's structure and the learner's progress.
2) It offers the ability to graphically navigate within the content, including the convenient selection of learning content suggestions.

In the *editing mode*, the *knowledge graph* can be used by the teacher to parameterize the assistance process for the following purposes.

1) The specification of the metadata for the learning content
2) The definition of the content-related dependencies between the learning content

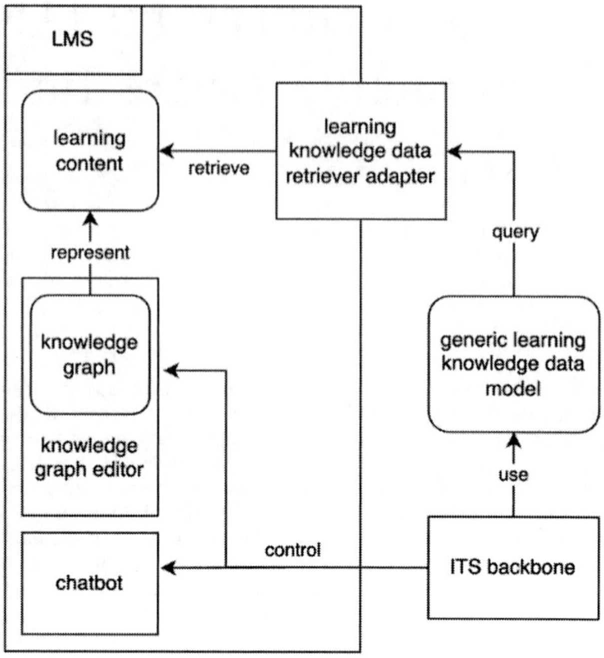

Fig. 1. Conceptual architecture of the proposed adaptive, structure-aware ITS.

B. Chatbot

The second component for providing assistance is a *chatbot*. It is integrated into the considered LMS and provides typical ITS functionalities such as suggesting learning content. This component is controlled by the *ITS backbone*, which processes the data from the *generic data model* (see Section III-C). The *ITS backbone* is also coupled to the knowledge graph editor, so that it can influence the content representation. This means that it can cause the representation to be restructured according to the learning content suggestions accepted by the learner, or it can cause the adaptation of the representation to the learner's state of knowledge.

C. Generic Data Model

With regard to the intended assistance functionalities, the presented components require two types of data, the so-called *learning knowledge data*. First, information about what content the learner is studying and how this content is structured is required for the composition of the knowledge graph. Second, information about the learner's interaction with the system is needed to adapt the knowledge graph to the learner's progress and to determine appropriate assistance mechanisms.

Since the learning knowledge data must be system-independent, a *generic learning knowledge data model* is proposed that is used for two different purposes. On the one hand, it is responsible for the system-independent provision of data for the algorithms that determine which assistance processes are required and when. On the other hand, it is used for the automatic provision of the ITS components that are integrated into the LMS under consideration. This is necessary to ensure that the ITS is as system-independent and therefore as adaptive as possible.

D. Data Retriever Adapter

The information stored in the generic learning knowledge data model is queried by a thin adaptation layer, which is responsible for the coupling between the adaptive ITS and the considered LMS. This layer is implemented by a *learning knowledge data retriever adapter*. In order to minimize dependencies on the LMS, and because the adapter must be system-specific, it encapsulates no more functionality than retrieving the required data.

IV. CONCLUSION AND FUTURE WORK

To overcome two major drawbacks of current ITS for LMS, the architectural design of an adaptive, structure-aware ITS was presented. This system provides assistance using a chatbot and a graphical representation of the learning content structure. The data required for the respective assistance scenarios is retrieved through a thin adaptation layer and stored and processed in a generic, LMS-independent data model. Although the adaptation layer has to be system-specific, it encapsulates no more functionality than the plain data retrieval and is therefore easy to implement for an appropriate LMS. The actual ITS functionality is implemented system-independently, depending on the data that can be delivered by the LMS-specific adaptation layers. In addition to the parameterization of the assistance components, the data from this model is also used for the automatic provision of these components.

In summary, using the ITS with the proposed architecture, the learning content of diverse LMS can be adapted to the user's needs. The approach will be evaluated in terms of applicability and effectiveness considering a subset of appropriate state-of-the-art LMS.

REFERENCES

[1] N. S. Aldahwan and N. I. Alsaeed, "Use of artificial intelligent in learning management system (lms): A systematic literature review," *International Journal of Computer Applications*, vol. 175, no. 13, pp. 16–26, 2020.

[2] V. M. Bradley, "Learning management system (lms) use with online instruction," *International Journal of Technology in Education (IJTE)*, vol. 4, no. 1, pp. 68–92, 2021.

[3] J. R. Carbonell, "Ai in cai: An artificial-intelligence approach to computer-assisted instruction," *IEEE transactions on man-machine systems*, vol. 11, no. 4, pp. 190–202, 1970.

[4] P. Giuffra, E. Cecilia, and R. A. Silveira, "A multi-agent system model to integrate virtual learning environments and intelligent tutoring systems," 2013.

[5] C. E. Giuffra Palomino, R. Azambuja Silveira, and M. K. Nakayama, "An intelligent lms model based on intelligent tutoring systems," in *International Conference on Intelligent Tutoring Systems*, Springer, 2014, pp. 567–574.

[6] C. E. Giuffra. P, R. A. Silveira, and M. K. Nakayama, "An intelligent tutoring systems integrated with learning management systems," in *Highlights on Practical Applications of Agents and Multi-Agent Systems: International Workshops of PAAMS 2013, Salamanca, Spain, May 22-24, 2013. Proceedings 11*, Springer, 2013, pp. 316–327.

[7] R. Krauße and H. Körndle, "Tee-the electronic exercise," *Marktplatz Internet: Von e-Learning bis e-Payment, 13. Leipziger Informatik-Tage (LIT 2005)*, 2005.

[8] K. Mangaroska and M. Giannakos, "Learning analytics for learning design: A systematic literature review of analytics-driven design to enhance learning," *IEEE Transactions on Learning Technologies*, vol. 12, no. 4, pp. 516–534, 2018.

[9] K. Mangaroska, B. Vesin, and M. Giannakos, "Cross-platform analytics: A step towards personalization and adaptation in education," in *Proceedings of the 9th international conference on learning analytics & knowledge*, 2019, pp. 71–75.

[10] K. Mangaroska, B. Vesin, V. Kostakos, P. Brusilovsky, and M. N. Giannakos, "Architecting analytics across multiple e-learning systems to enhance learning design," *IEEE Transactions on Learning Technologies*, vol. 14, no. 2, pp. 173–188, 2021.

[11] E. Mousavinasab, N. Zarifsanaiey, S. R. Niakan Kalhori, M. Rakhshan, L. Keikha, and M. Ghazi Saeedi, "Intelligent tutoring systems: A systematic review of characteristics, applications, and evaluation methods," *Interactive Learning Environments*, vol. 29, no. 1, pp. 142–163, 2021.

[12] J. Paladines and J. Ramírez, "A systematic literature review of intelligent tutoring systems with dialogue in natural language," *IEEE Access*, vol. 8, pp. 164 246–164 267, 2020.

[13] V. M. Ramesh, N. Rao, and C. Ramanathan, "Implementation of an intelligent tutoring system using moodle," in *2015 IEEE Frontiers in Education Conference (FIE)*, IEEE, 2015, pp. 1–9.

[14] G. Rößling *et al.*, "Enhancing learning management systems to better support computer science education," *ACM SIGCSE Bulletin*, vol. 40, no. 4, pp. 142–166, 2008.

Enhancing Digital Learning: A User Management and Access System for Remote Laboratories

Marek Achilles, Emilia Weinhold, Kathleen Hallmann, Debora Beger, Chantal König, Florian Matthes, Celina Scholz, Max Schweizer, Rico Beier-Grunwald, Alexander Lampe, Marc Ritter, Matthias Vodel, Christian Roschke
University of Applied Sciences Mittweida
Mittweida, Germany
{machille, eweinhol, kkeilber, dbeger, ckoenig, fmatthe2, cscholz6, mschwei1, beier1, lampe, ritter, vodel, roschke}@hs-mittweida.de

***Abstract*—The digitization of teaching and education is continuously increasing and numerous management systems for digital courses are available. However, the limits of these systems are quickly reached or the systems are too expensive when remote interaction with real laboratory hardware is required. We present a web-based Remote Lab System (RLS) created with open-source tools, which can be integrated flexibly into the existing university infrastructure and realizes the administration, planning and control of the online access to laboratory devices.**

***Index Terms*—Distance learning, user management system, remote/online hardware access, web application**

I. Introduction

Remote web-based teaching provides flexibility and can be facilitated by open source or commercial learning management systems (LMS) and tools like Moodle, Adobe Captivate, MS Teams etc. for the majority of lecture formats. However, for engineering students, laboratory work with physical devices is an essential part of their education that must also be available online. While some laboratory hardware can be accessed via web user interfaces, it is often difficult to integrate them into standard LMSs and ensure that only authorized users operate the devices. Commercial solutions are available from the device manufacturers [1], but can be expensive and difficult to integrate into existing university IT infrastructure. To address these challenges, we developed an open-source web-based RLS with key LMS functions and the flexibility to later integrate with web interfaces of different devices. Our system was designed to be cost-effective and to leverage existing university IT infrastructure to maximize efficiency.

In the following sections, we provide a detailed explanation of the architecture and software components used and conclude with examples of potential applications and extension points to demonstrate the versatility of our approach.

II. System architecture and data model

The RLS software architecture is presented in Fig. 1. The management module includes a frontend for user interaction, which communicates with the backend through an API that encapsulates business logic and database communication. The hardware accessibility module consists of proxy servers for both HTTP and WebSocket requests that provide access to the lab hardware. A reverse proxy server is used to add security features such as connection encryption and authorization via the university's single sign-on system Shibboleth. Choosing an appropriate network configuration is crucial for preventing users from bypassing the system through direct access.

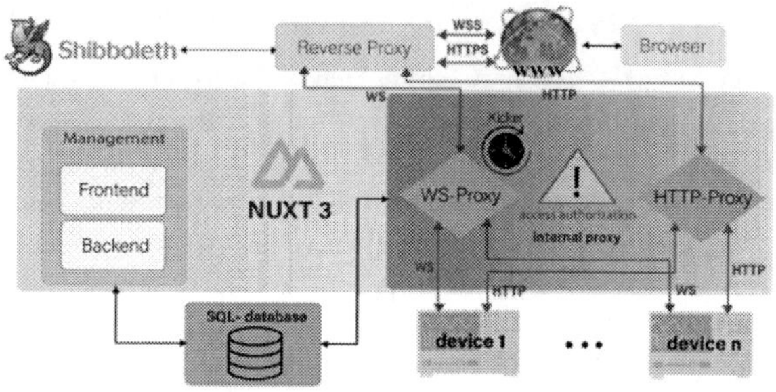

Fig. 1. System architecture of the RLS.

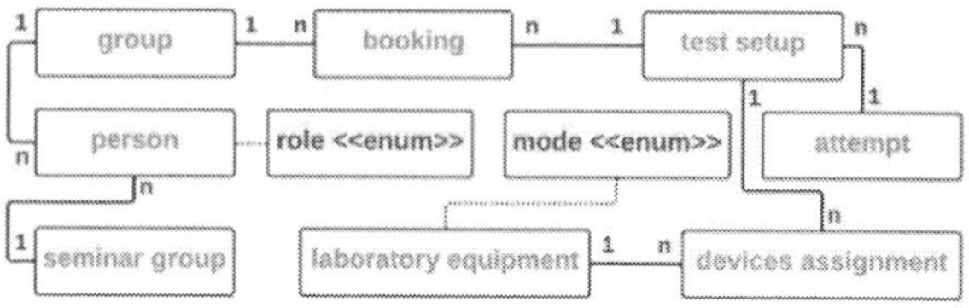

Fig. 2. Data model of user management subsystem.

The data model of the user management subsystem is depicted in Fig. 2. The system is designed for groups of people with assigned roles of either student or lecturer. Student groups have the ability to reserve timeslots for experimental setups. Each setup consists of devices assigned by the lecturer based on the specific experiment to be conducted. The number of available physical devices determines how many setups can be booked in parallel. Lab devices can be assigned to multiple experiments, as long as these experiments cannot be performed simultaneously.

III. Implementation

Various frameworks were utilized for the implementation of the RLS to expedite development and enhance reliability,

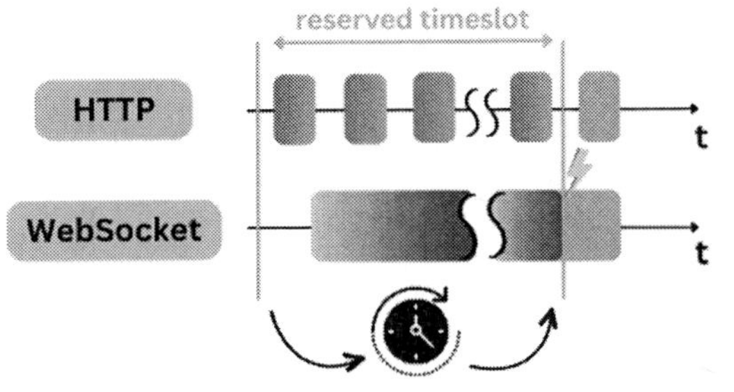

Fig. 3. Hardware access handling: the system verifies permission at the start of each connection, since HTTP connections are short-lived, they can only slightly exceed the time limit; in contrast, WebSocket connections are long-lived and require active termination to comply with the time limit.

allowing us to concentrate on addressing the core issues rather than common problems. To achieve a consistent design and seamless functionality across the user interface, the frontend was build using the Javascript framework Vue in conjunction with Primevue, a library of modern and customizable UI components. The full-stack web application framework Nuxt was utilized to implement the backend and enable communication between the frontend and backend components through an API, which facilitates smooth integration and efficient communication. Special attention was given to secure data manipulation and explicit error handling. To streamline communication with the database, we utilized the schema-driven Object-Relational-Mapping library, Prisma. This library provides a fully-typed object-based abstraction over a relevant subset of SQL, enabling developers to work with the database in a more intuitive and efficient manner. Authentication and authorization are handled by the modular reverse proxy server, which, in our case, utilizes a plugin for the Shibboleth system. This design provides a flexible and modular approach, allowing for easy integration with other authentication systems with minimal impact on the application code. The system will therefore accommodate the varying authorization procedures across different universities.

The most challenging aspect of the development process was implementing redirection and access control of the existing hardware user interfaces. This required careful inspection and a deep understanding of the devices' software architecture and functionality. The development process required the implementation of two separate proxy server components. The first component was an HTTP proxy server responsible for access control and redirecting requests to the appropriate devices' start pages based on internal routing data. Achieving seamless integration of the system required intercepting responses and adjusting link paths accordingly. To enable interactive monitoring and control of the lab hardware through the device user interface, a long-lived WebSocket connection is established. As a result, a WebSocket proxy had to be implemented as the second component to forward real-time communication between the devices and the user. Due to the long-lived nature of WebSocket connections, it was necessary to give special attention to terminating open socket connections once they reached the reserved time limit (see Fig. 3).

IV. Quality Assessment and Evaluation

To ensure the integrity and reliability of our API, each individual endpoint was subjected to extensive automated testing using a variety of test cases, including positive, negative, and edge cases. To facilitate fine-grained control of test cases, programming standards were established that require distinguishable error messages. By adhering to these standards, test cases can differentiate between different error causes, enabling more thorough and detailed assessment. The testing process was automated using the open-source tool Vitest with a separate database in a containerized environment to help avoiding any potential conflicts with the production database.

To evaluate the usability of the software, various user tests were conducted including a prototype evaluation with 45 students who tried out functions such as group registration and appointment booking, as ll as an evaluation of experiment configuration by 3 lecturers. To gather feedback and identify areas for improvement, the open-source tool AttrakDiff was used in conjunction with individual questionnaires. The derived portfolio representation of this evaluation is shown in Fig. 4 indicating that the developed application was considered to possess a high hedonic as well as pragmatic quality.

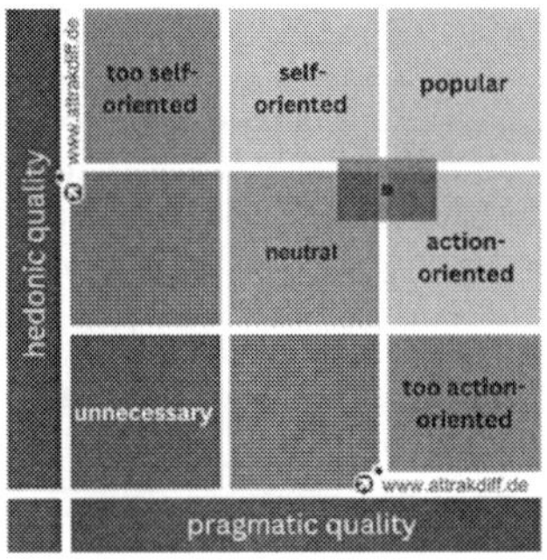

Fig. 4. Portfolio representation of hedonic (perceived stimulation and user identification) and pragmatic quality (usability and goal achievement).

V. Summary

Our system supports laboratory work for students, regardless of location. Users can register and access assigned devices during booked time slots. Instructors can manage devices, users, bookings, and experimental scheduling. The software has already been implemented for remote control of function generators and oscilloscopes, and can be easily adapted for other lab equipment or standard embedded systems with a web user interface, such as Raspberry Pi. Future extensions to the software may include a chat function and document management, providing additional value and enhancing user experience.

References

[1] KEYSIGHT Technologies, "PathWave Lab Operations für Remote Learning, PW9112EDU"

Leveraging Learning by Doing in Online Psychology Courses: Replicating Engagement and Outcomes

Martha Hubertz
Psychology Department
University of Central Florida
Orlando, USA
email: martha.hubertz@ucf.edu

Rachel Van Campenhout
Learning Science
VitalSource Technologies
Raleigh, USA
email: rachel.vancampenhout@vitalsource.com

Abstract—**For two upper-level online psychology courses—Psychology of Sex & Gender and Forensic Psychology—the instructor used adaptive courseware as the primary digital learning resource. This courseware was designed to integrate formative practice with textbook content in a learn-by-doing method known to generate the doer effect—a learning science principle shown to have six times the effect on learning than reading alone. The doer effect research provides confidence in the efficacy and generalizability of this learning method. However, it is imperative to investigate the practical implication of this learning method on student outcomes in natural learning contexts. How does doing practice while reading help students' exam scores? This instructor applied similar courseware implementation practices to both courses and was able to create similarly high engagement within the courseware as well as increased exam scores. These results show the importance of combining learning science methods with instructor expertise to provide an optimal learning environment for students, as well as the ability to replicate results across semesters and courses.**

Keywords-online learning; learn by doing; courseware; learning outcomes; replication, teaching and learning.

I. Introduction

Online learning has been a focus of higher education for decades with an increasing number of online courses offered, as well as entire online degree programs. However, the COVID-19 pandemic focused attention on the need for online learning options more than ever before. In the fall of 2020, 75% of all undergraduates (11.8 million) in the United States had at least one online class and 44% of undergraduates were exclusively enrolled in distance education (7 million) [1]. These numbers are especially impactful compared to those prior to the start of the pandemic in 2019. Undergraduates enrolled in distance education was 97% higher than in 2019 while those enrolled exclusively online rose 186% compared to 2019 [1]. This dramatic change in learning conditions has sparked significant conversation on effective teaching and learning online. Teaching models are not all equally effective [2] and neither are digital learning resources. In this paper, we describe online Psychology courses taught at the University of Central Florida (UCF) to illuminate both the teaching practices and the learning resources that produced positive learning outcomes. These examples of successful online teaching and learning practices are particularly beneficial to share given that increased student outcomes were repeated in multiple semesters and across multiple courses.

Along with various forms of online and distance learning, there are many types of digital learning resources and environments. Learning science research has long investigated how best to learn in digital learning environments. Researchers at Carnegie Mellon University's Open Learning Initiative identified that courseware environments that combined frequent formative practice with expository text and media in objective-aligned lessons helped students learn the same or more information and retain it for longer than their peers in traditional courses [3]. This combination of formative practice with reading content became the focus of an area of learn-by-doing research. Koedinger et al. [4][5] found through correlational investigation that doing practice while reading had about six times the effect size on learning than just reading. Calling this learning by doing method the doer effect, they were also able to model this relationship to infer causality [5][6]. The doer effect research was replicated using similar courseware environments at different universities and found the same correlational and causal results [7][8][9]. In the field of education in particular, research on learning methods is all too often not replicated, and results are cited that could not be replicated [10]. The replication of the doer effect research confirms that this learning by doing method is generalizable across contexts and should be broadly applied.

The doer effect learning science principle proves doing practice is causal to learning, yet this research does not indicate the impact it will have to student learning outcomes in a practical sense (i.e., how much will doing practice increase exam scores?) [9]. Carvalho et al. [11] expressed the need to investigate this in natural learning contexts and, using data from MOOCs, identified that more doing did lead to higher quiz and exam scores. Their research also reported that students often overestimated the benefit of reading and underestimated that of doing practice. To further understand how the learn by doing method benefits students on course outcomes, this approach was applied in a large online Psychology course at UCF. The instructor found that student exam scores increased after they were assigned the practice as an integrated part of their core reading content [12].

In this paper, we extend the prior classroom research by investigating two different Psychology courses taught by the same instructor at UCF. The goal of this paper is to identify if the same learn by doing courseware environment with the same implementation practices can produce similar improved exam scores for two different courses over multiple semesters.

II. METHODS

The courseware learning environment employed in these courses was automatically generated through a process called SmartStart. The textbook was used as the primary learning text and natural language processing and machine learning tools were applied to identify learning objectives in the text, chunk content into shorter lessons, and generate formative practice [13]. Two types of practice questions were generated: matching and fill-in-the-blank. A large-scale analysis of these questions using student data from natural learning environments found that they performed as well as human-authored questions on engagement, difficulty, and persistence [14]. In addition to these automatically generated questions, the instructor added human-authored questions as additional formative practice to the lesson pages, and wrote adaptive activities for four of the most challenging topics in the courseware.

The students included in this analysis selected these courses as part of their coursework in Psychology. The majority of students were juniors and seniors and taking these courses as electives in their major. The student population at UCF consists of a high proportion of first generation (25%) and transfer students (70%). Both Psychology of Sex and Gender and Forensic Psychology were taught as entirely online courses with synchronous weekly class periods. The instructor used the learning management system to organize week by week instructions for students, post reminders, and link the learning resources for the course. The courseware was also linked in the learning management system to open to each week's chapter of the course.

The application of learning science in the classroom is a complex task for teaching and learning, as context matters when considering the needs of students and the most appropriate method of implementing technology for learning [15]. In this case, the instructor applied implementation practices augmented over several semesters that included a clear introduction of the courseware, frequent reminders in the learning management system, and assigned points for the completion of the practice questions. Incentivizing the practice holds students accountable for using their learning materials, but also *places value on the process of learning*, not just the outcomes. Each course had 20% of the assigned points for completing a minimum of 85% of the total formative practice questions. The points were only dependent on completion—not on first-attempt accuracy—to maintain the formative nature of the practice.

III. RESULTS

A. *Psychology of Sex & Gender*

To see how these courseware implementation practices impacted students, engagement data from the courseware platform was combined with student outcome data from the course exams. The platform engagement data was plotted on graphs to provide a visual of how many students read and did practice on each page of the courseware. An engagement graph for the initial semester (2020) for Psychology of Sex and Gender is shown for comparison, as it had 2% points assigned for practice and shows a more typical student engagement and overall attrition [12]. In this example (Figure 1), the vertical space between the blue reading dots and red practice dots indicates that some students were reading and not doing any practice on those pages. This vertical space is called the reading-doing gap. Figure 1 also shows a very typical trend for overall engagement—attrition both within chapters and over the entire course.

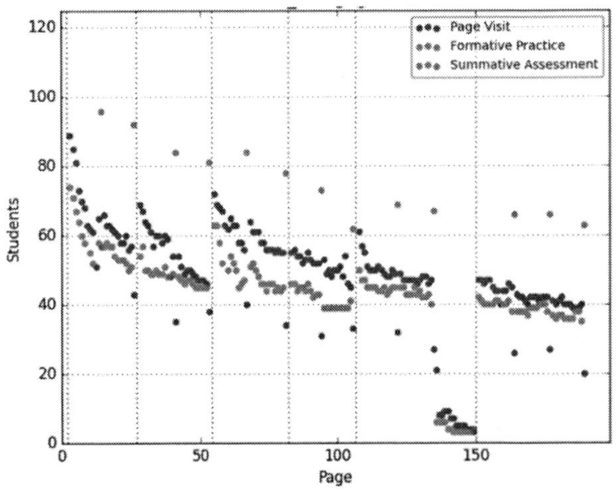

Figure 1. 2020 Psychology of Sex & Gender engagement.

The following two semesters of the Psychology of Sex and Gender course (Figure 2 and 3) had 20% of the grade assigned for completing 85% of the formative practice. By comparison, both of these graphs have no visible reading-doing gap, and there is very little attrition during the course. Compared to Figure 1, these two engagement graphs show a dramatically improved student engagement pattern in the courseware.

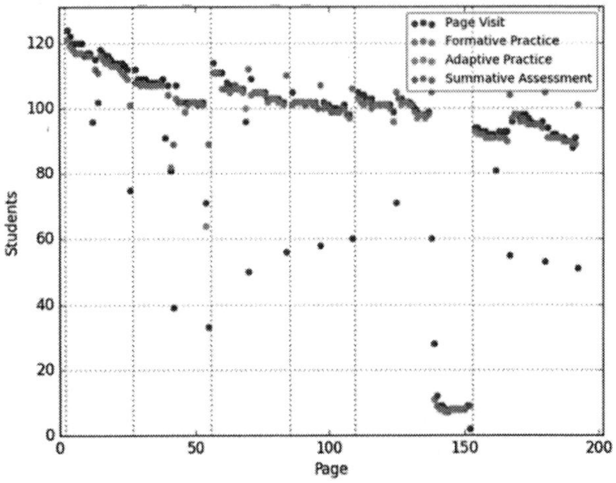

Figure 2. 2021 Psychology of Sex & Gender engagement.

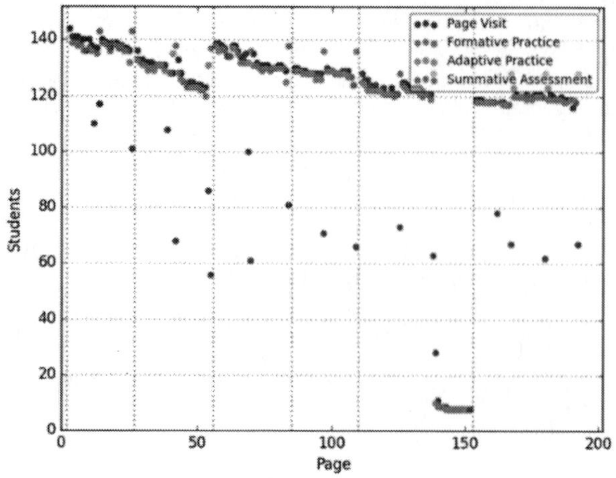

Figure 3. 2022 Psychology of Sex & Gender engagement.

Data from the three course exams is included in Table 1 to compare across several years. The exam data from 2019 was included as a comparison as this was a semester that used the same digital textbook without the learning by doing method. The spring 2020 semester was the first semester with courseware and the 2% for practice, and spring 2021 and 2022 had the 20% for practice. The mean exam scores increased between 5 and 10 points the first semester using courseware (2020) and increased again another 7 to 10 points in 2021 for exams 1 and 2. The mean exam scores for 2021 and 2022 remained close, showing a consistency in outcomes for each of these semesters.

TABLE I. EXAM SCORES FROM PSYCHOLOGY OF SEX AND GENDER ACROSS FOUR YEARS.

		Exam 1	Exam 2	Exam 3
Fall 2019	Mean Score	59%	66%	71%
	Score Range	39–101%	12–104%	19–103%
	n Students	64	66	66
Spring 2020	Mean Score	70%	68%	84%
	Score Range	23–98%	24–104%	39–104%
	n Students	98	86	71
Spring 2021	Mean Score	77%	78%	79%
	Score Range	43–102%	42–102%	42–99%
	n Students	106	105	104
Spring 2022	Mean Score	75%	78%	80%
	Score Range	30-104%	39-104%	15-104%
	n Students	130	130	127

B. Forensic Psychology

Forensic Psychology was selected for the SmartStart courseware process after the initial semester of Psychology of Sex and Gender was completed. For this course, both the 2021 and 2022 semesters had 20% of the course grade assigned to the formative practice. The engagement graphs for each semester (Figure 4 and 5) mirror those seen for the Psychology of Sex and Gender course, with a minimal reading-doing gap and very little attrition across the course. It is also notable that while all courses presented here are large sections, the 2021 Forensic Psychology course had more than 250 students and still maintained consistent engagement.

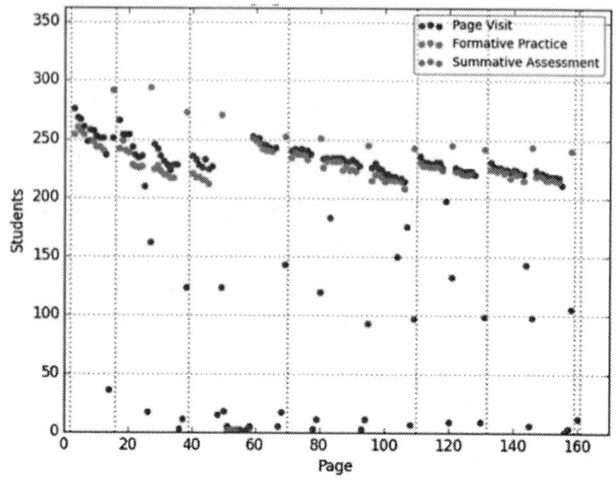

Figure 4. 2021 Forensic Psychology engagement.

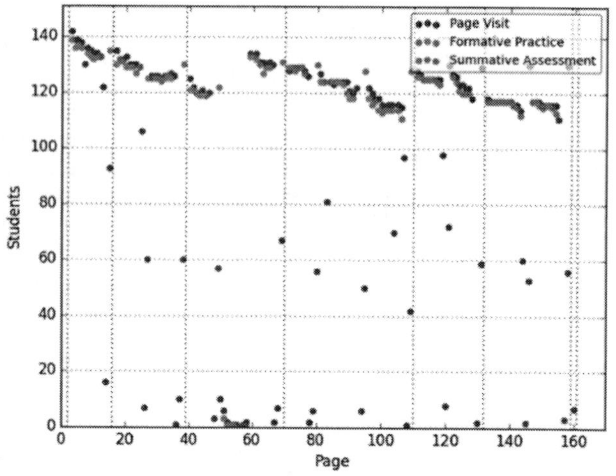

Figure 5. 2022 Forensic Psychology engagement.

The Forensic Psychology spring 2021 and 2022 mean exam scores are within a few points of each other and are within a similar range as Psychology of Sex and Gender. While there was no historical section for comparison, they are consistent in engagement and outcomes.

TABLE II. EXAM SCORES FROM FORENSIC PSYCHOLOGY.

		Exam 1	Exam 2	Exam 3
Spring 2021	Mean Score	75%	80%	83%
	Score Range	35-103%	26-102%	32-105%
	n Students	249	248	242
Spring 2022	Mean Score	77%	81%	82%
	Score Range	41-102%	39-104%	52-103%
	n Students	134	133	129

IV. Conclusion

As online learning continues to become increasingly prevalent in a post-pandemic world, identifying effective teaching and learning strategies and tools that benefit students is key. Yet even more important is to ensure these methods and results are reproduceable. This instructor applied the same teaching practices to two different online Psychology courses over multiple semesters, both of which utilized the same courseware platform as the primary learning by doing resource. The incentivization of the practice questions in the courseware increased student engagement dramatically. In both sections of both courses, attrition in the units and course was reduced to a minimal amount. The reading-doing gap was also nearly eliminated as students consistently did the practice as they read. Maximizing student engagement by incorporating formative practice into the course grade helped students take advantage of the doer effect's learning benefits. The practical outcome of maximizing student learning by doing was increased exam scores. That these outcomes were from multiple sections over different years, as well as from different courses, shows a particularly important outcome: these instructor practices and learning outcomes can be replicated. Research in teaching and learning needs more cases of learning interventions that can be replicated in natural learning contexts in order to recommend practices at scale.

Future research should work to extend the generalizability of these findings by investigating if similar implementation strategies can increase student engagement with formative practice and increase learning outcomes in a variety of subjects and institutions. Follow up research is also planned to investigate how completing formative practice in this courseware environment may benefit first generation and at-risk students specifically. As a school with a large first generation and transfer student population, approaches that benefit and support these student populations is important to UCF. Online learning will continue to grow at UCF and other higher education institutions and effective, reproducible teaching and learning methods will need to be researched and adopted.

References

[1] National Center for Education Statistics. Undergraduate Enrollment. *Condition of Education.* U.S. Department of Education, Institute of Education Sciences. Retrieved May 31, 2022, from https://nces.ed.gov/programs/coe/indicator/cha

[2] L. E. Margulieux, W. M. McCracken, and R. Catrambone,. Mixing in-class and online learning: Content meta-analysis of outcomes for hybrid, blended, and flipped courses. *Computer-Supported Collaborative Learning Conference*, CSCL, 1, 2015, pp. 220–227.

[3] M. Lovett, O. Meyer, and C. Thille. The Open Learning Initiative: Measuring the effectiveness of the OLI statistics course in accelerating student learning. *Journal of Interactive Media in Education*, (1), 2008, pp. 1-16. http://doi.org/10.5334/2008-14

[4] K. Koedinger, J. Kim, J. Jia, E. McLaughlin, and N. Bier, "Learning is not a spectator sport: doing is better than watching for learning from a MOOC." In: Learning at Scale, pp. 111–120, 2015. Vancouver, Canada. http://dx.doi.org/10.1145/2724660.2724681

[5] K. Koedinger, E. McLaughlin, J. Jia, and N. Bier, "Is the doer effect a causal relationship? How can we tell and why it's important." Proceedings of the Sixth International Conference on Learning Analytics and Knowledge, LAK 2016, pp. 388-397. http://dx.doi.org/10.1145/2883851.2883957

[6] K. R. Koedinger, R. Scheines, and P. Schaldenbrand, "Is the doer effect robust across multiple data sets?" Proceedings of the 11th International Conference on Educational Data Mining, EDM 2018, pp. 369–375. http://dx.doi.org/10.1145/2883851.2883957

[7] R. Van Campenhout, B. G. Johnson, and J. A. Olsen. The doer effect: replicating findings that doing causes learning. *Proceedings of eLmL 2021: The Thirteenth International Conference on Mobile, Hybrid, and On-line Learning. ISSN 2308-4367,* 2021, pp. 1–6. https://www.thinkmind.org/index.php?view=article&articleid=elml_2021_1_10_58001

[8] R. Van Campenhout, B. G. Johnson, and J. A. Olsen. The doer effect: Replication and comparison of correlational and causal analyses of learning. *International Journal on Advances in Systems and Measurements, 15*(1&2), pp. 48–59, 2022).

[9] R. Van Campenhout, B. Jerome, and B. G. Johnson. The Doer Effect at Scale: Investigating Correlation and Causation Across Seven Courses. *In LAK23: 13th International Learning Analytics and Knowledge Conference (LAK 2023)*, pp. 357–365, 2023. https://doi.org/10.1145/3576050.3576103

[10] M. Serra-Garcia, and U. Gneezy, "Nonreplicable publications are cited more than replicable ones," In Science Advances, vol. 7, pp. 1–7, 2021. http://doi.org/10.1126/sciadv.abd1705

[11] P. F. Carvalho, E. A. Mclaughlin, and K. R. Koedinger. Is there an explicit learning bias? Students beliefs, behaviors and learning outcomes. *Proceedings of the 39th Annual Conference of the Cognitive Science Society (Eds. Gunzelmann, G. et al.)*, pp. 204–209, 2017.

[12] Hubertz, M. & Van Campenhout, R. (2022). Teaching and iterative improvement: The impact of instructor implementation of courseware on student outcomes. *The IAFOR International Conference on Education – Hawaii 2022 Official Conference Proceedings.* https://doi.org/10.22492/issn.2189-1036.2022.19

[13] B. Jerome, R. Van Campenhout, and B. G. Johnson. Automatic Question Generation and the SmartStart Application. *Learning at Scale, 2021.* https://doi.org/10.1145/3430895.3460878

[14] R. Van Campenhout, J. S. Dittel, B. Jerome, and B. G. Johnson, "Transforming textbooks into learning by doing environments: an evaluation of textbook-based automatic question generation." In: Third Workshop on Intelligent Textbooks at the 22nd International Conference on Artificial Intelligence in Education, 2021. Retrieved June 30, 2022 from: https://intextbooks.science.uu.nl/workshop2021/files/iTextbooks_2021_paper_6.pdf

[15] R. Van Campenhout and A. Kessler. Developing Instructor Training for Diverse & Scaled Contexts: A Learning Engineering Challenge. *Proceedings of eLmL 2022: The Fourteenth International Conference on Mobile, Hybrid, and On-line Learning*, pp. 29–34, 2022. https://www.thinkmind.org/index.php?view=article&articleid=elml_2022_2_40_58010

Promoting Interactive Learning Using 5G Networks and Synchronous Immersive Contents: the DI5CIS Project

Flavio Manganello
Institute for Educational Technology
National Research Council
Genoa, Italy
E-mail: manganello@itd.cnr.it

Chiara Fante
Institute for Educational Technology
National Research Council
Genoa, Italy
E-mail: chiara.fante@itd.cnr.it

Fabrizio Ravicchio
Institute for Educational Technology
National Research Council
Genoa, Italy
E-mail: fabrizio.ravicchio@itd.cnr.it

Giannangelo Boccuzzi
Hypex
Monopoli, Italy
E-mail: a.boccuzzi@hypex.video

Riccardo Boccuzzi
Hypex
Monopoli, Italy
E-mail: r.boccuzzi@hypex.video

Cinzia Campanella
Vodafone Italia
Milan, Italy
E-mail: Cinzia.Campanella@vodafone.com

Giuseppe Gammariello
Capgemini Engineering
Rome, Italy
E-mail: giuseppe.gammariello@capgemini.com

Paolo Quaranta
Prodea Group
Turin, Italy
E-mail: paolo.quaranta@prodeagroup.com

Abstract— **The DI5CIS project seeks to address the challenges faced by multimedia learning designers in providing advanced interactive mobile content that requires massive data streams and low latency. To achieve this, the project aims to explore the potential of 5G networks in enabling mobile enjoyment of highly sophisticated audiovisual content created through a gamified interactivity production methodology applied to live-action film material. The project will enact this experiential format in two use cases, related to the teaching of STEM disciplines. The impacts of 5G infrastructure on the technical mobile enjoyment of content, such as fluidity and audiovisual quality, will be investigated, as well as the effects on specific indicators such as engagement, motivation and learning outcomes in the educational context. By improving the quality of experience and learning, the DI5CIS project is highly relevant for e-learning and mobile learning challenging innovative educational and technical aspects.**

Keywords-Digital Game-Based Learning; Gamification; Digital Storytelling; Interactive Narrative Learning; 5G.

I. INTRODUCTION

The project “Interactive Learning in 5G: Synchronous Immersive Contents” (Didattica Interattiva in 5G: Contenuti Immersivi Sincroni, DI5CIS) aims to explore innovative ways of using interactive visual content centered on narrative and video-ludic mechanics and created through an innovative methodology and technology. The 5G architecture is a decisive enabling factor for the realization of highly immersive educational content for mobile devices, opening up interesting possibilities for the use of Digital Game Based Learning (DGBL) [1] and Digital Storytelling (DST) [2]. The DI5CIS project, funded by the Ministry of Enterprises and Made in Italy (MIMIT) under the “Progetto 5G audiovisivo (2022)” grant, involves five partners: PRODEA Group, HYPEX, Capgemini engineering, Vodafone Italia, and the Institute for Educational Technology of the Italian National Research Council (CNR-ITD).

This poster first presents the two main objectives of the project (Section II). Then the four main pillars on which the project is based on are detailed (Section III). Furthermore, the process to realize the educational digital artefacts (Section IV) and to test them in real educational settings (Section V) is presented briefly. Finally, Sections VI highlights some relevant preliminary considerations for the implementation of the project.

II. PROJECT OBJECTIVES

The DI5CIS project exploits the 5G architecture [3] to produce edutainment content based on pioneering interaction patterns covered by an industrial patent, capable of enabling real-time interactive cooperation within the experience between multiple users. In this perspective, DI5CIS aims at pursuing the following two objectives: a) research and identify use cases that utilize real-time interaction and co-operation between multiple users, merging technological advancement with the impacts of cooperative learning; b) measure the related impact on the Quality of Experience within the use cases thus investigated. In this direction, the project makes use of high-level assets: structural, such as Multi-Access Edge Computing provided by Vodafone Italia and Capgemini Engineering; patenting, both process and method, for the creation of interactive and branched live-action video content, provided by HYPEX (with the support of PRODEA Group for video production); and methodological-scientific as well of educational technology research, provided by CNR-ITD.

III. THE FOUR PILLARS OF THE PROJECT

At the macro level (Pillar 1), the DI5CIS project shows an interpenetration between the game and the narrative dimension, aimed at motivating and engaging students [4]. Then, the disciplinary dimension (Pillar 2) is translated into the development of interactive multimedia content for learning physics and chemistry, based on the fundamental elements of the STEM approach [5]. Furthermore, it is possible to find development choices (Pillar 3), defined by the grammars of the multimedia products, and the user's possibility of interacting by elements coherent with the content of the scene they are viewing. This element leads to the technological layer (Pillar 4), that is the integration of different elements to provide a true immersive experience: from devices integrated sensors to the 5G network infrastructure. More in depth the uninterrupted flow of the story and a user-narrative interaction reinforce its sense of presence in the plot [6].

IV. ARTEFACT DEVELOPMENT PROCESS

The development of the artefacts tends to harmonize the learning approach with the technical development choices, supported by the technological infrastructure described. The combination of the disciplinary, the playful, the narrative and the interactive elements supports the student's learning activities based on the multimedia artefact exploration. The realization of this 'common thread' is possible thanks to the involvement of teachers (in a perspective of Stakeholder Engagement) in the design and development phases of the products and the creation of an action-research group in which all the actors are involved. Two artefacts will be implemented in the educational case study: PhysiGame, dealing with Physics' topics (i.e., state functions, equations of state, first and second laws of thermodynamics, etc...), and ChemiGame, about Chemistry's topics (i.e., phase transition, latent heat, thermal expansion, etc...).

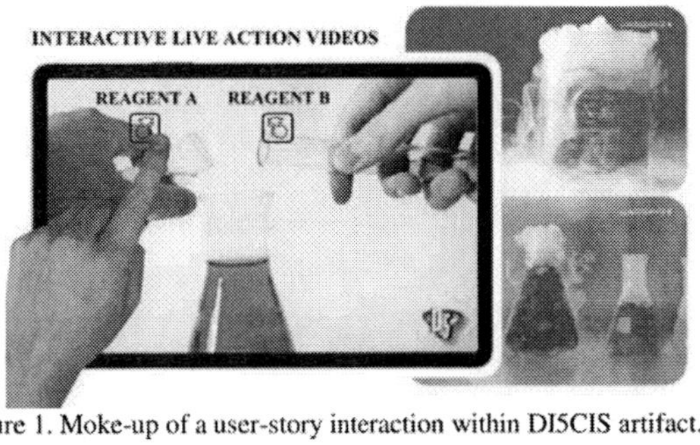

Figure 1. Moke-up of a user-story interaction within DI5CIS artifact.

V. EXPERIMENTATION

The artefacts will be initially tested within three classrooms, 4th grade of high school, in co-located situated learning activities [7], in which students will use the artefacts as a learning activity. The experimentation goal will be to understand how the interactive and playful artifacts are used and what are their effects on learning. engagement, behaviour and motivation. These elements will also be read in the light of the students' profiles, to understand to what extent personal characteristics can have a moderating effect on the previously mentioned dimensions. To detect the elements useful for the research, tools such as standardized tests and observation grids, as well as a user behavior tracker integrated within the interactive stories, will be used.

VI. PRELIMINARY CONSIDERATIONS

The process of developing interactive and engaging stories is complex and requires coordination between teachers and the development team. Modern technologies such as 5G and mobile devices offer new opportunities to create immersive experiences with learner-narration and peer interaction, which can advance learning of STEM disciplines through DGBL and DST.

REFERENCES

[1] M. Prensky, Digital game-based learning, Columbus: McGraw-Hill Education. 2001.

[2] J. Lambert, Digital storytelling: Capturing lives, creating community 4th ed., New York, NY: Routledge, 2013

[3] L. Xingqin and N. Lee, 5G and Beyond: Fundamentals and Standards. Cham: Springer International Publishing AG, 2021.

[4] S. Göbel, A. de Carvalho Rodrigues, F. Mehm, and R. Steinmetz, "Narrative game-based learning objects for story-based digital educational games". The 1st International Open Workshop on Intelligent Personalization and Adaptation in Digital Educational Games, Oct. 2009, pp 43-53.

[5] OECD , PISA 2018 Assessment and Analytical Framework, Paris: PISA, OECD Publishing, 2019

[6] B. G. Witmer, and M. J. Singer, "Measuring presence in virtual environments: A presence questionnaire," Presence, vol 7.3, pp 225-240, Jun. 1998.

[7] B. K., Litts, G. W., Smith, D. J., Gagnon, J. Martin, and J. Mathews, "Situated Learning and Mobile Technologies: Connecting Theory to Design" The Ninth Annual Games, Learning, Society Conference, 2013, pp 210-21.

Scan to Learn: A Lightweight Approach for Informal Mobile Micro-Learning at the Workplace

Katharina Frosch
Department of Business Management
Brandenburg University of Applied Sciences
Brandenburg an der Havel, Germany
email: frosch@th-brandenburg.de

Abstract— **Informal learning at the workplace is a crucial ingredient in updating and upskilling today's workforce, but in many jobs, informal learning opportunities are scarce. Bite-sized learning via mobile devices (Mobile Micro-Learning, MML) can be a powerful means to enhance informal work-related learning also in such learning-deprived fields. Based on good practices of recent MML implementations, a lightweight approach is developed. It involves an instructional blueprint and an open-source, low-threshold technology for MML, and meets the specific needs of workers in learning-deprived fields. The main idea is a scan-to-learn system where Quick Response (QR) codes are attached to physical objects in the work environment. Workers can scan the QR codes to learn and are directed to short, interactive learning nuggets. For evaluation, a proof-of-concept is provided.**

Keywords-work-based learning; informal learning; mobile learning; micro-learning; QR code; instructional design; open source.

I. Introduction

Work-based learning is seen as a powerful means for continuously updating workers' qualifications on the job [1], with the lion's share of learning being informal [2]. Informal learning takes place outside a prescribed learning framework (no organized event or package) and without a professional trainer [3]–[5]. It may be conceived as learning *in* work [6]: Embedded ("situated") in daily work routines [1][5], informal learning is initiated in a self-directed manner by workers and triggered by "an internal or external jolt" [4], i.e., on demand when a specific work task is requiring it. Typical examples are observing, seeking help or feedback from others, discussing, experimenting (learning by just doing the job), trial and error, reflecting or searching the intra- or Internet for information [1][4]. Informal learning can hence rely on the interaction with others ("social learning"), or on self-initiated study, practice and experimentation ("learning by doing") [4].

However, in many occupational fields, the conditions for informal learning at work limited: In decentralized work settings (e.g., train, trucks or delivery drivers, mobile care workers), there is little direct interaction between workers. The same is true in highly mechanized settings with large physical distances between workers, and in work environments with a lot of noise or high language diversity among workers – all of which is rather typical for blue-collar work [7][8]. This hampers learning by observing, asking questions and receiving feedback [9].

Due to tight schedules or high degrees of automation, many jobs offer little autonomy, which is seen as a crucial condition for experimentation on-the-job or other self-directed learning activities [8][10]. Finally, access to codified organizational or external knowledge from the Internet [11] is difficult for those who have no permanent access to a stationary desktop computer. "Learning-deprived" jobs [9] typically suffer from reduced speed and intensity of informal learning at the workplace and jeopardize workforce upskilling.

Such limited opportunities for informal learning at work weight all the heavier as often, the knowledge or skills needed to continue one's work or to start with learning-by-doing would not require extensive educational content, but rather a little tweak. Learning based on bite-sized learning nuggets has been termed micro-learning or Mobile Micro-Learning (MML) as it is typically delivered by mobile devices [12].

This paper shows to what extent MML can help to improve work-related learning in learning-deprived environments. We propose a lightweight approach to situate MML units in daily work routines with QR codes affixed to physical objects in the work environment (mobile tagging). The rest of the paper is structured as follows: Section II illustrates existing concepts and good practices of micro-learning at the workplace and explores its potential for informal learning. We then sketch our lightweight approach for informal MML at the workplace and illustrate it with a proof-of-concept based on a combination of freely available open-source tools (Section III). In Section IV, we discuss our findings, critically reflect on our approach and conclude with an outlook.

II. Related Work and Good Practices

A. Mobile Micro-Learning

Micro-learning typically consists of short learning nuggets (1-5 minutes) that are focused on one narrow topic and that are provided in rich, interactive media formats [12]–[14], e.g., (animated) videos, podcasts, job aids, cheat sheets, flashcards, quizzes or even gamified elements [15] and virtual reality nuggets [16]. Micro-learning is undertaken just-in-time when needed ("on demand") [12]. In this context, mobile technologies are found to naturally match the concept of micro-learning and play an important role in its delivery [17][18]. The use of mobile devices (e.g., smartphones, tablets) for learning anytime without being tied to a tightly-delimited physical location [19] is termed mobile learning [20][21]. In what follows, we subsume the above-mentioned learning practices under Mobile Micro-Learning (MML) [13][14]. Note that in the context of informal learning at the workplace, the concepts of micro-learning and micro-training are often used interchangeably, as both refer to short, often digital training or learning activities that can be easily integrated in daily work routines [22][23]. In this paper, we stick to the term (mobile) micro-learning because it favors somewhat more the notions of self-directed learning that go beyond the mere acquisition of knowledge and skills.

MML has been found to increase learners' motivation, improved knowledge retention thanks to reduced cognitive load and repetition [14][18][24]. A the same time, it is an efficient strategy to integrate learning into busy schedules, also for employees working in distributed settings [24][25].

MML seems appropriate for and widely used in informal learning settings [15], also if implemented at the workplace [14]. It stimulates self-directed learning, allowing learners to consume learning nuggets on-demand when they get aware of a problem or question in a specific situation [26], [27]. MML can be easily embedded in daily work routines and allows for informal work-related learning, also in deprived work settings as described in Section I (decentralized work, limited opportunities for interaction, lack of access to desktop computers). If properly designed, MML is not limited to the acquisition of narrow knowledge or skills, but may also enable higher-order learning [26] which is particularly relevant for the experimental and reflective dimensions of informal work-related learning [28].

B. *Examples of Mobile Micro-Learning at the Workplace*

Researchers and practitioners highlight the potential of MML for onboarding, ongoing professional qualification, and just-in-time learning [29]–[32]. Typical applications of MML at the workplace are compliance training in occupational safety [33] or information system security [34][35], building knowledge on new and existing products [36]–[38], or improving customer service [32]. Other, albeit less frequent are providing procedural work instructions e.g., for installing or technical equipment [37] or in medical care [39], and machine use [40]–[42], as well as improving soft skills such as team management or goal setting [44][45]. Prominent examples from the industry are micro-learning initiatives for occupational safety at Walmart or Bloomingdale's that came with high participation rates and considerable savings [24] or the case of InterContinental Hotels Group to improve the management of complex customer service requests based on micro-learning which helped to reduce onboarding time for new employees from five to two weeks [45].

Recent scientific cases and evaluation studies on MML in real-life work settings cover a great variety of topics, e.g., how to keep costs in large building projects [46], dementia-friendly approaches for staff in neighborhood convenience stores [48][49], methods and approaches in pharmacovigilance [49] as well as a great number of examples from health and medical care [40][51]. Further attempts have been made in the hospitality sector [32], in logistics [51], in ICT [53][54], for public administration and NATO staff [30][55], for librarians [55], for school and university teachers [57][58] as well as for childcare workers [58], and even for employees of dairy farms [59]. However, these examples are either not validated in a real-world setting, contain little information about the actual approach, rely on relatively lengthy learning units, or were published before 2020. Recent topical reviews provide even more examples for MML [17][21][24][29][57][61]–[63]. However, many of these studies were tested in an educational setting, only.

Six studies were analyzed in-depth (S1 – S6, see Table 1) to investigate how companies and public organizations implement MML. All were conducted in real-work settings, underwent scientific evaluation, and contained sufficient details about implementation. The examples chosen rely on short learning nuggets (< 5 min) and primarily draw on rich, interactive media. Looking at studies published not later than 2020 allows us to get an overview of the state-of-the-art.

As the focus of this paper is to study the potential of MML for informal learning in learning-deprived work settings, four aspects are central:

- To what extent can learners self-direct their learning activities?
- Are forms of higher-order learning such as practice, experimentation, feedback, and reflection sufficiently triggered?
- How are learning activities "situated" in actual work routines?
- Do media formats and instructional strategies enable learning among workers who are not used to consuming longer verbal explanations or engaging in self-directed learning?

TABLE I. SELECTED MML STUDIES IN REAL WORKPLACE SETTINGS

Study	*Country no. of learners*	*Topic and learners*
S1 [49]	>100 countries (N>2000)	Pharmacovigilance (pharmacists, medical doctors, others)
S2 [46]	Norway (N=334)	Cost-efficiency in construction projects (project managers, engineers, architects and other)
S3 [47][48]	Japan (N=62)	Dementia-friendly customer care" (employees in neighborhood convenience stores)
S4 [39]	Australia (N>2000)	Clinical care and no-clinical topics (nurses, medical staff, non-clinical staff)
S5 [56]	USA (N/A)	Teaching skills and learning science (faculty at academic health centers)
S6 [50]	USA (N=26)	Point-of-care training for high-risk, low volume therapies (nurses)

Three of the six examples analyzed come with a prescribed learning curriculum to improve specific competencies. S1 to S3 fall in this category. S1 consists of four modules, each comprising 6 to 8 short (2-3 min) videos and a final quiz at the end of every module [49]. Here, learning nuggets are not self-containing as content, practice, and quizzes are separated from each other [48][50]. In such a setting, learners are less expected to engage in self-directed learning but directed toward the predefined learning objectives in small steps.

The three other studies, both from the medical and health care field, allow for more self-directed learning: In S4 [39], a group of Australian hospitals provides the micro-learning format "Take 5 – learning for busy people" to their care, medical and non-clinical staff. Learners go through slide decks with condensed information about clinical and non-clinical topics. A learning nugget could explain the procedure in case of a "code blue" (a patient having a medical emergency such as cardiac arrest). Learning bites last about five minutes. Delivery happens browser-based by the internal website so that staff can search for learning nuggets whenever a problem or question arises during the work process. S5 applies an almost identical approach ("Take 5" on teaching skills and learning science for faculty members in academic health centers [56]): A website contains 41 Take-5 videos, jointly with other resources for learning and development. The videos were professionally recorded, prepared in conversational language, and not longer than 800 words. A blueprint suited for just-in-time learning was suggested and used: A teaser with statistics, an expert testimonial, a question, or a call for action pointing out why the topic is relevant. Then evidence from the literature, expert advice, or tips and tricks were provided. Integrating animations helped to improve the retention of central issues.

In S6 [50], nurses can access point-of-care training for high-risk, low volume-therapies based on Quick Response (QR) codes affixed to work equipment. Scanned with a smartphone, they link to short training videos (2-3 minutes).

The preferred format used in the five examples of MML is slide desks, short video clips (sometimes animated), and quizzes. Only one study additionally uses animated videos and mini-simulation games [47]. Text-based information still plays an important role, as in some work situations, learners cannot play the audio, and videos have to come with transcripts, then [49].

The focus of the analyzed MML seems to be more on information and learning and less on practice, experimentation and reflection. In study 1 [49], learners explicitly point out that they see included quizzes as a valuable instrument for self-assessment, feedback and reflection, but would like to get more opportunities to practice. In S4 to S6, MML primarily relies on static microsites and video clips and does not offer quizzes or other activities related to reflection or practical exploration. A higher degree of self-directedness in learning seems to imply fewer opportunities for higher-order learning and vice versa.

To conclude, the potential of MML for informal, work-related learning depicted in Subsection II is realized only very selectively. The first three studies use MML as the little brother or sister of e-learning: "e-learning courses [...] based on micro-learning" [49, p. 1171] seem to be the method of choice to meet the requirements of a remote, distributed workforce that has little leeway for learning when at work. There is only low potential for informal learning while at work, as micro-learning is neither self-directed nor anchored in the work tasks employees perform when learning. In contrast, in S4 and S5 (website with an index of self-contained learning nuggets), learners use learning nuggets as needed when administering a specific work task. Moreover, applying the same instructional blueprint and format for the learning nuggets to meet the needs of the learners appears to be a viable strategy.

However, searching indexes of available learning nuggets using a mobile phone is unlikely to be effective in settings where workers tend to be less savvy in the self-directed use of large amounts of digital information. A promising approach seems to be letting learners access learning nuggets just in time at the workplace by linking them to QR codes in the physical work environment. So far, this approach is not widespread in the workplace. More MML implementations of that kind can be found in work-related laboratory settings [40] and education [62] or again in health and medical care to quickly access guidelines [63].

The instructional strategy adopted in the examples mainly underlines the use of (very) short learning nuggets, often based on videos or text-based information. Workers in noisy settings or with limited skills in verbal comprehension will, however, be less apt to understand spoken or written text. Furthermore, apart from using quizzes to self-assess learning progress, the examples analyzed do not provide novel insight into how we could enhance practice, experimentation, and reflection beyond the mere acquisition of knowledge and skills. This being a general problem in the design of MML [26], it constitutes a particular challenge when MML shall enhance informal work-related learning in very hands-on (and less academic) fields.

Informal work-related learning based on MML requires a concise implementation strategy that allows for self-directed learning, anchors learning nuggets in work, allows for practice, experimentation, reflection, and feedback, and lowers learning barriers for less savvy users. Given that this is quite a challenge, it is not surprising that apart from a few applications in occupational safety training in large corporations and some examples from the hospitality sector, farming, and convenience stores, the majority of empirical studies on MML still refer to (higher) education and often related to science in general or medical and health services in particular, or foreign language acquisition.

III. APPROACH

Based on our findings in Section II and general design principles for MML [15][26][27], we provide recommendations on instructional strategy and technical implementation for a lightweight MML that fosters informal work-related learning in learning-deprived occupational contexts.

A. Suggestions for Design and Implementation

A good point of departure for designing and implementing MML are the four principles for MML design summarized from earlier research by [26] and validated in a pilot test by [27].

- *Principle 1*: MML content should fit on the small screens of mobile devices.
- *Principle 2*: MML should address learners in the moment they feel the need to learn something. Connected to this, MML content should be short (no longer than 5 minutes).
- *Principle 3a*: MML learning nuggets should be designed following an instructional flow that starts with an information snippet to provide an aha moment about the relevance (step 1), followed by instructional snippets with short exercises (quizzes, micro games, ideas for practice and experimentation at the workplace) and instant feedback (step 2). This instructional flow is based on an earlier model of Gagne [64], as cited in [27].
- *Principle 4a*: MML content should be designed in a way that triggers interaction between the learner and the content (e.g. using practical and/or gamified activities).

These four principles are an excellent starting point to design MML for informal work-related learning. To make them even more suited to support and trigger informal workplace-related MML in learning-deprived occupational contexts, the following clarifications and additions are put forth:

- *Principle 2a (revised):* We favor short learning nuggets covering a single topic (1-2 minutes) to fit tight schedules, meet a single, specific question arising from the work context and to reduce cognitive load for learners. This is particular important in the workplaces we focus that often are characterized by high time pressure (e.g. in health and care services) or a noisy work environment [42].
- *Principle 2b (Mobile tagging system).* To trigger learning from within work processes, several approaches [40], [62], [63] have found QR codes affixed to work equipment and locations to be a good practice to link to learning nuggets that might be useful in the respective work context.
- *Principle 3a (revised):* The instructional flow suggested helps to design learning nuggets that go beyond the mere acquisition of knowledge and that are still self-contained. However and as pointed out already by [26], besides opportunities for experimentation and practice, learning nuggets for effective workplace-learning should also contain practices for reflection, which further enhances higher order learning.
- *Principle 4b:* Animated videos or visual, interactive work aids should be preferred over text-based and verbal information to enable learners who are less used to consume large amounts of texts or speak another language.

Revising and complementing the four original principles for designing MML content by [26] makes MML more lightweight: First of all, short videos preferably with visualizations and animations lower the barrier for learning for those with less favorable prerequisites for effective informal workplace-learning. Second, self-containing learning nuggets that also comprise reflective activities help to enhance higher order learning processes that are vital for successful workplace learning. Third and last, mobile tagging based on QR codes are a strong trigger to engage in informal learning activities when encountering questions and challenges in the work process.

Similarly, implementing MML for informal workplace learning should be also lightweight from a company perspective. This is captured in two additional recommendations:

Recommendation 1 refers to an easy-to-use authoring tool: Learning managers should be able to generate learning nuggets without too much effort, as studies show that time constraints, a lack of technical skills and inadequate infrastructure are major barriers for the implementation of digitally-supported learning activities [65]. Content types should support the instructional scheme suggested above and support mobile display. H5P allows the user to create HTML5 interactive content and publish it in learning or content management systems such as Moodle, Canvas, WordPress, or Drupal [66]. It is free and open source, appears easier to use than most commercial e-learning authoring tools, and offers many predefined interactive formats that support active learning [67]. Moreover, H5P content can be shared and reused, and open licensing is encouraged [66]. An example of MML that uses H5P to implement interactive content is [52], whereas others use authoring tools such as Articulate Storyline 360 [51] or iSpring Suite [49], or simple video recording and editing software [40][51][57].

Recommendation 2 refers to a secured platform to manage, store and distribute learning nuggets: In most cases, developing a custom micro-learning platform will not be viable. Instead, many companies use a Learning Management Tool (LMS) with support for eLearning [68]. Most LMS support authoring and distribution of H5P content. However, introducing and operating a fully-fledged LMS exclusively for MML might be perceived as too high an investment. This will often be the case for Smaller and Medium-Sized Enterprises (SME). As an alternative, a more lightweight Content Management System (CMS) such as WordPress seems to be sufficient: It supports H5P content generation and storage, comes with user authentication and offers an appropriate structure to manage modular learning nuggets [68][69].

To conclude, the proposed principles and recommendations are considered effective in supporting our learners: They need short learning nuggets anchored in the work process that foster engagement in knowledge acquisition, practice, experimentation, and reflection. The low-threshold approach benefits learners in learning-deprived work contexts who may be less adept at self-directed learning. Similarly, creating and distributing learning nuggets is kept simple so that barriers to adoption are low, even for SMEs or companies with little experience with digital learning.

B. Proof-of-Concept

As a proof-of-concept, we use a simple website based on WordPress with an H5P plugin as a micro-learning platform. It comes with role-based authentication to protect learning nuggets against non-authorized viewing or editing.

Figure 1 shows how learning managers would generate a learning nugget and attach the automatically generated QR code to a physical object in the work environment, where learners "Scan to learn" with their smartphone camera.

An exemplary learning nugget has been developed and automatically equipped with a QR code. Hereby, an H5P content type "interactive video" is wrapped into a H5P element "KewAR Code" which auto-generates a QR code linking to the readily designed learning nugget when saved. Note that to reference H5P content instead of an URL or other text content, the content type "KewAR Code" has to be extended as suggested by [71]. The H5P plugin in Wordpress offers this combination of content types by default and provides comfortable authoring for such learning nuggets.

The learning nugget has been structured as suggested above, following a blueprint that allows triggering higher-order learning (see Figure 2). The example refers to using a car polishing machine in a garage. Starting point is a short video where learners see an employee operating the machine and explaining the most important do's and don'ts, which comes close to "learning by observing".
Visual overlays to the video present key aspects, so that verbal or written text is not a main mode of presentation. The video integrates quiz questions with immediate feedback to allow learners to assess their progress. The example you see in Figure 2 is a visual true and false activity the angle at which the machine must be placed on the coating surface. Learners provide their answers by dragging the correct and the wrong option in the respective places.

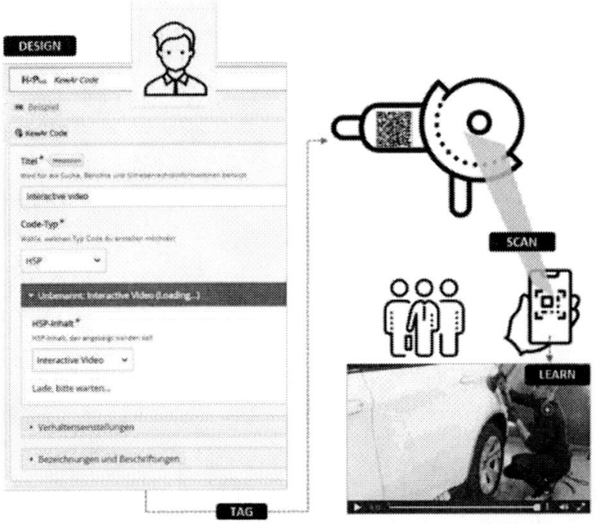

Figure 1. Scan to learn system

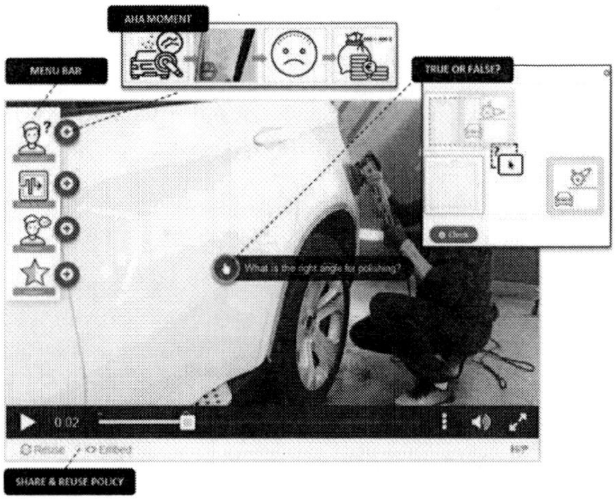

Figure 2. Example for micro-learning nugget

A sidebar with four activity buttons was added to the video. The first refers back to the relevance of the topic. In our example, an infographic provides an aha moment, showing how expensive it can be if workers apply the polishing machine to the car at the wrong angle and cause scratches to the paint. The second button contains ideas for practice and experimentation at the workplace. The third button offers starting points to reflect about the topic of the learning content. Workers can hit the last button to provide feedback on the learning nugget (optional). The activity buttons remain displayed throughout the video, and learners can freely decide whether and when to use it. freely decide whether and when they make use of it or not.

IV. DISCUSSION AND CONCLUSIONS

In the future, we need even more informal learning to support the tremendous level workforce upskilling as we face major transformation processes related to climate change, population aging as well as ongoing digitization and automation. However, many jobs offer limited opportunities for informal learning, in particular if human-human interaction is scarce, access to stationary desktop computers is difficult, and workers are less experienced in self-directed learning. In Section II, we have shown that the concept of MML closely overlaps with the characteristics of informal learning. The anytime-anywhere options of mobile technology might help to foster informal learning in learning-deprived work settings. However, there are barely some examples for MML programs launched for workers in blue-collar, non-academic fields. Drawing upon good practices in MML, this paper offers suggestions for the design and implementation of MML in such "atypical" settings.

The proof-of-concept in Section III shows that based on a lightweight approach using a website with a simple CMS system, H5P interactive technology and QR codes, the design and distribution of short but engaging MML nuggets is achievable even for novices in the field of micro-learning and SME with limited resources for workforce training. Using short videos as a basis, placing visuals and animations over "verbals", designing stand-alone learning nuggets with integrated quizzes and other activities that foster experimentation and reflection should help to reduce barriers for learning, and to allow reaping the full benefits of MML for informal work-related learning – also in learning-deprived settings.

The approach suggested comes, however, with some drawbacks. Learning managers who design, curate and manage the learning nuggets may dislike the specific nature and structure of H5P content and the way authoring is organized in our lightweight approach. Furthermore, our approach is a self-hosted solution. Considering this, one might argue that a commercial micro-learning platform would be a more viable option. Indeed, platforms like EdApp [70] offer all needed functionality for our lightweight approach for MML even in its cost-free version (authoring tool for interactive micro-content, automated generation of QR codes). However, the size of video uploads is limited, and learners who wish to quickly access a micro-learning content might, however, dislike the fact that more clicks are needed for learning as compared to our scan-to-learn approach. Platforms like EdApp also require learners to register.

Moreover, due to its anytime-anyplace nature, MML offers by nature only limited potential for learning through experimentation and practice at the workplace ("learning-by-doing") and even fewer opportunities for "social learning" through direct interaction in terms of observation, feedback, or help-seeking. When implementing MML for informal work-related learning, adequate instructional strategies should be adopted to – at least partly – make up for these drawbacks. Some authors point out that it is still an open question of how this can be best achieved [26]. Here we could argue that in the specific work context featured in this paper, social interaction is limited, anyway.

The biggest challenge, however, in helping MML to spread in order to reap its full potential for informal learning at the workplace is the generation of content. Content creation can be cumbersome and is time-consuming. The production of one 5-minute learning nugget can cost € 5000 or more if professionally produced [56]. The lightweight approach suggested in this paper tries to keep it as simple as possible for those designing MML instructional content. In this context, we also suggest to abstain from Virtual Reality or Augmented Reality (VR/AR) applications, even if advancements in mobile technology nowadays allow to implement AR-based MML at the workplace as shown by [71]. However, creating such learning nuggets is particularly challenging with little or no technical expertise in this field [72]. Indeed, the exemplary learning nugget has been produced in less than one hour (excluding video recording) thanks to the existing blueprint and the user-friendly authoring tool in the H5P plugin. The hope of the author of this paper is that the lightweight approach suggested and evaluated in a first proof-of-concept lowers the threshold for both – companies and learners from fields where learning while working with the help of digital and mobile technologies are not yet "daily business". The "scan to learn" system also offers potential to implement lean onboarding processes.

As a next step, the suggested approach should be implemented and evaluated in a real-life work setting, to identify potential improvements. Looking further, the integration of gamified elements and the use of augmented reality in the sense of "marker-based AR" [71] in MML will be promising paths to consider [71][72] – as soon as these rather complex technologies do not induce new barriers for companies and learners, in particular if companies are small and work is of rather non-academic nature.

REFERENCES

[1] K. Smet, I. Grosemans, N. D. Cuyper, and E. Kyndt, "Outcomes of Informal Work Related Learning Behaviours: A Systematic Literature Review," *Scandinavian Journal of Work and Organizational Psychology*, vol. 7, no. 2, pp. 1–18, doi: 10.16993/sjwop.151.

[2] A. Clardy, "70-20-10 and the Dominance of Informal Learning: A Fact in Search of Evidence," *Human Resource Development Review*, vol. 17, no. 2, pp. 153–178, Jun. 2018, doi: 10.1177/1534484318759399.

[3] M. Eraut, "Informal learning in the workplace," *Studies in Continuing Education*, vol. 26, no. 2, pp. 247–273, Jul. 2004, doi: 10.1080/158037042000225245.

[4] A. Manuti, S. Pastore, A. F. Scardigno, M. L. Giancaspro, and D. Morciano, "Formal and informal learning in the workplace: a research review," *International Journal of Training and Development*, vol. 19, no. 1, pp. 1–17, 2015, doi: 10.1111/ijtd.12044.

[5] M. Le Clus, "Informal learning in the workplace: A review of the literature," *Australian Journal of Adult Learning*, vol. 51, no. 2, pp. 355–373, 2011.

[6] S. Sambrook, "Factors Influencing the Context and Process of Work-Related Learning: Synthesizing Findings from Two Research Projects," *Human Resource Development International*, vol. 8, no. 1, pp. 101–119, Mar. 2005, doi: 10.1080/1367886052000342591.

[7] D. Hovens, "Workplace Learning through Human-Machine Interaction in a Transient Multilingual Blue-Collar Work Environment," *Journal of Linguistic Anthropology*, vol. 30, no. 3, pp. 369–388, 2020, doi: 10.1111/jola.12279.

[8] J. Decius, N. Schaper, and A. Seifert, "Work Characteristics or Workers' Characteristics? An Input-Process-Output Perspective on Informal Workplace Learning of Blue-Collar Workers," *Vocations and Learning*, vol. 14, no. 2, pp. 285–326, Jul. 2021, doi: 10.1007/s12186-021-09265-5.

[9] S. Skule, "Learning conditions at work: a framework to understand and assess informal learning in the workplace," *International Journal of Training and Development*, vol. 8, no. 1, pp. 8–20, 2004, doi: 10.1111/j.1360-3736.2004.00192.x.

[10] C. P. Cerasoli et al., "Antecedents and outcomes of informal learning behaviors: A meta-analysis," *Journal of Business and Psychology*, vol. 33, pp. 203–230, 2018.

[11] D. Song and C. J. Bonk, "Motivational factors in self-directed informal learning from online learning resources,"

Cogent Education, vol. 3, no. 1, p. 1205838, Dec. 2016, doi: 10.1080/2331186X.2016.1205838.

[12] J. Thillainadesan, D. G. Le Couteur, I. Haq, and T. J. Wilkinson, "When I say … microlearning," *Med Educ*, vol. 56, no. 8, pp. 791–792, Aug. 2022, doi: 10.1111/medu.14848.

[13] T. Hug, "Mobile Learning as 'Microlearning': Conceptual Considerations towards Enhancements of Didactic Thinking," *International Journal of Mobile and Blended Learning*, vol. 2, no. 4, pp. 47–57, Oct. 2010, doi: 10.4018/jmbl.2010100104.

[14] Y.-M. Lee, "Mobile microlearning: a systematic literature review and its implications," *Interactive Learning Environments*, Sep. 2021, doi: 10.1080/10494820.2021.1977964.

[15] A. Taylor and W. Hung, "The Effects of Microlearning: A Scoping Review," *Education Tech Research Dev*, vol. 70, no. 2, pp. 363–395, Apr. 2022, doi: 10.1007/s11423-022-10084-1.

[16] R. Horst, R. Naraghi-Taghi-Off, L. Rau, and R. Dorner, "Bite-Sized Virtual Reality Learning Applications: A Pattern-Based Immersive Authoring Environment," *jucs*, vol. 26, no. 8, pp. 947–971, Aug. 2020, doi: 10.3897/jucs.2020.051.

[17] K. Leong, A. Sung, D. Au, and C. Blanchard, "A review of the trend of microlearning," *Journal of Work-Applied Management*, vol. 13, no. 1, pp. 88–102, Jan. 2020, doi: 10.1108/JWAM-10-2020-0044.

[18] M. S. Shail, "Using Micro-learning on Mobile Applications to Increase Knowledge Retention and Work Performance: A Review of Literature," *Cureus Journal of Medical Science*, vol. 11, no. 8, p. e5307, Aug. 2019, doi: 10.7759/cureus.5307.

[19] C. Pimmer and N. Pachler, "Mobile learning in the workplace: Unlocking the value of mobile technology for work-based education," *Increasing access through mobile learning*, pp. 193–203, 2014.

[20] M. M. Grant, "Difficulties in defining mobile learning: analysis, design characteristics, and implications," *Education Tech Research Dev*, vol. 67, no. 2, pp. 361–388, Apr. 2019, doi: 10.1007/s11423-018-09641-4.

[21] D. Yu, Z. Yan, and X. He, "Capturing knowledge trajectories of mobile learning research: A main path analysis," *Educ Inf Technol*, vol. 27, no. 5, pp. 7257–7280, Jun. 2022, doi: 10.1007/s10639-021-10869-6.

[22] R. C. Peebles, I. K. Nicholson, J. Schlieff, A. Peat, and D. J. Brewster, "Nurses' just-in-time training for clinical deterioration: Development, implementation and evaluation," *Nurse Education Today*, vol. 84, p. 104265, Jan. 2020, doi: 10.1016/j.nedt.2019.104265.

[23] H. Lukosch and P. de Vries, "Supporting Informal Learning at the Workplace," *International Journal of Advanced Corporate Learning (iJAC)*, vol. 2, no. 3, pp. 39–44, Aug. 2009.

[24] R. Sankaranarayanan, J. Leung, V. Abramenka-Lachheb, G. Seo, and A. Lachheb, "Microlearning in Diverse Contexts: A Bibliometric Analysis," *TechTrends*, Oct. 2022, doi: 10.1007/s11528-022-00794-x.

[25] Y. Y. Ho, E.-Y. Yeo, and D. S. B. M. Wijaya, "Turning Coffee Time into Teaching Moments Through Bite-Sized Learning for Adult Learners," *The Journal of Continuing Higher Education*, pp. 1–16, Mar. 2022, doi: 10.1080/07377363.2021.2024000.

[26] I. Jahnke, Y.-M. Lee, M. Pham, H. He, and L. Austin, "Unpacking the Inherent Design Principles of Mobile Microlearning," *Tech Know Learn*, vol. 25, no. 3, pp. 585–619, Sep. 2020, doi: 10.1007/s10758-019-09413-w.

[27] Y.-M. Lee, I. Jahnke, and L. Austin, "Mobile microlearning design and effects on learning efficacy and learner experience," *Education Tech Research Dev*, vol. 69, no. 2, pp. 885–915, Apr. 2021, doi: 10.1007/s11423-020-09931-w.

[28] R. Helyer, "Learning through reflection: the critical role of reflection in work-based learning (WBL)," *Journal of Work-Applied Management*, vol. 7, no. 1, pp. 15–27, Jan. 2015, doi: 10.1108/JWAM-10-2015-003.

[29] Y.-M. Lee, "Mobile microlearning: a systematic literature review and its implications," *Interactive Learning Environments*, vol. 0, no. 0, pp. 1–16, Sep. 2021, doi: 10.1080/10494820.2021.1977964.

[30] A. Dolowitz, J. Collier, A. Hayes, and C. Kumsal, "Iterative Design and Integration of a Microlearning Mobile App for Performance Improvement and Support for NATO Employees," *TechTrends*, vol. 67, no. 1, pp. 143–149, Jan. 2023, doi: 10.1007/s11528-022-00781-2.

[31] P. S. Hogle, "Microlearning in Corporate Settings," in *Microlearning in the Digital Age*, New York: Routledge, 2021, pp. 139–154.

[32] M. J. Dolasinski and J. Reynolds, "Microlearning: A New Learning Model," *Journal of Hospitality & Tourism Research*, vol. 44, no. 3, pp. 551–561, Mar. 2020, doi: 10.1177/1096348020901579.

[33] A. M. Selko, "Is Micro Learning a Better Way to Train Our Workforce?" Jul. 2019. [Online]. Available: https://www.industryweek.com/talent/article/22027877/is-micro-learning-a-better-way-to-train-our-workforce [retrieved: March 22, 2023].

[34] J. Kävrestad and M. Nohlberg, "Context-Based Micro Training: A Framework for Information Security Training," in *Human Aspects of Information Security and Assurance*, N. Clarke and S. Furnell, Eds. Cham: Springer International Publishing, 2020, pp. 71–81.

[35] J. Kävrestad, "Context-Based Micro-Training: Enhancing cybersecurity training for end-users," University of Skövde, School of Informatics, Skövde, 2022. [Online]. Available: http://urn.kb.se/resolve?urn=urn:nbn:se:his:diva-21819 [retrieved: March 20, 2023].

[36] K. Govender and M. Madden, "The effectiveness of micro-learning in retail banking," *South African Journal of Higher Education*, vol. 34, no. 2, pp. 74–94, 2020.

[37] A. Hoberg, C. Piele, and J. Veit, "Mobiles Lernen für Smart Home/Smart Grid," *HMD Praxis der Wirtschaftsinformatik*, vol. 50, pp. 80–94, 2013.

[38] G. Dutton, "Game To Train." 2018. [Online]. Available: https://pubs.royle.com/article/Game+To+Train/3177437/523001/article.html [retrieved: March 23, 2023].

[39] N. May, J. Young, and L. Gillman, "Take 5: Designing and evaluating 5-minute eLearning for busy hospital staff," *Focus on Health Professional Education*, vol. 22, no. 2, pp. 60–71, May 2021, doi: 10.3316/INFORMIT.120475124591839.

[40] S. Jaschke, "Mobile learning applications for technical vocational and engineering education: The use of competence snippets in laboratory courses and industry 4.0," in *2014 International Conference on Interactive Collaborative Learning (ICL)*, Dec. 2014, pp. 605–608. doi: 10.1109/ICL.2014.7017840.

[41] M. S. Billert et al., "Vocational Training With Microlearning—How Low-Immersive 360-Degree Learning Environments Support Work-Process-Integrated Learning," *IEEE Transactions on Learning Technologies*, vol. 15, no. 5, pp. 540–553, Oct. 2022, doi: 10.1109/TLT.2022.3176777.

[42] T. Weinert, M. Billert, M. T. de Gafenco, A. Janson, and J. M. Leimeister, "Designing a Co-creation System for the Development of Work-process-related Learning Material in Manufacturing," *Comput Supported Coop Work*, vol. 32, pp. 5–53, 2023, doi: 10.1007/s10606-021-09420-5.

[43] I. Goller, C. Kobe, R. Tscharner, S. Jud, and C. Hertach, "Using Micro Interventions to Develop Team Competencies," presented at the ISPIM Conference Proceedings, 2021, pp. 1–9.

[44] Zavvy, "Creating a training routine for leaders at Freeletics." [Online]. Available: https://www.zavvy.io/case-studies/freeletics [retrieved: March 19, 2023].

[45] Grovo, "InterContinental Hotels Group." [Online]. Available: https://www.grovo.com/resources/case-studies/intercontinental-hotels-group [retrieved: March 24, 2023].

[46] T. Beste, "Knowledge Transfer in a Project-Based Organization Through Microlearning on Cost-Efficiency," *The Journal of Applied Behavioral Science*, p. 00218863211033096, Jul. 2021, doi: 10.1177/00218863211033096.

[47] H. Matsumoto, Y. Hagiwara, N. Yamamoto-Mitani, and A. Igarashi, "A randomized control trial for ReDeSign: A dementia-friendly mobile microlearning training for store workers in Japan," *The Gerontologist*, vol. XX, no. XX, pp. 1–11, 2023, doi: 10.1093/geront/gnac182.

[48] H. Matsumoto, A. Igarashi, Y. Hagiwara, and N. Yamamoto-Mitani, "Relational Design for Dementia and Job Significance (ReDeSign): Study protocol for a randomized controlled trial of an online dementia training for retail workers," *Contemporary Clinical Trials Communications*, vol. 26, p. 100896, Jan. 2022, doi: 10.1016/j.conctc.2022.100896.

[49] A. Hegerius, P. Caduff-Janosa, R. Savage, and J. Ellenius, "E-Learning in Pharmacovigilance: An Evaluation of Microlearning-Based Modules Developed by Uppsala Monitoring Centre," *Drug Saf*, vol. 43, no. 11, pp. 1171–1180, Nov. 2020, doi: 10.1007/s40264-020-00981-w.

[50] M. Robalino, "Intervention Development: Quick Response Code Implementation for Point-of-Care Training Needs in the Emergency Department," *Journal of Emergency Nursing*, vol. 47, no. 6, pp. 938–943, Nov. 2021, doi: 10.1016/j.jen.2021.08.003.

[51] H. Lukosch, S. Kurapati, D. Groen, and A. Verbraeck, "Microgames for Situated Learning: A Case Study in Interdependent Planning," *Simulation & Gaming*, vol. 47, no. 3, pp. 346–367, Jun. 2016.

[52] U. Zandbergs, J. Judrups, E. Plane, and R. Uscins, "Improvement of microlearning with help of learning analytics in enterprises," presented at the 20th International Scientific Conference Engineering for Rural Development, May 2021, pp. 1584–1589. doi: 10.22616/ERDev.2021.20.TF338.

[53] L. Butgereit, "Gamifying mobile micro-learning for continuing education in a corporate IT environment," in *2016 IST-Africa Week Conference*, May 2016, pp. 1–7. doi: 10.1109/ISTAFRICA.2016.7530597.

[54] J. I. Criado, C. Herranz, and J. Villodre, "Informal Virtual Learning in the Public Sector: Educating Public Servants in Digital Social Innovation Environments," in *The Palgrave Handbook of the Public Servant*, H. Sullivan, H. Dickinson, and H. Henderson, Eds. Cham: Springer International Publishing, 2020, pp. 1–18. doi: 10.1007/978-3-030-03008-7_46-1.

[55] I. Isibika and C. Zhu, "Microlearning training intervention for librarians: design and development: 16th annual International Technology, Education and Development Conference," *INTED2022*, pp. 7432–7440, 2022.

[56] L. N. Dyrbye, A. L. Bergene, A. N. L. Hunderfund, and H. A. Billings, "Reimagining Faculty Development Deployment: A Multipronged, Pragmatic Approach to Improve Engagement," *Acad. Med.*, vol. 97, no. 9, pp. 1322–1330, Sep. 2022, doi: 10.1097/ACM.0000000000004688.

[57] T. Shamir-Inbal and I. Blau, "Micro-learning in designing professional development for ICT teacher leaders: The role of self-regulation and perceived learning," *Professional Development in Education*, vol. 48, no. 5, pp. 734–750, Oct. 2022, doi: 10.1080/19415257.2020.1763434.

[58] E. Pölzl-Stefanec and C. Geißler, "'Micro-steps' on the route to successful online professional development for Austrian Early Childhood Educators," *International Journal of Educational Research*, vol. 115, p. 102042, Jan. 2022, doi: 10.1016/j.ijer.2022.102042.

[59] A. Hesse et al., "Short communication: Microlearning courses are effective at increasing the feelings of confidence and accuracy in the work of dairy personnel," *Journal of Dairy Science*, vol. 102, no. 10, pp. 9505–9511, Oct. 2019, doi: 10.3168/jds.2018-15927.

[60] S. Nanjappa, V. Ghosh, S. Acharya, H. S. Mukerjee, and V. Stl, "Microlearning in corporate settings: practitioner perspectives," *Human Resource Development International*, pp. 1–8, Dec. 2022, doi: 10.1080/13678868.2022.2160688.

[61] C.-L. Lai, "Trends and research issues of technology-enhanced self-regulated learning in the mobile era: a review of SSCI journal articles," *International Journal of Mobile Learning and Organisation*, vol. 16, no. 2, pp. 150–172, Jan. 2022, doi: 10.1504/IJMLO.2022.121879.

[62] S. M. Hirsch, E. Bueno, and K. C. Tenure, "Quick Response Codes: An Innovative Approach to Just-in-Time

Education," *Journal of Neuroscience Nursing*, vol. 52, no. 6, pp. 308–310, Dec. 2020, doi: 10.1097/JNN.0000000000000550.

[63] C. T. Karia, A. Hughes, and S. Carr, "Uses of quick response codes in healthcare education: a scoping review," *BMC Med Educ*, vol. 19, no. 1, p. 456, Dec. 2019, doi: 10.1186/s12909-019-1876-4.

[64] R. M. Gagne, L. Briggs, and W. W. Wager, "Principles of Instructional Design Fort Worth," *TX: HBJ College Publishers*, 1992.

[65] D. O'Doherty, M. Dromey, J. Lougheed, A. Hannigan, J. Last, and D. McGrath, "Barriers and solutions to online learning in medical education – an integrative review," *BMC Medical Education*, vol. 18, no. 1, p. 130, Jun. 2018, doi: 10.1186/s12909-018-1240-0.

[66] M. Fischer, M. Rohweder, and P. Dewan, "H5P (product review)," vol. 42, no. 3, pp. 178–180, Dec. 2021.

[67] G. Kiryakova, "Engaging Learning Content for Digital Learners," *TEM J.*, vol. 11, no. 4, pp. 1958–1964, Nov. 2022, doi: 10.18421/TEM114-65.

[68] R. P. Díaz Redondo, M. Caeiro Rodríguez, J. J. López Escobar, and A. Fernández Vilas, "Integrating micro-learning content in traditional e-learning platforms," *Multimed Tools Appl*, vol. 80, no. 2, pp. 3121–3151, Jan. 2021, doi: 10.1007/s11042-020-09523-z.

[69] T. Javorcik, "Content Management System for Creating Microlearning Courses," in *2021 International Symposium on Educational Technology (ISET)*, Aug. 2021, pp. 223–227. doi: 10.1109/ISET52350.2021.00053.

[70] S. Bratt, "Essential strategies for developing mobile-based micro-learning," presented at the EdMedia+ Innovate Learning, 2020, pp. 17–25.

[71] K. Larson, "Using Augmented Reality in the Corporate Environment: A Proposed Study Protocol," in *2019 Eighth International Conference on Educational Innovation through Technology (EITT)*, Oct. 2019, pp. 245–249. doi: 10.1109/EITT.2019.00054.

[72] L. Rau, R. Horst, Y. Liu, and R. Dörner, "A Nugget-Based Concept for Creating Augmented Reality," in *2021 IEEE International Symposium on Mixed and Augmented Reality Adjunct (ISMAR-Adjunct)*, Oct. 2021, pp. 212–217. doi: 10.1109/ISMAR-Adjunct54149.2021.00051.

[73] A. Putri Septiani and Y. Rosmansyah, "Features, Frameworks, and Benefits of Gamified Microlearning: A Systematic Literature Review," in *2021 3rd International Conference on Modern Educational Technology*, New York, NY, USA, Sep. 2021, pp. 130–135. doi: 10.1145/3468978.3469000.

[74] D. R. Santos, C. R. Cordon, and M. Palomo-Duarte, "Extending H5P Branching Scenario with 360° scenes and xAPI capabilities: A case study in a local networks course," in *2019 International Symposium on Computers in Education (SIIE)*, Nov. 2019, pp. 1–6. doi: 10.1109/SIIE48397.2019.8970117.

Designing Principles and Guidelines for a Pedagogical Framework of STEM Learning Through Mobile Serious Games

Ignace M. Kasiama
Department of Educational Technology
Laval University
Quebec, Canada
ignace.kasiama-mupalanga.1@ulaval.ca

Laurence Capus
Department of Computer Science and Software Engineering
Laval University
laurence.capus@ift.ulaval.ca

Abstract— **The urgency of improving science, technology, engineering, and mathematics (STEM) learning has been internationally recognized. However, the views on the nature and development of proficiencies in STEM education are diverse, and increased focus on integration raises new concerns and needs for further research. The complexity of these factors reaches beyond just helping students achieve high scores in STEM topics assessments. In practice, teachers struggle and lack cohesive understanding of STEM education. Also, students are most of the time disinterested in some STEM subjects and do not understand how STEM knowledge is applied to real-world problems. Connecting ideas across disciplines is challenging when students have little or no understanding of the relevant ideas in the individual disciplines. Therefore, a STEM education conceptual framework is needed to build a research agenda that will in turn inform stakeholders to realize the full potential of integrated STEM education. In this paper, we present key concepts to build an integrated STEM education framework through mobile serious games which reflect design principles created based on the theoretical understanding of teaching and learning.**

Keywords- STEM; Mobile Educational serious games; Pedagogical framework; Design principles; Mobile learning environment

I. INTRODUCTION

Science, technology, engineering and mathematics fosters students' creativity and design thinking [7][12]. Globally, educators hope to improve student learning outcomes, such as participation, interest, engagement, persistence, and aspiration in STEM (science, technology, engineering, and mathematics) and STEM-related fields. For Taylor (2016), STEM education is a key factor in preparing young people to deal positively and productively with 21st century global challenges that are impacting the economy and the environment. The focus of our paper will be on science, technology, engineering, and mathematics (STEM) related studies at primary and secondary school levels. As we will deal throughout this paper with the design principles and guidelines for the pedagogical framework for STEM learning through mobile serious games, recommendations, and guidelines for considering these design principles in the STEM learning design environment using mobile serious games and how these principles will be applied including concrete examples within the complete framework, will be subject of our next research work. As stated by Martin et al. [17], it has been widely argued that more active instructional methods must be implemented in classrooms. The authors refer to the general proposition of Bonwell et al. [3] to define these more active instructional methods for students to be engaged in usual tasks such as listening, reading, writing, discussing, or solving problems but also, and most importantly, to be engaged in higher-order thinking tasks such as analysis, synthesis, or evaluation and for which an inquiry-based approach to STEM subjects can produce good results.

In this context, serious games can play a special role because the quantitative and predictive models of STEM topics can be used to generate interactive environments that can be freely experienced. Serious games have great potential to catalyze and support inquiry-based approaches to STEM instruction, over-coming curricular and logistical barriers [20]. Despite a decade of research emphasis on STEM education, there has not been much game-based learning for STEM, and the existing one are not consistent in terms of activities being monitored and learning outcomes assessed [35]. Serious games as a teaching aid can stimulate students interest and improve their understanding in STEM learning. The use of serious game on STEM learning analytics provides assessment data to measure student performance and achievement of pre-defined learning out-comes [36]. The concept of STEM education is an effort to engage students in learning about science, technology, engineering, and mathematics [10].

Today, digital games are considered a popular form of activity for children and even for adults. Most students cannot imagine a world without mobile technology [31]. As the process of technological change in education evolves, it must be recognized that mobile technology is part of the new education system. They provide personalized distance learning and automatic learning using mobile devices for students of all ages and backgrounds [5]. STEM learning through Mobile devices allows interaction, collaboration, and learning in a variety of ways: through apps, videos, online presentations, and other interactive tools [15]. The added value of STEM learning games through mobile serious games is that they appeal to many players.

Students can bring knowledge with them wherever they go. The growth rate of the mobile gaming market is a force to be reckoned with. Currently, there is a lack of high quality and critically evaluated interactive educational materials or tools available for teacher's use [9]. There is a need for student-centered and design-based approaches to STEM education to engage students in STEM fields and develop skills basics needed to succeed in a technological society. Educational games have been used for decades, their affordances serving as primary vehicles of learning, but their benefits are limited by their constructivist pedagogy. According to McDonald [18], game design as an educational tool can meet the needs of contemporary STEM educators and become an essential part of future science, technology, engineering, and math education initiatives.

These principles and guidelines for a pedagogical framework of STEM learning through mobile serious games will be useful for primary and secondary teachers in the design of STEM lessons, for example, choices of types of tasks and activities, ways of learning, teaching, and learning content in the context of STEM subjects. Teachers will be able to choose the design principles they deem most relevant to consider each time, depending on the specific learning objectives, instead of trying to keep all the principles in mind. Obviously, Teachers may also choose to focus on specific design principles based on their personal professional development needs.

II. State of the Art

Throughout this section will present principles to inform the design of innovative learning environments using mobile technologies. We will discuss how such design principles are an important outcome of creating a learning framework using mobile devices.

A. *The role of mobile technology in serious game*

As the world has become a global village because of the technological advancement in the world, mobile teaching and learning in recent years has become a valuable and real contribution to learning environment rather than what it used to be in previous years as a theory, academic exploration, and technological idea [1]. Obviously, with the rapid development of mobile communication technology and wireless internet technology, a new learning mode named mobile learning is quietly emerging. The characteristics of personalized learning at anytime and anywhere attract the attention of many scholars at home and abroad. However, it has become an urgent problem to ensure learners to focus on learning in a mobile learning environment for a long time, and that fragmentation learning can be effectively integrated into system learning. It is a meaningful attempt to integrate edutainment into mobile learning. For Husheng et al. [8], with the implementation of 4G technology, mobile games have made great leaps both in the game quality and the game platform. It also provides great opportunities for the combination of serious games and mobile learning.

Mobile serious game is serious game in the mobile device on the realization of the carrier. It has the characteristics of mobile games and serious games and has unique advantages in portability and entertainment. Users can use mobile phones to play games at any time and place, actively acquiring knowledge and skills, and achieving changes in attitudes and behaviors.

Given the fact that there is no single definition for mobile learning and stressing that mobile learning has not yet been defined, many researchers have put forth proposed definitions of the concept. Mobile learning has been described as a subdivision or subset of electronic learning [22]. Therefore, mobile learning focuses on the mobility of the learners, interacting with portable technologies and learning that reflects a focus on how society and its institutions can accommodate and support an increasingly mobile population.

B. *Design principles for mobile learning*

For van den Akker [32], design principles can refer to characteristics of a planned learning design (what it should look like), or its procedure (how it should be developed). Above all, design principles must be expressed in a way that can inform practice [33]. Design principles are best expressed in active terms that enable their ready use by teachers and designers presented with similar contexts and problems. They are often presented in a form that lists criteria of particular learning environments and outcomes, and when presented this way, often start with a verb. Again, design principles are not fixed, and are offered as advice on how others might benefit from the findings of a particular development and research endeavour. As noted by Reeves [24]: 'Instructional technologists engaged in [design-based] research are above all reflective and humble, cognizant that their designs and conclusions are tentative in even the best of situations'.

Herrington et al. [6] have outlined design principles for mobile learning and the following characteristics are recommended for the incorporation of mobile learning into an education learning environment:

TABLE I. DESIGN PRINCIPLES FOR MOBILE LEARNING

PRINCIPLES	DESCRIPTION
REAL WORLD RELEVANCE	USE MOBILE LEARNING IN AUTHENTIC CONTEXTS
MOBILE CONTEXTS	USE MOBILE LEARNING IN CONTEXTS WHERE LEARNERS ARE MOBILE.
EXPLORE	PROVIDE TIME FOR EXPLORATION OF MOBILE TECHNOLOGIES
BLENDED	BLEND MOBILE AND NON-MOBILE TECHNOLOGIES
WHENEVER	USE MOBILE LEARNING SPONTANEOUSLY
WHEREVER	USE MOBILE LEARNING IN NON-TRADITIONAL LEARNING SPACES
WHOMSOEVER	USE MOBILE LEARNING BOTH INDIVIDUALLY AND COLLABORATIVELY
AFFORDANCES	EXPLOIT THE AFFORDANCES OF MOBILE TECHNOLOGIES
PERSONALISE	EMPLOY THE LEARNERS' OWN MOBILE DEVICES
MEDIATION	USE MOBILE LEARNING TO MEDIATE KNOWLEDGE CONSTRUCTION.
PRODUCE:	USE MOBILE LEARNING TO PRODUCE AND CONSUME KNOWLEDGE.

III. PEDAGOGICAL FRAMEWORK FOR STEM LEARNING AND DESIGN PRINCIPLES

STEM education is the preparation for STEM fields and encouragement of STEM literacy. A commonly accepted definition of STEM education is provided by Tsupros et al. [30]: STEM education is an interdisciplinary approach to learning where rigorous academic concepts are coupled with real-world lessons as students apply science, technology, engineering, and mathematics in contexts that make connections between school, community, work, and the global enterprise enabling the development of STEM literacy and with it the ability to compete in the new economy. As stated earlier on, the importance of engaging and effective learning environments for science, technology, engineering, and mathematics (STEM) has been internationally recognised [27]. There is a need for learning environments that raise interest and motivation towards STEM studies and careers (Salmi et al., 2021) and better connect STEM competencies to cross-curricular, so-called twenty-first century skills, as well as to future workplace skills [27]. However, the creation of frameworks that gather and represent design principles [34], i.e. organisational units for synthesising design knowledge to guide the design of hybrid STEM learning environments is much needed [11].

Considering (a) the lack of a pedagogical conceptual framework to guide both educators and developers in the design of a learning environment, in the selection of effective teaching and learning, methods of teaching and learning, particularly in the context of STEM subjects; (b) the benefits of a participatory co-design approach for STEM educational serious games; (c) the impact of the pedagogical framework of STEM learning through mobile serious games. The following section will describe how design principles have been developed based on the research literature. These principles will serve as a research-based introduction to the topic after which priorities can be defined based on the concrete design target and goals.

A. Pedagogical Framework structure

The current state of research on the design of Digital Game Based Learning (DGBL) environments call for an updated review of the best practices in recent years for developing Digital Game based learning environments, which prompted our literature review. As outlined by Tetyana [30], it draws from successful examples of educators implementing STEM learning games in classes, and it highlights five key principles that facilitate the effectiveness of STEM learning: (1) interactivity; (2) immersiveness; (3) adaptive problem solving; (4) feedback, and (5) freedom of exploration. Practical examples are used to illustrate the effective implementation of these principles in STEM learning games environments and to underscore the significance of each component.

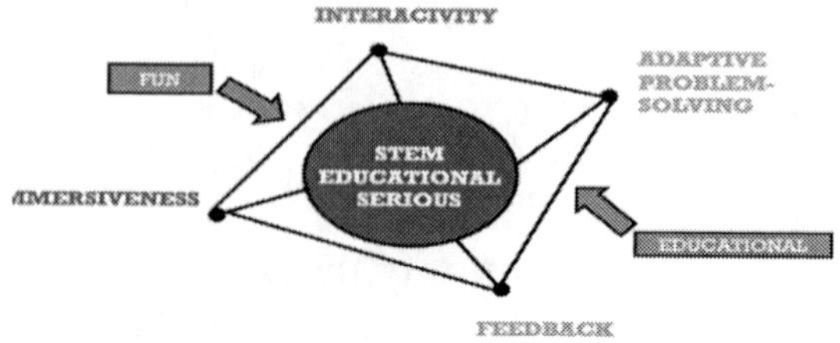

Figure 1. Principles in STEM learning games

Using the Pedagogical Framework for STEM Learning and Design Principles in the development of educational serious games can provide students with a more engaging and effective learning experience that helps them develop a deeper understanding of STEM concepts. As a result, it can help address the challenge of students having little or no understanding of the relevant ideas in individual STEM disciplines and can promote increased interest and participation in STEM fields. As stated by Martin et al., [17], it has been widely argued that more active instructional methods must be implemented in classrooms. The authors refer to the general proposition of Bonwell et al. [3] to define these more active instructional methods for students to be engaged in usual tasks such as listening, reading, writing, discussing, or solving problems but also, and most importantly, to be engaged in higher-order thinking tasks such as analysis, synthesis, or evaluation and for which an inquiry-based approach to STEM subjects can produce good results.

In this context, serious games can play a special role because the quantitative and predictive models of STEM topics can be used to generate interactive environments that can be freely experienced. Serious games have great potential to catalyze and support inquiry-based approaches to STEM instruction, over-coming curricular and logistical barriers [20]. Also, Young et al. [35] also noted that: Despite a decade of research emphasis on STEM education, there has not been much game-based learning for STEM, and the existing one are not consistent in terms of activities being monitored and learning outcomes assessed. According to Zaki et al. [36], the use of serious games as a teaching aid can stimulate students' interest and improve their understanding in STEM learning. The use of serious game on STEM learning analytics provides assessment data to measure student performance and achievement of pre-defined learning out-comes. As stated in the previous paragraph and similarly by Johnson et al. [10], the concept of STEM education is an effort to engage students in learning about science, technology, engineering, and mathematics. Today, digital games are considered a popular form of activity for children and even for adults.

Their ease of access and mobility allow people, young children to play on their smartphones. According to Sauvé et al. [26], although playing such games can be considered individualistic, studies indicate that online digital games allow individuals to connect with others in online virtual worlds. Currently, there is a lack of high quality and critically evaluated interactive educational materials or tools available for teacher's use. Again, for Jagoda [9], there is a need for student-centered and design-based approaches to STEM education to engage students in STEM fields and develop skills basics needed to succeed in a technological society. Educational games have been used for decades, their affordances serving as primary vehicles of learning, but their benefits are limited by their constructivist pedagogy. In fact, the game design as an educational tool can meet the needs of contemporary STEM educators and become an essential part of future science, technology, engineering, and math education initiatives [18].

These principles as outlined above, derived from successful implementation of digital gaming elements in learning, and they provide suggestions and strategies for incorporation of these elements based on real-life examples. The table below show how each of these elements are effectively adopted in STEM educational games and may offer ideas for the development of future STEM Digital game-based learning designs. Particularly learner-centred pedagogical principles have been guiding the framework development. The conceptualization of student-centered learning is influenced by authors such as Hayward, Dewey, Froebel, Piaget, Rogers, and Knowles [21]. All this, relate primarily to the constructivist view emphasizing the importance of places on activity, discovery, and independent learning but also cognitive theory highlighting the activity. It also has connections with social constructivist views emphasizing the importance of peer interaction in learning. O'Neill et al. [21] view student-centred and teacher-centred learning as a continuum:

- Low level of student choice - High level of student choice,
- Student passive - Student active,
- Power is primarily with teacher - Power primarily with the student.

In the table below, we will present general principles and description as well as some examples of how these aspects will be considered in the pedagogical framework of STEM learning through mobile serious games.

TABLE II. DESCRIPTIONS OF PRINCIPLES IN STEM LEARNING GAMES

Principle Indicator	Description
Interactivity	Games that offer meaningful interactions demonstratively maintain high levels of engagement in students and positively contribute to their performance on tests when compared to regular project-based instruction (e.g., An & Bonk, 2009; Barab et. al, 2007).
Immersiveness	Immersive details and students'' absorption in the activity may lead to the mental state of flow (Csikszentmihalyi, 1990), meaning that students would intrinsically enjoy the game and perceive the involvement in the game itself as its own reward (DeCharms, 1972; Deci, 1975; Nakamura & Csikszentmihalyi, 2002).
Adaptive problem solving	Many cognitive psychologists report that engaging students in solving real world problems positively affects their learning gains (e.g., Mayer, 1992; Merrill & Gilbert, 2008). The challenge to resolve these problems needs to be effectively aligned with the student''s ability and skill level to ensure effective learning. Therefore, I coined the term adaptive problem solving to accurately reflect this need. A well-designed DGBL should offer skill-level adjustments to the problems that students are facing which will ensure gradual learning for all students (Wilson et al., 2009) and create motivational tension (Driskell & Dwyer, 1984) when the challenge of the game is optimal for students'' skills.
Feedback	As in any form of learning, quality feedback helps students evaluate their progress, recognize their strengths, and identify areas that need improvement (Charles et al., 2009). Effective feedback should provide timely and relevant information on students'' progress towards their learning goals.

IV. CONCLUSION

Designing an effective STEM Learning environment using mobile serious games that can engage and motivate students as well as facilitate their learning is a challenging task. In many cases, teachers' pedagogical expertise does not directly translate into game design, and it leaves educators with no help regarding the effective ways to introduce STEM learning games in a class and what elements of games and learning should be prioritized. While there is no one correct way to design a digital game-based learning that would guarantee its effectiveness for all students, previous research can offer successful examples of digital games incorporated in classrooms that share common principles. The implementation and the effectiveness of these principles depend on students' goals, interests, subject matters, available resources, but they constitute a solid foundation for designing or adapting a digital game according to the desired learning objectives. The principles outlined in this paper provide insights into the potential to combine different STEM subjects, learning contexts, scenarios, and goals. As educational technologies continue to develop, more tools will be available for teachers to experiment with and uncover additional benefits and effective practices of using STEM digital-based games.

REFERENCES

[1] Alzaza, N.S., and A.R. Yaakub. (2011). Students' awareness and requirements of mobile learning services in higher education environment. American Journal of Economics and Business Administration 3(1): 95–100.

[2] Ball C, Huang K, Cotten SR, Rikard RV. (2018). Gaming the SySTEM: the relationship between video games and the digital and STEM divides. Games Cult Nov 29;15(5):501-528.

[3] Bonwell, JA Eison. (1991). Active Learning: Creating Excitement in the Classroom. Washington, DC: George Washington Univ.

[4] Fisher C. (2015). Designing Games for Children: Developmental, Usability, and Design Considerations for Making Games for Kids. New York: Focal Press.

[5] Grant, M. M., Tamim, S., Brown, D. B., Sweeney, J. P., Ferguson, F. K., & Jones, L. B. (2015). Teaching and learning with mobile computing devices: Case study in K-12 classrooms. TechTrends, 59(4), 32–45.

[6] Herrington, A.; Herrington, J.; and Mantei, Jessica (2009). Design principles for mobile learning. https://ro.uow.edu.au/edupapers/88

[7] Herro, D., Quigley, C. and Jacques, L.A. (2018), "Examining technology integration in middle school STEAM units", Technology, Pedagogy and Education, Vol. 27 No. 4, pp. 485-498

[8] Husheng, P., Chenjie, G., Junfu, Y., & Yuehua, C. (2017). Research on Design and Development of Mobile Serious Game under Mobile Learning Environment. 3rd Workshop on Advanced Research and Technology in Industry Applications (WARTIA 2017). Advances in Engineering Research (AER), volume 148

[9] Jagoda, P. (2020). Experimental Games: Critique, Play, and Design in the Age of Gamification (Chicago: University of Chicago Press, 2020), 386 pp

[10] Johnson, C. C., Peters-Burton, E. E., & Moore, T. J. (2015). STEM roadmap: a framework for integration. London: Taylor & Francis.

[11] Kali, Y., McKenney, S., & Sagy, O. (2015). Teachers as designers of technology enhanced learning Instruc- tional Science, 173–180

[12] Kang, N.H. (2019), "A review of the effect of integrated STEM or STEAM (science, technology, engineering, arts, and mathematics) education in South Korea", Asia-Pacific Science Education, Vol. 5 No. 1, pp. 1-22

[13] Kucher, T. (2021). Principles and best practices of designing digital game-based learning environments. International Journal of Technology in Education and Science (IJTES), 5(2), 213-223.

[14] Kukulska-Hulme A, Bossu C, Coughlan T, Ferguson R, FitzGerald E, Gaved M, et al (2021). Innovating Pedagogy: Open University Innovation Report 9. Milton Keynes: The Open University; 2021:1-51.

[15] Leontyeva, I., Pronkin, N., & Tsvetkova, M. (2021). Visualization of learning and memorization: Is the mind mapping based on mobile platforms learning more effective? International Journal of Instruction, 14(4), 173–186.

[16] Mäkelä, T., & Leinonen, T. (2021). Design Framework and Principles for Learning Environment Co-Design: Synthesis from Literature and Three Empirical Studies. Buildings, 11(12), Article 581.

[17] Martin Riopel, Lucian Nenciovici, Patrice Potvin, Pierre Chastenay, Patrick Charland, Jérémie Blanchette Sarrasin & Steve Masson (2020). Impact of serious games on science learning achievement compared with more conventional instruction: an overview and a meta-analysis, Studies in Science Education, 55:2, 169-214.

[18] McDonald, C. V. (2016). STEM Education: A Review of the Contribution of the Disciplines of Science, Technology, Engineering and Mathematics. *Science Education International, 27(4)*, 530–569.

[19] Motiwalla, L.F. (2007). Mobile learning: A framework and evaluation. Computers & Education 49(3): 581–596.

[20] National Research Council. (2011). Learning science through computer games and simulations. In M. A. Honey & M. L. Hilton (Eds.), Committee on science learning: computer games, simulations, and education. Washington, DC: The National Academies Press.

[21] O'Neill, G. & McMahon, T. (2005). Student-centred learning: What does it mean for students and lecturers? in G. O'Neill, G. Moore and B. McMullin (Eds.), Emerging Issues in the Practice of University Learning and Teaching. Dublin: AISHE.

[22] Peters, K. (2007). m-Learning: Positioning educators for a mobile, connected future. International *Journal Of Research in Open and Distance Learning, 8*(2), 1-17.

[23] Prensky, M. (2001). Digital game-based learning. New York: McGraw-Hill Education.

[24] Reeves, T. (2000). Enhancing the worth of instructional technology research through "design experiments" and other development research strategies. Paper presented at the Annual AERA Meeting, April 24-28, New Orleans.

[25] Salmi, H., Thuneberg, H., Bogner, F. X., & Fenyvesi, K. (2021). Individual creativity and career choices of pre-teens in the context of a math-art learning event. Open Education Studies, 3(1), 147–156.

[26] Sauvé, L; Renaud, L; Kaufman, D.(2010). Games, simulations and simulations games for learning: Definitions and distinctions. In D. Kaufman & L. Sauvé. Educational gameplay and simulation environments: Case studies and lessons learned, 1-26.

[27] Struyf, A., De Loof, H., Boeve-de Pauw, J., & Van Petegem, P. (2019). Students' engagement in different STEM learning environments: Integrated STEM education as promising practice? International Jour- nal of Science Education, 41(10), 1387–1407

[28] Taylor, P.C. (2016). "Session N: why is a STEAM curriculum perspective crucial to the 21st century?", 2009-2016 ACER Research Conferences. Paper 6, Australian Council for Educational Research (ACER), Melbourne

[29] Tetyana Kucher (2021). Principles and Best Practices of Designing Digital Game-Based Learning Environments. International Journal of Technology in Education and Science. Vol. 5, No. 2, 213-223

[30] Tsupros, N., Kohler, R., & Hallinen, J. (2009). STEM Education: A Project to Identify the Missing Components. Pittsburgh, PA: Intermediate Unit 1 and Carnegie Mellon.

[31] Tyurina, Y., Troyanskaya, M., Babaskina, L., Choriyev, R., & Pronkin, N. (2021). E-learning for SMES. International Journal of Emerging Technologies in Learning, 16(2), 108–119.

[32] van den Akker, J. (1999). Principles and methods of development research. In J. van den Akker, N. Nieveen, R. M. Branch, K. L. Gustafson & T. Plomp (Eds.), *Design methodology and developmental research in education and training* (pp. 1-14). The Netherlands: Kluwer Academic Publishers.

[33] Wang, F., & Hannafin, M. J. (2005). Design-based research and technology-enhanced learning environments. *Educational Technology Research and Development, 53*(4), 5-23.

[34] Warr, M., Mishra, P., & Scragg, B. (2020). Designing theory. Educational Technology Research and Development, 68, 601–632.

[35] Young, M. F., Slota, S., Cutter, A. B., Jalette, G., Mullin, G., Lai, B., Yukhymenko, M. (2012). Our princess is in another castle: A review of trends in serious gaming for education. Review of Educational Research, 82(1), 61–89.

[36] Zaki, N. A. A., Zain, N.Z.M., Noor, N.A.Z., & Hashim, H. (2020). Developing a conceptual model of learning analytics in serious game for STEM education. *Science Education Study Program FMIPA UNNES Semarang*.in serious game s for STEM education. *Science Education Study Program FMIPA UNNES Semarang.*

Design Thinking in the Era of Digital Transformation: A Conceptual Framework of Smart Learning Environment for Teacher Professional Development

Ali Gohar Qazi
Institute of Education, University College London, UK & Institute for Educational Development, The Aga Khan University (AKU-IED), Karachi London, UK
e-mail: ali.gohar.21@ucl.ac.uk

Muhammad Yasir Mustafa
Smart Learning Institute, Beijing Normal University, Beijing, China
e-mail: yasirpaf@gmail.com

Huang Ronghaui
Smart Learning Institute, Beijing Normal University, Beijing, China
e-mail: huangrh@bnu.edu.cn

Michael Agyemang Adarkwah
Smart Learning Institute, Beijing Normal University, Beijing, China
e-mail: adarkwahmichael1@gmail.com

***Abstract*—In the era of digital transformation, teacher professional development has become an essential part of education. The emergence of new technologies and the changing learning environment have made it necessary to reevaluate the traditional approach to professional development. In this study, we explore the concept of design thinking and its application in the creation of a smart learning environment for teacher professional development. We argue that design thinking offers a unique approach to problem-solving and can help educators develop innovative solutions to the challenges they face. We propose a framework for the design of a smart learning environment based on the principles of design thinking, and we discuss the potential benefits of this approach for teacher professional development.**

Keywords—Educational Technology; Pedagogical innovations; Teacher development; PD; Design

I. INTRODUCTION

In the era of digital transformation, the field of education has witnessed a significant shift in the way learning takes place. With the advent of technology, traditional teaching methodologies are being reevaluated and new teaching and learning approaches are being developed [1][2]. Among these, design thinking has emerged as a popular problem-solving methodology that is being adopted in various domains, including education [3]. In the context of education, design thinking offers a unique approach to developing innovative solutions to the challenges faced by educators in the digital age [4].

The use of design thinking in education is not new, and there is a growing body of research that highlights the benefits of applying design thinking to various educational contexts [5][6]. However, despite its potential, the use of design thinking in teacher professional development is still a relatively unexplored area [4][7][8]. Teacher professional development plays a crucial role in improving the quality of education and ensuring that teachers are equipped with the necessary skills and knowledge to meet the evolving needs of their students [9][10][11][12]. Therefore, it is essential to explore the potential of design thinking in developing a smart learning environment that can facilitate teacher professional development in the digital age.

The traditional approach to teacher professional development typically involves workshops, seminars, and conferences, which are often a "one-size-fits-all" approach and lack personalization [13]. Moreover, they are often time-bound and cannot be accessed at the teacher's convenience. In contrast, a smart learning environment can provide personalized and flexible learning opportunities that can be accessed anytime and anywhere. It can also promote collaboration and community building among teachers, which can help to foster a culture of continuous learning and improvement [14].

The aim of this research is to explore the potential of design thinking in developing a smart learning environment for teacher professional development in the digital age. The study proposes a framework for a smart learning environment that is based on the principles of personalization, flexibility, collaboration, and innovation. It also discusses the benefits of a smart learning environment for teacher professional development and highlights its potential to promote innovation and experimentation in the classroom. The given below research question guided the researchers to carry out this study.

RQ: How to promote teacher professional development in smart learning environments using design thinking principles?

Overall, this research contributes to the growing body of literature on design thinking in education and highlights the potential of a smart learning environment to support teacher professional development in the digital age. The conducted study provides insights into the application of design thinking principles in developing a smart learning environment and highlights the benefits of such an environment for teachers and their students.

The remainder of the paper is structured as follows. In Section II, the theoretical framework for smart learning environments is presented, which includes an overview of design thinking models and smart learning environment frameworks. Section III describes the methodology used to develop the proposed conceptual framework for a smart learning environment for teacher professional development. This includes a description of the research design, data collection methods, and analysis techniques used. Finally, in Section IV, the proposed conceptual framework for a smart learning environment for teacher professional development is presented, which integrates the principles of design thinking, personalization, flexibility, collaboration, and innovation. The section also includes a discussion of the potential benefits of the framework for teacher professional development in the digital age.

II. THEORETICAL FRAMEWORK

A. Design Thinking

Design thinking is a human-centered problem-solving methodology that emphasizes empathy, ideation, prototyping, and testing. In the context of education, design thinking offers a unique approach to developing innovative solutions to the real-life challenges faced by educators in the digital age. According to [15], design thinking provides a framework for educators to develop personalized and flexible learning opportunities that are tailored to the needs of their students [16].

The use of design thinking In education is not new, and there is a growing body of research that highlights the benefits of applying design thinking to various educational contexts. For example, in a study by [17] the authors explored the use of design thinking in a teacher professional development program. The study found that design thinking helped to promote innovation and experimentation among teachers, leading to improvements in their teaching practices and the quality of education. On the other hand, design thinking models are essential in education because they offer a structured, user-centered approach to problem-solving that can lead to more engaging and effective learning experiences for students, promote innovation and experimentation among educators, and help develop intuitive and user-friendly educational technology products. Prominent design thinking models include the 4D model, 3I model, and the widely-used d.school model. These models provide a structured and human-centered approach to problem-solving, generating innovative solutions that are tailored to the needs and experiences of users.

In the context of a smart learning environment, design thinking can provide a framework for developing personalized and flexible learning opportunities that can be accessed anytime and anywhere. A smart learning environment can incorporate adaptive learning technologies and learning analytics to provide personalized feedback and support for teachers. According to [18], a smart learning environment can facilitate collaboration among teachers, enabling them to share best practices and work together on common challenges. Moreover, the use of a smart learning environment for teacher professional development can help to promote a culture of continuous learning and provide opportunities for teachers to experiment with new teaching methodologies and technologies, resultantly promoting innovation and creativity in the classroom.

Several studies have explored the use of design thinking in teacher professional development. For example, [19][20] applied design thinking principles to the development of a teacher professional development program in Malaysia. The program was designed to promote creativity and innovation in the classroom, and it included elements of collaboration, prototyping, and feedback. The authors found that the program was effective in promoting creativity and innovation among participating teachers. According to [21], a smart learning environment can help to promote self-directed learning and enable teachers to take ownership of their professional development. Similarly, [22] explored the use of design thinking and developed a design thinking curriculum that included hands-on activities, collaboration, and feedback. The authors found that the curriculum was effective in improving teacher'' problem-solving skills and promoting innovation in the classroom.

Other studies have explored the use of smart learning environments in teacher professional development. For example, [23][24][25] developed a smart learning environment that included elements of personalization, flexibility, and collaboration. The environment was designed to support the professional development of mathematics teachers in China. The authors found that the smart learning environment was effective in promoting collaboration and improving teachers' problem-solving skills.

In responding to identifying various elements in SLEs, various SLE frameworks are introduced in the wide body of literature to structure for the development and implementation of effective and engaging learning experiences based on the principles of personalization, flexibility, collaboration, and innovation. For instance, the Smart Learning Ecosystem (SLE) framework, developed by researchers at the University of Illinois, incorporates elements of personalization, adaptability, and collaboration, and utilizes learning analytics to provide feedback and support for teachers. The Personal Learning Environment (PLE) framework emphasizes learner autonomy and control over their learning experiences, using a variety of tools and resources. The Intelligent Tutoring System (ITS) framework incorporates artificial intelligence and machine learning algorithms to provide personalized instruction and feedback to learners, with learning analytics for monitoring progress and teacher support. The Community of Inquiry (COI) framework focuses on collaborative learning, emphasizing social presence, cognitive presence, and teaching presence. These frameworks provide a useful structure for meeting the diverse needs of learners in the digital age.

Thus, from the above literature, we can construe that the use of design thinking in a smart learning environment can provide a unique approach to developing innovative solutions to the challenges faced by educators in the digital age. The use of a smart learning environment for teacher professional development can provide personalized and flexible learning opportunities that are tailored to the needs of individual teachers. It can also promote collaboration and experimentation among teachers, fostering a culture of continuous learning and improvement in the classroom. The proposed framework for a smart learning environment for teacher professional development based on the principles of design thinking, personalization, flexibility, collaboration, and innovation can provide a foundation for the development of innovative solutions in teacher professional development in the digital age.

B. Design Thinking and Smart Learning Environment

Design thinking is a problem-solving approach that has gained popularity in recent years. The approach is characterized by a focus on empathy, creativity, and innovation. Design thinking involves understanding the needs of the user, developing a deep understanding of the problem, and then generating innovative solutions. Design thinking has been successfully applied in many fields, including business, healthcare, and education. Additionally, design thinking can be applied in the creation of a smart learning environment for teacher professional development.

- The first step in the design thinking process is to understand the needs of the user. In the case of teacher professional development, the user is the teacher. The designer must understand the specific needs of the teacher, including their knowledge, skills, and experience.
- The second step in the design thinking process is to define the problem. In the case of teacher professional development, the problem is to provide a flexible and personalized approach to professional development that is tailored to the specific needs of the teacher.
- The third step in the design thinking process is to generate ideas. In the case of teacher professional development, the designer must generate innovative solutions that meet the needs of the teacher. This could involve the creation of online learning resources, the development of a mentorship program, or the creation of a social learning platform.
- The fourth step in the design thinking process is to create a prototype. In the case of teacher professional development, the designer must create a prototype of the smart learning environment. The prototype can be a simple version of the final product that allows the designer to test and refine the design. This could involve developing a small-scale pilot program to test the effectiveness of the smart learning environment.
- The fifth and final step in the design thinking process is to test and iterate. In the case of teacher professional development, the designer must test the smart learning environment with a group of teachers and iterate based on their feedback. This process allows the designer to refine the design and make improvements based on the needs of the user.

III. METHODOLOGY

The study aims to develop a conceptual framework to explore the relationship between design thinking, smart learning environments, and teacher professional development in the era of digital transformation. To achieve this aim, a comprehensive methodology was employed, which involved a rigorous and systematic literature review [26][27].

The literature review was conducted using the two main scientific databases, Web of Science and Scopus, and other academic databases such as ERIC, ScienceDirect, and SpringerLink. The academic search engine, Google Scholar, was used in locating additional relevant literature. A literature search strategy was employed using the relevant keywords "design thinking," "design-based learning," "learning by design," "smart learning," "smart learning environment," and "teacher professional development." For a study to be included, it had to be in English, full-text, and a journal article and had to be aligned with the objective of this study by focusing on using design practices to build a smart learning milieu to promote teacher professional development.

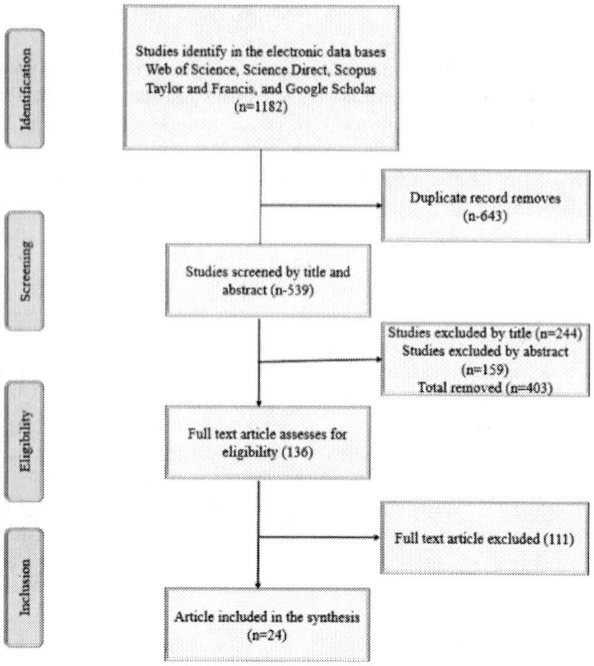

Figure 1. PRISMA Diagram

The inclusion and exclusion criteria were employed to select relevant articles and publications. The 24 research articles were included in the analytic process in accordance with PRISMA [28] the quality of the sources was assessed using established criteria for critical appraisal [29]. This helped to ensure that the literature reviewed was both comprehensive and high-quality..

The literature review focused on exploring key concepts, theories, and best practices related to the use of design thinking and smart learning environments in teacher professional development, as well as the impact of digital transformation on the teaching and learning process. This allowed for a deep understanding of the theoretical background of the study, and provided a solid foundation for the development of the conceptual framework.

A thematic approach was used to analyze the data collected from the literature review, which involved identifying key themes and concepts, and organizing them into a logical framework. This helped to ensure that the conceptual framework was grounded in the relevant literature and accurately reflected the key theoretical concepts and themes related to the research questions.

The limitations of this methodology were carefully considered and addressed. For instance, the potential for bias in the selection and interpretation of the literature was minimized by using established inclusion and exclusion criteria, and by critically appraising the quality of the sources. Additionally, the potential for gaps in the literature was addressed by conducting a comprehensive search across multiple sources and using a variety of search terms.

IV. Proposed Framework for a Smart Learning Environment for Teacher Professional Development

The rapid pace of digital transformation has had a significant impact on education, and teacher professional development has become an essential part of the process. The emergence of new technologies and the changing learning environment have made it necessary to reevaluate the traditional approach to professional development. The traditional approach to professional development has typically involved attending workshops, conferences, and other training sessions. However, in the era of digital transformation, there is a need for a more flexible and personalized approach to professional development. Therefore, based on the principles of design thinking, we propose a framework for the design of a smart learning environment for teacher professional development. The framework is based on four key principles: personalization, flexibility, collaboration, and innovation, as shown in Figure 1.

- Personalization: The smart learning environment must be tailored to the specific needs of the teacher. This could involve the creation of personalized learning paths, the development of customized learning resources, or the provision of individualized coaching and mentorship.
- Flexibility: The smart learning environment must be flexible and accessible. This could involve the creation of online learning resources that can be accessed anytime and anywhere, or the provision of virtual coaching and mentorship.
- Collaboration: The smart learning environment must promote collaboration and community building. This could involve the creation of social learning platforms, the development of peer mentoring programs, or the provision of opportunities for teachers to collaborate on projects and share ideas.
- Innovation: The smart learning environment must promote innovation and experimentation. This could involve the provision of opportunities for teachers to experiment with new teaching strategies, the development of innovation challenges, or the creation of incubators for new ideas.

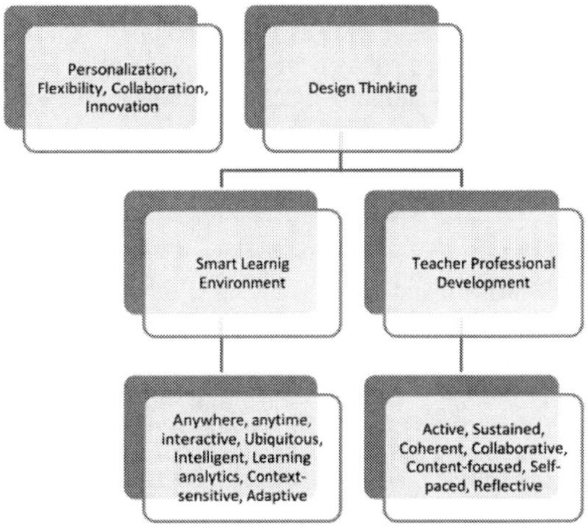

Figure 2. Proposed Conceptual Framework

The proposed conceptual framework illustrates that TPD programs with active and situated learning approaches have shown to be effective in enhancing teacher competencies and skills. Active learning involves hands-on activities, experiential learning, and interactive teaching methods that promote engagement and participation. Situated learning refers to learning that takes place in a real-world context, providing teachers with opportunities to apply their knowledge and skills in authentic situations. Collaborative learning, where teachers work together to share their knowledge and experiences, can also enhance TPD outcomes. Content-focused TPD programs are designed to deepen teachers' knowledge of specific subject areas or instructional strategies, and self-paced TPD programs allow teachers to learn at their own pace, providing flexibility and autonomy. Finally, reflective learning involves self-reflection on teaching practices, which can help teachers identify areas for improvement and enhance their teaching effectiveness. Overall, TPD programs that incorporate these characteristics can be effective in improving teacher competencies and ultimately enhancing student learning outcomes.

On the other hand, relationship between TPD, design thinking, and Smart Learning Environments can be strengthened through the use of technology-mediated TPD platforms. These platforms can provide anytime, anywhere access to interactive, intelligent, and adaptive learning activities that are content-sensitive and personalized to the needs of individual teachers. By incorporating these technologies into TPD, educators can promote a culture of continuous learning and improvement, enabling them to develop innovative solutions to challenges faced in the digital age.

V. Conclusion

The era of digital transformation has made it necessary to reevaluate the traditional approach to teacher professional development. Design thinking offers a unique approach to problem-solving that can help educators develop innovative solutions to the challenges they face. A smart learning environment can provide a flexible and personalized approach to professional development that meets the specific needs of the teacher. By adopting a design thinking approach, educators can create a smart learning environment [30] that promotes collaboration, innovation, and continuous learning and improvement.

REFERENCES

[1] P. Mishra and M. J. Koehler, "Technological pedagogical content knowledge: A framework for teacher knowledge," *Teachers college record,* vol. 108, no. 6, pp. 1017-1054, 2006.

[2] T. Wang, "ICTs and the Education of Design Professionals," in *2009 International Association of Computer Science and Information Technology-Spring Conference*, 2009: IEEE, pp. 126-130.

[3] K. Roth, D. Globocnik, C. Rau, and A. K. Neyer, "Living up to the expectations: The effect of design thinking on project success," *Creativity and Innovation Management,* vol. 29, no. 4, pp. 667-684, 2020.

[4] S. Panke, "Design thinking in education: Perspectives, opportunities and challenges," *Open Education Studies,* vol. 1, no. 1, pp. 281-306, 2019.

[5] L. Kimbell, "Rethinking design thinking: Part I," *Design and culture,* vol. 3, no. 3, pp. 285-306, 2011.

[6] J. Liedtka, "Why design thinking works," *Harvard Business Review,* vol. 96, no. 5, pp. 72-79, 2018.

[7] R. Lor, "Design thinking in education: A critical review of literature," 2017. ACEP ISBN 978-986-5654-50-4

[8] K. Phusavat, A. N. Hidayanto, P. Kess, and J. Kantola, "Integrating Design Thinking into peer-learning community: Impacts on professional development and learning," *Journal of Workplace Learning,* vol. 31, no. 1, pp. 59-74, 2019.

[9] B. Basma and R. Savage, "Teacher professional development and student literacy growth: A systematic review and meta-analysis," *Educational Psychology Review,* vol. 30, no. 2, pp. 457-481, 2018.

[10] L. Darling-Hammond *et al., Empowered educators: How high-performing systems shape teaching quality around the world.* John Wiley & Sons, 2017.

[11] L. Darling-Hammond, "Teacher learning that supports student learning," *Educational Leadership,* vol. 55, no. 5, pp. 6-11, 1998.

[12] A. G. Qazi and F. J. Mtenzi, "The Conceptual Framing, Design, and Development of Mobile-Mediated Professional Development for Primary Mathematics Teachers," *International Journal of Mobile and Blended Learning (IJMBL),* vol. 15, no. 2, pp. 1-19, 2023.

[13] H. K. Bett, "The cascade model of teachers' continuing professional development in Kenya: A time for change?," *Cogent Education,* vol. 3, no. 1, p. 1139439, 2016.

[14] A. Gohar, "Designing an Innovative Mobile-Enabled Continuous Professional Development Solution for Teachers," *EDULEARN22 Proceedings,* pp. 6862-6867, 2022, doi: 10.21125/edulearn.2022.1613.

[15] J. S. Gero and J. Milovanovic, "A framework for studying design thinking through measuring designers' minds, bodies and brains," *Design Science,* vol. 6, p. e19, 2020.

[16] M. G. Luchs, "A brief introduction to design thinking," *Design thinking: New product development essentials from the PDMA,* pp. 1-12, 2015.

[17] S. Lee, T. Kim, J. Kim, S. Kang, and J. Yoon, "The effect of a design thinking-based maker education program on the creative problem solving ability of elementary school students," *Journal of The Korean Association of Information Education,* vol. 23, no. 1, pp. 73-84, 2019.

[18] P. A. García-Tudela, P. Prendes-Espinosa, and I. M. Solano-Fernández, "Smart learning environments: a basic research towards the definition of a practical model," *Smart Learning Environments,* vol. 8, no. 1, pp. 1-21, 2021.

[19] C.-M. Yang, "Applying Design Thinking as a Method for Teaching Packaging Design," *Journal of Education and Learning,* vol. 7, no. 5, pp. 52-61, 2018.

[20] R. Wahab, A. Abdullah, M. Abu, N. Atan, M. Mokhtar, and M. Hamzah, "A learning 3D geometry through sketchup make (SPPD-SUM) to enhance visual spatial skills and the level of geometric thinking," *Journal of Fundamental and Applied Sciences,* vol. 10, no. 6S, pp. 1005-1039, 2018.

[21] G.-J. Hwang and Q.-K. Fu, "Advancement and research trends of smart learning environments in the mobile era," *International Journal of Mobile Learning and Organisation,* vol. 14, no. 1, pp. 114-129, 2020.

[22] T. M. Kessner *et al.,* "(Design) thinking out loud: adolescents' design talk in a library makerspace tabletop game design camp," *Information and Learning Sciences,* vol. 122, no. 9/10, pp. 651-670, 2021.

[23] S. K. Cheung and F. L. Wang, "The continuous pursuit of smart learning," *Australasian Journal of Educational Technology,* vol. 37, no. 2, pp. 1-6, 2021.

[24] B. Gao, Q. Wan, T. Chang, and R. Huang, "A framework of learning activity design for flow experience in smart learning environment," in *Foundations and Trends in Smart Learning: Proceedings of 2019 International Conference on Smart Learning Environments,* 2019: Springer, pp. 5-14.

[25] Y. Rosmansyah, B. L. Putro, A. Putri, N. B. Utomo, and Suhardi, "A simple model of smart learning environment," *Interactive Learning Environments,* pp. 1-22, 2022.

[26] Y. Xiao and M. Watson, "Guidance on conducting a systematic literature review," *Journal of planning education and research,* vol. 39, no. 1, pp. 93-112, 2019.

[27] A. K. Akobeng, "Understanding systematic reviews and meta-analysis," *Archives of disease in childhood,* vol. 90, no. 8, pp. 845-848, 2005.

[28] D. Moher *et al.,* "Preferred reporting items for systematic review and meta-analysis protocols (PRISMA-P) 2015 statement." *Systematic reviews, vol. 4, no. 1, pp. 1-9, 2015.* https://doi.org/10.1186/2046-4053-4-1

[29] H. Arksey and L. O'Malley "Scoping studies: towards a methodological framework." *International journal of social research methodology,* vol. 8, no. 1, pp. 19-32, 2005.

[30] R. Huang, M. Y. Mustafa, A. Tlili, R. Zhuang, T. Chang, and D. Burgos, "Design of Online-Merge-Offline (OMO) learning environments in the post-COVID-19 era: case study analysis," in *International Encyclopedia of Education (Fourth Edition),* R. J. Tierney, F. Rizvi, and K. Ercikan Eds. Oxford: Elsevier, 2023, pp. 296-304.

A Systematic Literature Review of Design Thinking in Education in Korean Publications

Cheng Fei
Smart Learning Institute,
Beijing Normal University
Beijing, P.R.China
e-mail: feicheng@bnu.edu.cn

Boulus Shehata
Smart Learning Institute,
Beijing Normal University
Beijing, P.R.China
e-mail: boulus.shehata@qq.com

Ronghuai Huang
Smart Learning Institute,
Beijing Normal University
Beijing, P.R.China
e-mail: huangrh@bnu.edu.cn

Abstract— **Design Thinking (DT) has the potential to enhance products, services, and processes as a human-centered approach and has been recently used in education. While most of the literature on design thinking is dominated by English-published papers, and has a 'Western' perspective, it does not identify the state of research in other cultures. This systematic review addresses research on DT in education published in the Korean language due to its long history and considerable experience. It aims to identify the key trends, challenges, and future directions of DT in education as presented in peer-reviewed articles published between 2013 and 2022 in Korean journals. The study highlights the importance of cultural considerations, such as the self-concept and sociocultural background, in designing solutions that serve the community. The findings are useful for multicultural design centers, research institutes, and enterprises that are involved with the exploration of cultural characteristics related to DT for better intercultural human communication.**

Keywords-Design Thinking; Education; Korean publications; Systematic literature review.

I. INTRODUCTION

The origins of Design Thinking (DT) can be traced back to the late 1960s when design began to be seen as a scientific approach to problem-solving [1]. The term DT was first introduced in 1969 in the American book "Artificial Science" "Design is a way of Thinking". And its diffusion began in 2000 when SAP, a German software company, started to strongly support research. Since then, its meaning has expanded to include management's ability to lead innovation by effectively solving the company's current and difficult problems [2]. DT utilizes both analytical and intuitive thinking and is a process of divergence and integration, analysis, and consolidation through inspiration, conception, and execution [3]. It is a good choice for problem-solving in many fields because it allows for multiple perspectives on complex problems during execution [4]. Thus, DT can be redefined as a human-centered, higher-order thinking skill based on experimentation and a positive attitude that strives to imagine, collaborate, exchange different opinions, and restructure cognitive processes to find the best solutions to difficult and complex real-world problems faced by individuals and organizations. In teaching and learning, the strengths of DT lie in engaging learners, enhancing their understanding of content, facilitating learning by creating opportunities for application through tasks, and developing not only conceptual understanding but also functional and practical aspects through repeated practice. Koh et al. present a comprehensive conceptualization and application of design thinking in teaching and learning [5]. They present old and new concepts, as well as critical perspectives related to three major design theorists, namely Herbert Simon, Donald Schön, and Nigel Cross. In addition, in design thinking classes, teacher intervention is minimized and learners engage in team project activities under their own direction, which naturally develops self-directed learning skills as well as communication and collaboration skills. The process of DT involves intuition, analysis, analogy, and reasoning, enabling learners to solve creative problems, and through this problem-solving experience, learners gain a sense of purpose and take ownership of the project [6]. Based on the results of previous research on design thinking in teaching and learning, design thinking has been used as a pedagogical approach to foster creativity, which is important for sustainable development goals. With the extensive publication on DT education, Panke [7] provided a systematic literature review of case studies, reports, theoretical reflections, and several scholarly works to draw perspectives, opportunities, and challenges [7]. Her summary of previous literature reviews highlights the broad amount of studies that has been published and analyzed. Meinel and Leifer [8] stated that "with a deep belief that design must be rooted in people, culture and human values, ERGO believes in the power of Design Thinking in bringing innovation to one of the most culturally sensitive regions in the world." For example, Traifeh et al. [9] reported the early adoption of design thinking in Arabic-speaking countries, based on an analysis of Twitter data, which revealed differences in the rank order of countries tweeting about design thinking in Arabic and English. Based on the design education process, Chen [10] helped teachers to use the design thinking approach as a strategy for innovative change teaching and learning by integrating design literacy and disciplinary literacy as cultivation goals and instructing students to use the design thinking approach to complete practical activities in a diverse and pervasive curriculum, demonstrating that the design thinking approach to teaching and learning can promote the development of students' innovative abilities.

Most literature reviews of DT Education focus on English published papers [11] [12] [13] and are from a 'Western' perspective. To the best of our knowledge, there is no systematic literature review that covered DT research in Korean language. Therefore, this paper presents a systematic literature review of top Korean journals for their trends in research on DT education, the processes and models of DT, the challenges of DT education and future research recommendations. Furthermore, with the rise of globalization, it is important to uncover non-Western cultural diversity and bring it to light, especially when it comes to art and design [14] [15] [16]. For instance, Kim M. [15]writes about non-Western perspectives on human communication, which involves cultural variations in self-concept and the sociocultural ground for the self. Collinge et al. [14] further explore this field by discovering the quality of life assessment in non-Western cultures. Ito et al. [16] provided a systematic review of non-Western and cross-cultural/national leisure research. This inspired us to find out if different cultures have different design thinking approaches. Therefore, this paper presents a systematic literature review to answer these questions:

RQ1. What is the trend of Design Thinking in education in terms of publication year, research methods, target groups and subjects/domains involved in Korean publications?

RQ2. What are the processes of Design Thinking in education according to Korean publications?

RQ3. What are the challenges for Design Thinking in education and future research directions according to Korean publications?

This study is divided into six sections where the introduction is in Section 1, methodology is in Section 2, findings and discussion is in Section 3, future recommendations is in Section 4, conclusion is in Section 5 and references is in Section 6.

II. METHODOLOGY

This study synthesizes quantitative and qualitative studies to review DT education according to Korean publications. Since the reporting of systematic reviews can be prone to being biased, and the interpretation of results is inclined to be subjective [17], Preferred Reporting Items for Systematic Reviews and Meta-Analyses (PRISMA) guidelines will be followed to produce this systematic review [18]. The flow chart in Figure 1 shows the process of selecting studies for this review.

A. Searching the databases

The first step of the review was by one of the authors to search the Web of Science database using the strings "design thinking (topic)" and "education (topic)," while limiting the search results to the Korea Citation Index (KCI) database. KCI is a Korean citation index released by the National Research Foundation of Korea (NRF) in 2008 and is also known as the Korean core journal indexing system. The KCI database on Web of Science provides access to more than 1.4 million articles from more than 2,500 multidisciplinary journals covered by the Korea Journal Database and contains bibliographic information on scholarly literature published in Korean language. The data for this study included scholarly research published before December 31, 2022, the date when the literature was searched in the database, with a total of 2858 relevant articles by over 200 authors from 1999 to 2022.

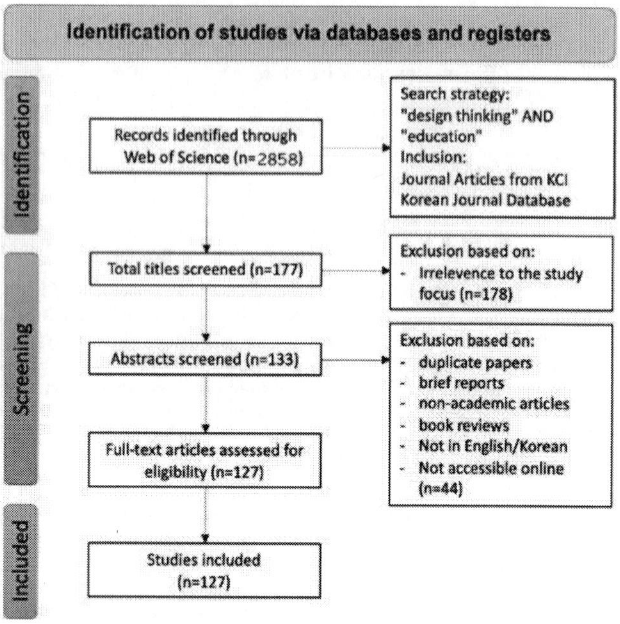

Figure 1. PRISMA chart for study identification and selection process

B. Selecting the studies

966 records were identified, and after initial screening, the author identified 177 records and 789 records were excluded because they were not relevant to the focus of the study. After re-screening of abstracts, 127 records were identified, of which 50 were excluded because they were duplicate papers, brief reports, non-academic articles, book reviews, not in English or Korean, or they were not accessible online.

III. FINDINGS AND DISCUSSION

In this section, we present the findings according to each research question.

RQ1. What is the trend of Design Thinking in education in terms of publication year, research methods, target groups and subjects/domains involved in Korean publications?

In terms of publication year in Korean journals, there was a rise of published research on DT education from 2018 to 2019 as can be seen in Figure 2. Much of this rise covers studies on the topic of Maker Education (ME). This may be explained by the fact that the Korean government announced its ME policy in 2017 and 2018 [19]. It is also evident that design thinking is actively used as a pedagogical approach to develop future talent in various educational institutions including universities and companies. The number of DT research related to teaching and learning has steadily increased since 2016 and exploded in 2020, showing a blossoming academic journal, reflecting the interest in DT among various alternatives in the era of the fourth industrial revolution, when educational institutions, including universities, are thinking about how to develop and improve the core competencies that future talents should have through teaching methods. increased. The number of research subjects is dominated by the curriculum, while the number of research topics is dominated by the curriculum or curriculum development. Therefore, there is a need to recognize the importance of teachers as facilitators in design thinking pedagogy and to study it in more depth.

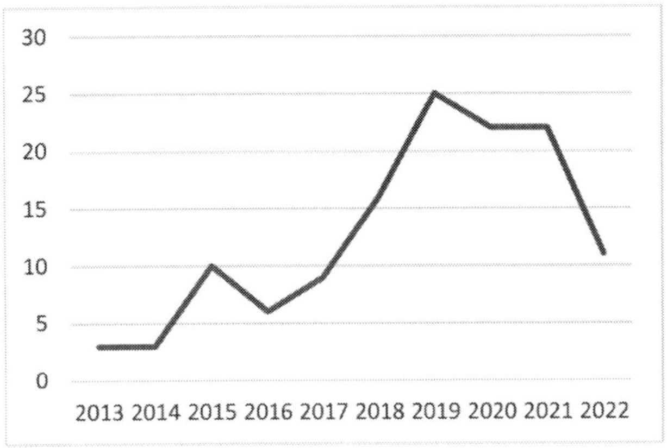

Figure 2. Distribution of DT education in Korean publications based on publication year

Figure 3 shows research methods used in the reviewed papers. The majority of the studies conducted Qualitative (30%) or Quantitative (28%) research. We also notice several theoretical studies (24%), review papers (7%) and articles using the Delphi method (2%). One study applied a meta-analysis [20] to calculate the overall Effect Size and ES for different variables of ME. Through the analysis, it was found that the most frequently mentioned tool for collecting data was observation, followed by interviews and survey. Due to the DT 'artistic' nature, we observe that a large portion of studies did not conduct experiments, except for a few. DT research in the field of teaching and learning published in Korean journals tends to focus on programs, with learners coming second. Among learners, a large number of studies were conducted on university students, while a similar proportion of studies were conducted on on-campus programs and off-campus programs. This is consistent with Kim's study that most DT research in design and the arts is about introducing concepts and applications, while most educational research using DT is about developing and applying curriculum in offline learning environments. This is also in line with the findings of Kim [21], who analyzed 85 design-related liberal arts courses offered as liberal arts programs at the top 33 universities in Korea from 2017 to 2019 and found that 25% of them were related to DT. Research on teaching DT in Korea is most often related to development, followed by validation of effectiveness. The most common topics were program development, curriculum development, and model and process development, suggesting that the use of design thinking in teaching and learning is widely present in all areas of the university, not just in the major disciplines. As for effectiveness validation research, we find that the most active are classroom effectiveness topics based on curriculum development and utilization. We can see that there is a trend to quickly diagnose and complement the actual effectiveness of the developed DT programs by validating their effectiveness, not just their development. Therefore, there is a need for more research on the educational effectiveness of collaborative activities through DT. In addition, in-depth theoretical research should be conducted to balance the development of DT research related to teaching and learning and to complete the construction of DT scholarship.

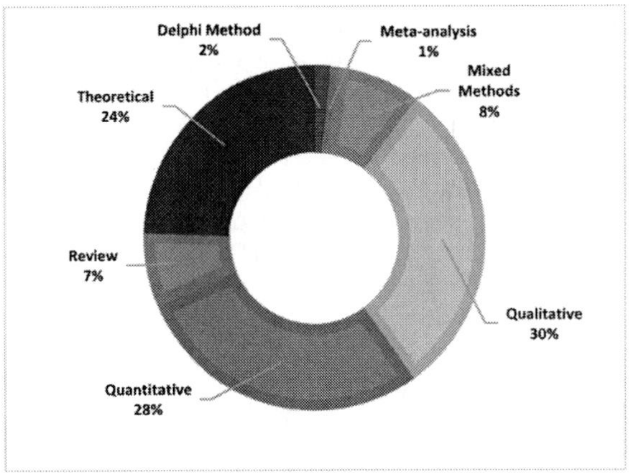

Figure 3. Distribution of DT education in Korean publications based on research methods

Findings also reveal target groups used in the DT education research (see Figure 4). In order not to present a fairly long list, only the top 5 groups are presented. The majority of studies involved college students (n = 53) followed by primary school students (n = 16), teachers (n = 15), secondary school (n = 13), secondary school (n = 13) and K-12 (n = 12). The findings show that DT can be applied in several college majors, such as robotics [22], engineering [23], medicine [24], nursing [25], entrepreneurship[26], and several others.

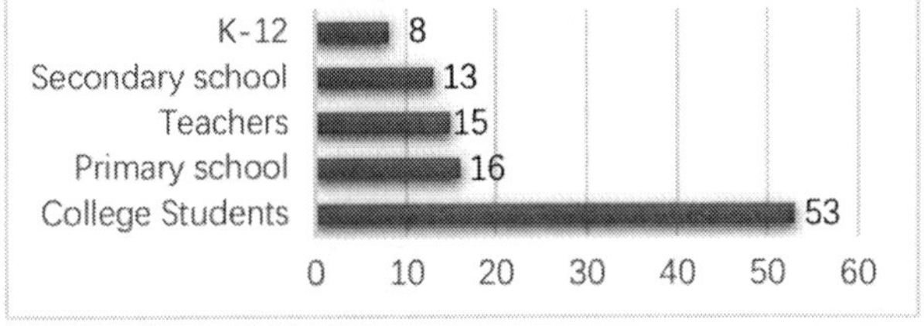

Figure 4. Distribution of DT education in Korean publications based on target group in the research

As can be seen in Table 1, DT education research within Korean journals covered several subjects ranging from general domains, such as multidisciplinary (n = 30) or teacher preparation (n = 24), to specific domains, such as in Maker Education (n = 14), STE(A)M subjects (n = 9), entrepreneurship (n = 9), or even dance programs (n = 1). In multidisciplinary domains, studies looked at how DT can develop 21st-century skills, such as creativity [6] of creative problem-solving [27]. In teacher preparation, studies looked at generic courses for pre-service or in-service teachers to design thinking for different purposes, such as with early childhood [28], with students' anxiety and resilience [29] or with teaching mathematics [30]. DT education in specific subjects seems to offer valuable findings. For instance, in STE(A)M education, Lee and Tae [31] exploded the effects related to DT on primary school students' problem-solving and interest in mathematics and science. In entrepreneurship, Jung and Kim [32] presented how DT can influence K-12 students' entrepreneurship skills. In languages, Bae [33] made action research for teachers to apply DT in improving early childhood language learning. Arts and Kim [21] suggested a framework for ceramics education. In addition, the active research variables related to DT in Korean education are design thinking literacy, step-by-step learning experiences in DT, DT-based teaching methods, DT-based team projects, and DT-based creative education curriculum. The dependent variables are mostly learner-related variables that can be subdivided into learning, competence, and affect. The learning category includes variables such as motivation, classroom satisfaction, and academic performance; the competency category includes problem-solving skills, articulation skills, self-directed learning skills, career development skills, creativity, collaboration, and teamwork efficiency. This is consistent with the findings of Hong, Ji-Myung, who found that a curriculum using DT helped to strengthen preschool teachers' emotional intelligence and creative personality, and Lee, Soo-Jin, and Yoon, Ok-Han [34], who found that a DT curriculum was meaningful for improving empathic problem-solving skills related to creative thinking and emotional intelligence. This confirms that the use of DT courses or programs has a direct impact on the development and improvement of various factors related to learners' learning, abilities, and emotions. Therefore, design thinking research on teaching and learning needs to focus more on the instructor. By its very nature, DT often implemented in the form of PBL(Project-Based Learning), focuses on the learner rather than the instructor. This does not mean that the role of the instructor is diminished, but rather that the role of the facilitator is increased, i.e., facilitating team projects and encouraging learner participation. In other words, the instructor in a DT classroom is an instructor who needs to develop learners' understanding of the concepts and processes of DT, a project manager who needs to coordinate and support the successful completion of each team's project, and a facilitator who helps learners learn to learn on their own through the process of experiencing a series of activities. Despite the important role of the instructor as a facilitator of DT, existing DT research on teaching and learning is biased toward the learner and the program. There is a need for more research on instructors in DT classrooms, including the competencies of DT instructors who value the learner experience, the achievements of DT instructors and learners, and the application and effectiveness of DT instructors and programs.

TABLE I. FREQUENCIES OF DT EDUCATION IN KOREAN PUBLICATIONS BASED ON SUBJECT/DOMAIN

Subject/domain	Frequency
Multidisciplinary	30
Teacher Preparation	24
Maker Education	14
Psychology-related	10
STE(A)M Education	9
Technology	9
Entrepreneurship	8
Science	5
Language	3
Arts (Music, Dance)	5
Environmental Issues	2
Medicine	2
Engineering	1
Management	1
Research Skills	1
N/A	3
Total	**127**

RQ2. What are the processes of Design Thinking in education according to Korean publications?

There are several DT processes/stages/phases/models, ranging from 3 to 9 process, as can be seen in Table 2. Three-step processes was seen in business or economics related programs [35]. Four-step processes was common with Maker Education that involves 'Tinkering – Making – Sharing – Improving' [36], or 'Word – Image – Prototype – Role playing' [37] which can be applied to objects of various backgrounds and can be used by extending basic models according to their field. Five-step processes was the most common DT models, specially the 'Empathize – Define – Ideate – Prototype – Test' model, with multidisciplinary, teacher education and STE(A)M education fields. Six-step processes are basically an extension of the five-step process by adding an extra stage, such as evaluation [38] or sharing [39] after testing the design. Seven, Eight, and Nine-step processes are further complex extensions of the five-step process. Studies that used longer processes were few. This is in accordance with Grönman and Lindfors [40] as they emphasized that DT process models are varied in their steps and has an iterative process. Therefore, it has four main phase categories, i.e., "empathy and user focus, problem, framing and defining, creating ideas and visualization, and experimentation and iteration". Thus, we can see that the influence of DT in the teaching field is slightly weaker in academia compared to other teaching methods, because it originated in the corporate world, where companies wanted to have an innovative organizational culture, improve their human resource capabilities, and develop new product development processes, such that the DT implementation process originated from the development of entrepreneurship. In recent years, there has been a growing interest in DT and active research on DT in teaching, but most of the research has focused on practical research on the development, use, and validation of solutions. In order for DT to be considered a distinct pedagogical approach and not just a team project class or problem-solving class, it is necessary to continue to conduct research using a variety of research methods. In addition, in order for the study of design thinking to have balance and academic depth, it is necessary to actively pursue research that builds theory through in-depth reflection and exploration, including not only practical research but also theoretical and philosophical discussions.

TABLE II. TYPES OF DT PROCESSES IN EDUCATION RESEARCH

DT Process type	Specific Design Thinking Processes	Examples
3 Steps	Inspiration – Ideation – Implementation	Choi, 2015
4 Steps	Tinkering – Making – Sharing – Improving	Lee, 2019
	Word – Image – Prototype – Role playing	Park & Nagan, 2020
5 Steps	Empathize – Define – Ideate – Prototype – Test	Lee & Tae, 2017
	Learn – Ideate – Design – Make – Share	Seo & Kim, 2018
6 Steps	Empathize – Define – Ideate – Prototype – Test – Evaluate/Share	Kim & Min, 2020
7 Steps	Orientation – Empathize – Define – Ideate – Prototype – Test – Summary	Shin et al., 2019
8 Steps	Tinkering – Finding issues – Empathizing – Planning – Making – Testing – Improving – Feedback	Yoon et al., 2019
9 Steps	Tinkering – Empathizing – Defining – Ideating – Prototyping – Sharing – Testing – Improving – Maker Fair	Choi & Bae, 2022

WITHIN KOREAN PUBLICATIONS

RQ3. What are the challenges for Design Thinking in education and future research directions according to Korean publications?

The findings revealed several challenges when it comes to DT in Education, which is mainly related to cultural traits, specifically the Confucian-heritage culture. Several studies pointed out that the Confucian-heritage culture is more assessment-driven, showing more reverence to authority, with less emphasis on higher order thinking, such as critical and creative thinking [41]. Affected by this culture, students may fear exhibiting different opinions or solutions that don't necessarily follow the norms [41], particularly in liberal arts [42]. In this sense, a common challenge to DT education in Korean culture is the complex design activities that demand higher order thinking. In such situations, the design process can be intimidating, and teachers may not be trained to ease an open and safe space for students to fully express their opinions without fear. This leads to another challenge, where DT leads to superficial embracing of form-centered designs, rather than human-centered design solutions. This may be a reason behind why some critics of DT mistakenly attribute the failure to use DT to the method itself, when it is the DT teaching and learning approaches. Other common challenges of incorporating design thinking into education with a focus on cultural aspects include the following:

1. Lack of cultural sensitivity: DT approaches may not be culturally sensitive, causing resistance and difficulties in implementation among diverse communities [43].
2. Resistance to cultural change: Incorporating cultural dimensions into DT may represent a departure from traditional approaches to education and may be met with resistance from educators and students who are accustomed to the status quo [44].
3. Inconsistent application across cultural contexts: DT may not be consistently applied across different cultural contexts, due to variations in cultural values, norms, and beliefs [45].
4. Limited cultural resources: Implementing DT in education in a culturally sensitive manner may require additional resources, such as specialized training on cultural competency and culturally responsive teaching [46].
5. Assessment and evaluation across cultural contexts: Assessing and evaluating the effectiveness of DT in diverse cultural contexts can be challenging, as cultural variations may impact DT outcomes [47].
6. Integration with existing curricula in a culturally responsive manner: Integrating DT into existing curricula in a culturally sensitive manner can be challenging, as it may require rethinking traditional teaching and learning approaches to be more culturally responsive [48].

Future direction of DT Education as highlighted in the reviewed papers point to the importance of establishing an educational 'learning community' to provide an open platform for teachers and project experts to exchange and discuss. This would facilitate the exchange of open and creative teaching and learning practices in the process of using design thinking. At the same time, it would offer students to reflect on their designs to promote their own culture, instead 'imitating' other cultures imported by the media (such as Hollywood). This can also uncover new approaches to design thinking, based on the Confucian culture within the Korean context. For instance, DT education can consider using Korean-inspired designs from the Hangul (Alphabet), Hansik (Food), Hanok (Traditional Housing), Hanbok (Clothing), and Hanguk-Eumak (Music). Another common highlight from the reviewed papers was the integration between schools and enterprises to set medium- and long-term educational projects, rather than short-term seminars or experimental- projects. This will provide an opportunity to conduct an in-depth, longitudinal study exploring the intrinsic motivations and interactions of the participants, which will enrich the industry-academia collaboration. In addition to this, there is a need to explore the importance and educational effectiveness of collaboration through pedagogical research in DT. In modern society, where there are increasingly complex problems that are not well defined, DT places a strong emphasis on unlocking the power of collective intelligence through collaboration. DT is a pedagogical approach that looks to leverage the strengths of teams by combining individual excellence with a collaborative attitude. Although there is some prior research on design thinking and team effectiveness, team collaboration effectiveness, and collegiality, there is a dearth of research on improving competencies through collaborative activities in DT team projects. Therefore, in addition to improving individual creativity and problem-solving skills, more research should be conducted on developing empathy, collaborative problem-solving, and collaborative creativity through design thinking.

IV. Future Recommendations

We conducted a systematic review on Korean published studies to explore trends, research methods, target groups and subjects/domains, as well as processes, challenges, and future research directions on DT Education. The reviewed papers reveal a lack of research on designs inspired from the Asian culture, such as Korea. According to the review findings, we suggest for future research to address the following recommendations:

- The role of cultural variations in self-concept and sociocultural background in DT:
  a. Understanding cultural differences in self-concept and identity.
  b. The influence of cultural values and norms on DT approaches.
  c. The impact of sociocultural background on DT outcomes.

Cultural dimensions play a significant role in shaping the design of solutions that serve a particular community. An understanding of cultural variations in self-concept and sociocultural background can inform DT approaches to better serve the needs of diverse communities.

- The limited focus on DT from non-Western perspectives:
  a. The dominance of Western perspectives in DT literature.
  b. The need for more research on DT from diverse cultural dimensions.
  c. The potential benefits of incorporating diverse cultural perspectives in DT education.

Most of the literature on DT has a Western perspective, and there is a need for more research on DT from other cultural dimensions, such as Arab, Chinese, Japanese, and Korean.

- The importance of considering cultural dimensions in DT education:
  a. Enhancing the effectiveness of DT in serving diverse communities.
  b. Improving intercultural communication in DT.
  c. Encouraging the development of culturally responsive DT approaches.

Incorporating cultural dimensions into DT education can enhance the effectiveness of DT in serving diverse communities and improve intercultural human communication.

- The need for further exploration of cultural characteristics related to DT:
  a. Uncovering variations in design approaches in different cultural contexts.
  b. Improving our understanding of the relationship between culture and DT.
  c. Encouraging the development of culturally sensitive DT practices.

Further exploration of cultural characteristics related to DT can uncover variations in design approaches in education, which will be crucial for understanding the relationship between culture and DT.

According to the review findings, we suggest to explore more DT educational approaches in atypical disciplines such as science, environmental studies, medicine, or management. Moreover, future research can utilize longer processes in different subjects/domains and conduct in-depth interviews or experimental research approaches to explore how these extra steps have an influence on design-thinking competence.

V. Conclusion and Future Work

This study covered that there a great attention to Design Thinking (DT) education, especially with the increasing use of educational technology platforms and tools such as the metaverse and robots. Though several literature reviews were made on DT education, the attention is mainly focused on the published studies in English. This study conducted a systematic review on DT research in education published in Korean language to explore trends, research methods, target groups and subjects/domains, as well as processes, challenges, and future research directions on DT Education. The reviewed papers reveal a lack of research on designs inspired from the Asian culture. We ask, how can design thinking in education uncover and teach characteristics of the Korean culture, such as Hangul (Alphabet), Hanok (Traditional Housing), Hanbok (Clothing), and many more elements rooted in the society? It is recommended that the research community explore cultural characteristics related to design thinking. This would uncover variations in design approaches in education that is vital for intercultural human communication. Systematic reviews can be made on publications from other languages as well, such as in Arabic or Chinese. In addition to this, we also suggest that the use of DT in teaching and learning needs to be widely used and studied as a curriculum for adults through continuing education institutions. Previous research has focused on university courses, such as developing DT programs for university course management and validating the effectiveness of classes for university students. In Asia, which has entered a rapidly aging society, the importance of establishing an appropriate lifelong learning system for adults and developing effective programs cannot be overemphasized. Therefore, DT should be applied not only to university students but also to adults in general, and design thinking research on teaching and learning should continue not only for university disciplines but also for adults in general.

REFERENCES

[1] Ahn, Youngsik (2021). Reflections on Design Thinking: Focusing on the processes of concept formation and meaning expansion. Research in Learner-Centered Instruction, 21(24), 647-665.

[2] Kelly, T. and Littman, J. (2001). The art of innovation, Lesoons in creativity from IDEOP, America's leading design firm. New York.

[3] Tim Brown (2009). Focus on design, book, Youngsa Kim, Seoul.

[4] Roger, S. Pressman. and Bruce, R. Maxim. (2020) Software engineering: a practitioners approach. New York: McGraw-Hill Education.

[5] Koh, J. H. L., Chai, C. S., Wong, B., and Hong, H. Y. (2015). Design thinking for education: Conceptions and applications in teaching and learning. Springer.

[6] Choi, H., and Park, J. (2014). Developing the design process in education to improve creativity based on design thinking. Journal of Digital Design, 14(4), 677-686

[7] Panke, S. (2019). Design thinking in education: Perspectives, opportunities and challenges. Open Education Studies, 1(1), 281-306.

[8] Meinel, C., and Leifer, L. (2012). Design thinking research (pp. 1-11). Springer Berlin Heidelberg.

[9] Traifeh, H., Bin Tareaf, R., Abou Refaie, R., Meinel, C., and Von Thienen, J. (2021). How Did Design Thinking Develop in the Arab World? Findings from Twitter Analysis. Journal of Design Thinking, 2(2).

[10] Chen, P., Huang, R. H. (2021) Exploring the paths and strategies of design education: a new perspective on the cultivation of innovative talents. 3(335),18-24.

[11] Razzouk, R., & Shute, V. (2012). What is design thinking and why is it important?. Review of educational research, 82(3), 330-348.

[12] Lor, R. (2017). Design thinking in education: A critical review of literature.

[13] McLaughlin, J. E., Wolcott, M. D., Hubbard, D., Umstead, K., & Rider, T. R. (2019). A qualitative review of the design thinking framework in health professions education. BMC Medical Education, 19, 98.

[14] Collinge, A., Rüdell, K., & Bhui, K. (2002). Quality of life assessment in non-Western cultures. International Review of Psychiatry, 14(3), 212-218.

[15] Kim, M. S. (2002). Non-Western perspectives on human communication: Implications for theory and practice. Sage.

[16] Ito, E., Walker, G. J., & Liang, H. (2014). A systematic review of non-Western and cross-cultural/national leisure research. Journal of Leisure Research, 46(2), 226-239.

[17] Sinha, M. K., & Montori, V. M. (2006). Reporting bias and other biases affecting systematic reviews and meta-analyses: a methodological commentary. Expert review of pharmacoeconomics & outcomes research, 6(5), 603–611. https://doi.org/10.1586/14737167.6.5.603

[18] Moher, D., Liberati, A., Tetzlaff, J., Altman, D. G., Prisma Group. (2010). Preferred reporting items for systematic reviews and meta-analyses: The PRISMA statement. International Journal of Surgery (london, England), 8(5), 336–341.

[19] Lee, Dongkuk & Kwon, Hyuksoo. (2022). Keyword analysis of the mass media's news articles on maker education in South Korea. International Journal of Technology and Design Education. 32. 10.1007/s10798-020-09615-9.

[20] Lee, D. K. (2019). A meta-analysis of the effects in maker education. The Journal of Educational Information and Media, 25(3), 577-600.

[21] Kim, Y. Y. (2021). Suggestion for creative idea frame of ceramic collaboration education through design thinking. 한국과학예술융합학회, 39(3), 69-75.

[22] Lim, D., & Ahn, J. (2019). A Case Study: Designeer Education Program and Application of Capstone Design-Focusing on Design Thinking Process of a Robot Vacuum Cleaner. Journal of Engineering Education Research, 22(2), 61-70.

[23] Kim, Y. A., & Han, Y. S. (2016). An Analysis of the Design Activities in Appropriate Technology based Engineering Design in order to utilize the Concept of Design Thinking. Journal of Engineering Education Research, 19(5), 25-34

[24] Yoo, J. Y. (2020). The effect of medical service design thinking teaching-learning on empathic problem solving ability: Convergence analysis of structured and unstructured data. Journal of Digital Convergence, 18(6), 311-321.

[25] Kim, J. S. (2020). The effect of design thinking-based nursing learning program in students.

[26] Kim, Hyun-Min (2015) Design Entrepreneurship in Visual Communication Design Education. Journal of Basic Design & Art.

[27] Young-Jae, J. (2021). Development of Design Thinking Class Program Applying Creative Problem Solving (CPS) in College Classes. Jounal of Fisheries and Marine Sciences Education, 33(5), 1153-1171.

[28] Lee, Jongman (2020) Case study of 'Subject Logic and Essay' class based on Design Thinking: Focused on critical thinking and creative attitude of pre-service early childhood teacher. Journal of Learner-Centered Curriculum and Instruction

[29] Seong, G. B. (2019). The effects of problem-based activities with the design thinking process on teaching anxiety, resilience, and creative problem-solving competence of pre-service English teachers. The Journal of Foreign Studies, 47, 41-80.

[30] Lee, J., & Kim, H. (2020). Analysis of pre-service mathematics teachers' experience on design thinking based teaching practicum. Communications of Mathematical Education, 34(3), 235-256.

[31] Lee, E., & Tae, J. (2017). The effect of STEAM program based on design thinking on primary school pupil's convergent problem solving & interest in math-science. Journal of Curriculum Integration, 11(1), 143-162.

[32] Jung, H. J., & Kim, C. O. (2018). A Study on the Entrepreneurship Education Framework for Youth based on Design Thinking. Journal of the Korean Entrepreneurship Society, 13(1), 176-200.

[33] Bae, J. H. (2021). Action Research to Improve the Curriculum for Early Childhood Language Education Based on Design Thinking for Prospective Kindergarten Teachers. The Journal of the Korea Contents Association, 21(12), 119-131.

[34] Yoon, Okhan (2017). A Study of the Instructional Systems Design Model for STEAM Education- Focus on Design Thinking. Korean Journal of General Education, 11(2), 443~474.

[35] Choi, W. (2015). The holistic startup business model development by lean startup and design thinking: startup methodology and education program development for designers in the creative economy. Hongik University.

[36] Lee, S., Kim, T., Kim, J., Kang, S., & Yoon, J. (2019). The effect of a design thinking-based maker education program on the creative problem solving ability of elementary school students. Journal of The Korean Association of Information

Education, 23(1), 73-84.

[37] Park, hyeyoung, & Nagan. (2020). '공예 대중화'를 위한 메이커 교육 프로세스 연구-디자인 씽킹 방법론 (WIPR) 과 전문가 인터뷰를 통하여. 한국디자인문화학회지, 26(2), 185-196.

[38] Kim, Kyoungeun & Min Seonghye (2020) Preschool Teacher's Perception of Design Thinking. Journal of Learner-Centered Curriculum and Instruction

[39] Lee, Yeong-Chan (2021) Exploring the Direction to Apply Design Thinking to Invention Education in Practical Arts Subject of Elementary School. [초등학교 실과의 발명교육 영역에서 디자인씽킹 적용 방향 탐색] The Journal of Korean Practical Arts Education.

[40] Grönman, S., & Lindfors, E. (2021). The process models of design thinking: A literature review and consideration from the perspective of craft, design and technology education. Techne serien-Forskning i slöjdpedagogik och slöjdvetenskap, 28(2), 110-118.

[41] Stankov, L. (2010). Unforgiving Confucian culture: A breeding ground for high academic achievement, test anxiety and self-doubt?. Learning and Individual Differences, 20(6), 555-563.

[42] Cheng, B., & Zhang, D. (2020). Cultivating citizens with Confucian cosmopolitanism: Defining the purpose of liberal arts education in the Asian context. Frontiers of Education in China, 15(4), 564-587.

[43] Sungae Kim(2019). Effects of Robotics Education Program based on the Design Thinking Process on the Creativity for Engineering College Students in the field of IT.

[44] Park, Suhong(2021). Development of Entrepreneurship Education Model Based on Design Thinking for Community Value Realization.

[45] Kwon, Young-kook(2017). A Study on Combined Education for Design Thinking - Focusing on Stanford D. School Curriculum.

[46] Dohyun Lee(2015).The Suggestion of Design Thinking Process and its Feasibility Study for Fostering Group Creativity of Elementary-Secondary School Students in Science Education.

[47] Kristen Koeun Nam(2022). An Educational Program of Design Thinking class for Creative Problem Solving- Focused on the practical project of multidisciplinary curriculum.

[48] Yoon Hye Jean (2013). Creative Thinking and Convergence Education for Innovative Design.